HANDWRITING: Theory, Research and Practice

Handwriting

Theory, Research and Practice

JEAN ALSTON and JANE TAYLOR

CROOM HELM
London & Sydney

NICHOLS PUBLISHING COMPANY
New York

© 1987 Jean Alston and Jane Taylor
Croom Helm Ltd, Provident House, Burrell Row,
Beckenham, Kent BR3 1AT

Croom Helm Australia, 44–50 Waterloo Road,
North Ryde, 2113, New South Wales

British Library Cataloguing in Publication Data

Alston, Jean
   Handwriting: theory, research and practice.
   1. Writing — Psychological aspects
   I. Title   II. Taylor, Jane
   152.3′845   QP310.W7

   ISBN 0–7099–0580–7
   ISBN 0–7099–5107–8 Pbk

First published in the United States of America in 1987
by Nichols Publishing Company, Post Office Box 96,
New York, NY 10024

Library of Congress Cataloging-in-Publication Data

Alston, Jean.
   Handwriting, theory, research, and implications for
practice.

   Includes index.
   1. Penmanship. 2. Penmanship — Remedial teaching.
I. Taylor, Jane. II. Title.
LB1590.A47 1987   372.6′34   87-14061
ISBN 0-89397-287-8

Filmset by Mayhew Typesetting, Bristol, England
Printed and bound in Great Britain
by Billing & Sons Limited, Worcester.

Contents

Authors and Contributors

AUTHORS

Jean Alston has an honours degree in psychology and a masters degree in education. She has taught children throughout the primary school age range and was a member of the Derbyshire Remedial Service in the years 1967 to 1972. She has published several articles on handwriting and its measurement and on the educational needs of brittle-boned children. She is Senior Lecturer in Special Education at Crewe and Alsager College of Higher Education, Cheshire, where she specialises in literacy skills, educational measurement and the education of physically handicapped children.

Jane Taylor has diplomas in occupational therapy and education. She has worked with children with cerebral palsy at Queen Mary's Hospital, Carshalton, Surrey, and with children with learning difficulties at the Dyslexia Clinic, St Bartholomew's Hospital and the Sheldon Children's Centre, King's College Hospital, London. She is currently employed at the Helen Arkell Centre in London. Both authors are founder members of the Handwriting Interest Group.

CONTRIBUTORS

Nusia de Feldman, Professor in the Department of School Psychology, Universidad Central de Venezuela, Caracas, Venezuela.
George Pasternicki, Educational Psychologist, Leicester Education Authority, England.
Muriel Tarnopol, Assistant Professor, Department of Counseling, San Francisco State University, San Francisco, USA.
Elizabeth Whitmarsh, Special Needs Teacher, Coppenhall High School, Crewe, Cheshire, England.
Jenny Ziviani, Senior Lecturer, Department of Occupational Therapy, University of Queensland, Australia.

Acknowledgements

Our thanks go to the children we have encountered in our work who, through their endeavours, have educated us to an extent that it became possible for us to write this text. We also thank our families, who have supported us during the sometimes difficult writing period, with special thanks to Robert Alston Junior, who so willingly completed the scribbles.

We are grateful to the many colleagues in the U.K. Handwriting Group who, with us, are excited about the current happenings in the field of handwriting, and to many friends from overseas who have been willing to send materials and share their views with us.

For graphics and calligraphy, we would like to thank Molly Richardson, Senior Lecturer, Central Resources, Crewe and Alsager College of Higher Education.

We would also like to thank the following:

(1) *British Journal of Special Education*, for permission to publish figures 14.1 and 14.5, and table 14.3.
(2) Department of Education, Western Australia, for permission to print figure 13.1
(3) Mayfield Publishing Company, Palo Alto, for permission to print figures 2.1 and 2.2 from R. Kellogg (1969) *Analyzing Children's Art*.
(4) Department of Education, Wellington, New Zealand, for permission to print figures 12.3 and 13.2.
(5) Support for Learning, for Permission to print figure 7.1.

Muriel Tarnopol and Nusia de Feldman wish to thank Jastak Associates, Inc., for permission to translate the Arithmetic and Spelling Tests for the Wide Range Achievement Test into Spanish, Japanese and Chinese; Keith Beery, for permission to translate the Developmental Test of Visual Motor Integration; and Elizabeth Koppitz, for permission to translate the Human Figure Drawing Test.

Preface

This book is the outcome of five years of collaboration, discussion and applied research by the two major authors. Many people have been consulted during those years and common platforms for interested professionals have been established through the United Kingdom Handwriting Interest Group and through its newsletter 'The Handwriting Review', for which the authors were key workers during the formative years. Chapters 10 and 11 have been written exclusively by Jane Taylor and she has been responsible for collating the information from Australia. Jean Alston has been responsible for interpreting legislation and much of the research and exclusively for the sections on research methods and physically handicapped children. Guest writers were invited for the importance of their particular areas of interest. George Pasternicki, for example, has considerably extended the research on lined or unlined paper and Elizabeth Whitmarsh, we believe, has important things to write about the special needs of secondary school pupils. Jenny Ziviani's research is well known at international level, and we invited her to bring together her own research and that of others for this text. Muriel Tarnopol was able to offer comparative research from a number of countries and we were pleased to welcome her as a writer from the United States of America, and as one who has an international reputation in the more general field of learning disabilities. She is pleased to acknowledge the help of Nusia de Feldman, who conducted the research in Venezuela.

The text has been written by specialists from different professions and although contributors have an interest in handwriting in common, they professionally regard it from different points of view. In the interests of dialogue, and in pursuance of individual arguments, overlapping of some topics inevitably occurs. The fact that this does occur helps to emphasise the importance of some of the basic principles.

To simplify the text, the pronouns 'she' for teachers and 'he' for pupils are used. However, we do not wish thereby to imply that all teachers are women or that all pupils with handwriting difficulties are boys.

1

The Current Situation

While in this text we refer principally to developments in the United Kingdom, we have made ourselves aware of the current situation in the United States and Australasia, and refer to them as appropriate. The contributions of Muriel Tarnopol from the United States of America and Jenny Ziviani from Australia also help us to present a more balanced view of developments principally though not exclusively in the English-speaking world.

It is evident that *reading* has received considerable attention during recent decades, both as an area of research and as one for discussion on theory and practice. Similarly, *writing* as a creative, expressive and communicating skill has been examined in detail. In Britain recently this is the focus of the 'Writing Project', initiated in 1985 by the United Kingdom's School Curriculum Development Committee. The Project reflects the increasing interest in pupils' writing for different purposes and in the manner in which it might be influenced by teachers. However, this text is concerned with the *physical* skill of writing, and has as its concern 'legibility' and economy of movement for correct letter, word and sentence formation. Interest in teaching handwriting is growing rapidly. However, the extent to which recommendations or formal guidelines for the teaching of handwriting in schools occur varies considerably. They have been introduced in New Zealand and Australia in recent years and tend to be quite prescriptive in their form and content. Their introduction is slow in the United Kingdom and the United States of America. However, the popularity of commercially produced handwriting schemes and the evidence that many teachers are now searching for teaching guidelines and for help for those pupils who have handwriting problems reflects a need for reappraisal of the situation in these countries.

Many educationalists regard handwriting as a small component of the wider arts of literacy, i.e. oral language, creative writing and reading. However, at its simplest level, handwriting is a physical skill requiring the adequate development of sensory-motor competence and co-ordination in the performer and a competent level of instruction in the components of the physical task from the instructor. Motor skills are resistant to change and the need for them to be developed accurately in the early stages of development is very important for handwriting, as this is the skill employed by our pupils throughout their school lives. The well-instructed teacher will be alerted to the young child who begins life in school with what might seem to her to be difficulties in fine motor skill and co-ordination. As with many basic educational skills, extra help in the early stages can often prevent failure as the child moves through his early years in school.

As well as bringing her own skills to the teaching of the hand-writing task, the teacher may need other professionals on whom she can call for help. The physiotherapist may be able to assist with recommendations for help with general body posture and may be able to identify weaknesses that can be influenced by simple exercises and activities. Such activities may be enjoyed by all children and incorporated in the movement and general physical activities normally employed in the infant school curriculum. The occupational therapist may advise on furniture, writing tools and other aspects of the writing environment. The teacher is the one who is able to co-ordinate the recommendations of other professionals and through observing these recommendations realise the importance of her own intervention in the teaching of this important physical skill. Ideally, we do not wish to raise attention to the mechanical hand-writing skill any more than is essential for adequate performance by children. The mastery of mechanical skills gives us freedom to explore the instructive and creative aspects of education. However, throughout the text, attention is drawn to the way in which hand-writing needs vary at different stages of the pupil's educational career. Recommendations to assist pupils as they encounter changes in handwriting needs are presented at appropriate points in the text.

A growth in the number of children being referred to the clinics of paediatric neurologists particularly because of difficulties in handwriting, suggests that a close look at this aspect of the curriculum is needed. Pupils also present at general practitioners' surgeries with what seem to be psychogenic sickness and alimentary disorders; a good proportion of them are eventually identified as having difficulty with writing and related school tasks. The evidence suggests that attention to this predominantly physical skill is long overdue. In this book we bring together contributions from other disciplines involved in helping those with problems, refer to current research that we deem to be of interest and applicable to the roles of the practitioners, and suggest guidelines for co-operation and intervention by the different professional groups.

CURRENT HANDWRITING STANDARDS

The publication of *A Language for Life* (Bullock 1975) proved to be an influential marker in education in the United Kingdom. Handwriting received only a cursory glance in this extensive publication but the committee did question teachers about their teaching of handwriting to six-year-old and nine-year-old children. They concluded that as many as 12 per cent of six-year-olds and 20 per cent of nine-year-olds spent no time on handwriting practice *per se*. From the positive point of view, however, the committee suggested that it could be recorded that most teachers did think the skill important and tended to devote anything up to half an hour each week to this activity. The committee, in their general examination of skill acquisition, concluded that 'If a child is left to develop his handwriting without instruction he is unlikely to develop a running hand which is simultaneously legible, fast flowing and individual and becomes effortless to produce.' In the survey conducted by Her Majesty's Inspectors, Department of Education and Science, *Primary Education in England* (1978), handwriting is referred to as being practised in at least 80 per cent of the schools surveyed. The authors conclude that the subject is considered to be of importance by the teachers they questioned.

English from 5 to 16: Curriculum Matters 1, from the Department of Education and Science (1984) states, as an objective for seven-year-olds, 'Write legibly' and for eleven-year-olds, 'Exercise sufficient control over spelling, punctuation, syntax, and handwriting to communicate meaning effectively.'

English 5 to 16: The Responses to Curriculum Matters 1 (1986) is a document presenting Her Majesty's Inspectors' response to the evidence they received from readers of the earlier document. Their suggestions on how the objectives for the teaching of English might be recast, indicate that although there is only brief reference to mechanical writing skill, its importance along with that for spelling, punctuation and sentence construction is recognised. A recast objective for seven-year-olds states the following:

> Children should also have had extensive experience of the teacher's attention and support, individually and in groups, which has included, generally and in relation to specific tasks, both diagnosis and assistance with the development of: clear handwriting, a grasp of spelling patterns, the establishment and extension of simple written sentence patterns and their elementary punctuation.

Objectives at the age of eleven include:

> All children should also have had extensive experience of planned intervention and support, in accordance with their individual needs and related to appropriate tasks and contexts, with regard to the development of their writing skills. In general these will encompass: handwriting, spelling, punctuation, the development of sentence variety, control and organisation, paragraphing, and the proof-reading, editing and re-drafting of some of their own work.

The report of White (1986; Assessment and Performance Unit) *The Assessment of Writing: Pupils Aged 11 and 15* makes no reference to handwriting as such, and reports, more generally, the range of writing activities that 11 to 15-year-olds encounter across the curriculum in school. The authors refer, in their assessment of pupils' writing, to content, organisation, appropriateness and style, knowledge of grammatical conventions and orthographic conventions. In assessment of ability to use orthographic conventions, the authors state that account is taken of '. . . a pupil's ability to use upper and lower case letters systematically and . . . to employ the conventions of word division'. When referring to writing in general, the authors state that 'About 3 per cent of each age group, excluding those in special schools, are in great difficulty with writing.' They also conclude that secondary school pupils voice negative attitudes towards writing more strongly than do primary pupils and that more boys than girls of both age groups show negative and reluctant attitudes towards writing. In addition, they note 'The presence of a group of pupils for whom writing is synonymous with the acquisition of motor skills, and fraught with problems about pens, pencils and access to rubbers . . .' and conclude that '. . . for some 11-year-olds writing is still a novel skill . . .', indicating that the statement applies to about 10 per cent of their sample. Among the seven general recommendations, no reference is made to a possible need for helping pupils to become competent in the mechanical writing task as an underpinning skill from which more positive attitudes to writing in general might develop.

Discussion of handwriting standards can refer to how teachers influence handwriting by their teaching or how pupils perform in the writing task. In the absence of educational guidelines, freedom of what or how one will teach is left to the individual school staff or even to the individual teacher. Rubin and Henderson (1982) in their survey of one London borough, found that a number of teachers in schools used 'no specific style' and one suspects may not have used a consistent method of instruction even within the same school. Alston's research (1985) in Cheshire primary schools also suggests that for some children a similar situation exists. Three of the seventeen county schools had staff who did not employ a consistent and comprehensive scheme and many teachers professed to employing eclectic methods and to dealing with children's handwriting problems as the need arose. Occasionally there were inconsistent teaching methods between teachers within the same school, and we might suggest that this inconsistency would make progress particularly difficult for the less able children. Teachers have the perpetual problem of being expected to teach large classes of children and are not usually offered the facility of being allowed to observe their children individually. For some reason it is assumed that other professionals need to do this but that class teachers do not. As long as this state of affairs exists, it will be difficult for us to ask class teachers to observe the letter movement patterns in the early stages of children's writing. This lack of observation and ensuing incorrect movement may lead to writing habits that have their ramifications throughout the child's school career. Group teaching of handwriting may help and could, if properly implemented, make the need for complex remedial measures for the child with persistent difficulties unnecessary. With regard to published handwriting schemes, one is dependent on the strength of the publishers' selling techniques rather than on the quality of their products. Implementation of the scheme is then dependent on management within the school. Worksheets may or may not be beneficial, as practice makes 'permanent' and may not make the handwriting any more perfect than it was before the exercise.

Rubin and Henderson (1982) found that, in the teachers'

opinions, 307 children (204 boys and 103 girls) in the nine- to ten-year age range, were experiencing serious handwriting problems. These figures represented 12 per cent of the children in the London borough where the research was conducted. The authors note that '. . . after at least four years of instruction . . . many children have still not acquired a level of competence in handwriting which is acceptable to their teachers'. In 1984, Alston completed a survey of third-year junior school pupils in Cheshire (nine- to ten-year-olds) engaging the assistance of five experienced special needs teachers from the Chester area. Their brief was to identify, in each batch of writing samples from 17 schools, those children who seemed, in handwriting, to be performing at a level that would probably be inadequate for them to meet the handwriting needs in secondary school education. (It was assumed that they would need to be able to vary speeds according to writing purposes, to maintain a legible script and avoid excessive fatigue.) In general this was intended to identify the pupils who were in need of assistance with handwriting in their last year of primary school education. The incidence of difficulty for these children was about 21 per cent; that for children from three of the more urban schools was much higher.

Briggs' research (1980) showed that for many pupils with handwriting difficulties the outcome can be serious, as their difficulties can influence grades in 16+ examinations. With support from the West Midlands Examinations Board, he was able to take essays that had already been awarded examination grades, have them rewritten in different handwriting scripts and show how there might be changes in the marking in consequence. The rewritten scripts were presented to experienced markers, who, using consistent marking criteria, remarked them. Differences in marks awarded were significantly related to handwriting quality at the 5 per cent level of significance. Briggs concluded that for scripts at the borderline 'pass' and 'fail' level, handwriting difference can influence the examiner to award 'fail' for some candidates. We may add to Briggs' assertions that, for the pupils identified in his research, the whole of the secondary school period may have been affected by slower-than-usual writing speeds, unnecessary difficulties with note taking, and adverse comments from teaching staff. The general effects of problems in this mechanical skill are likely to spill over into the child's level of success and failure throughout the curriculum.

6

APPLIED RESEARCH AND ITS INFLUENCE ON INITIAL AND CORRECTIVE TEACHING

One could assert that education has been bedevilled by authoritative assertion about what should be taught and how one should go about teaching. One might even refer to fashions in teaching that often seem to have considerable influence on the educational scene, despite the fact that there is little empirical foundation for their promotion. The Bullock committee stated, for example, '. . . the paper on which the children are to write should always be unlined and of sufficient size to be unrestricting . . .' Little, if any, research evidence had been available to the committee, yet it felt able to make a statement that was likely to influence the practices of teachers throughout the educational system. In the same year as the committee's publication, Burnhill *et al.* (1975) were to report research that could strongly contest the committee's statement, and there has been a growth in research on the use of lines for writing since that time. Pasternicki refers at length to this question later in this book (Chapter 7).

It is common for writers to refer to the 'correct' hold or writing tool grip and yet there is little research to show that any one writing tool grip is more beneficial than another. Developmental and experimental psychologists have observed children develop hand positions and strategies for different manipulative tasks and have looked at the implications for writing tool management. Other writers have classified writing tool grip and then examined the legibility and speed of subjects employing those tool holds and strategies. Speed and quality trials have, however, tended to be over a period of a few minutes, which, of course, is unlikely to relate to what would occur if the child were asked to write for say half an hour, and to do so after he had already been writing for a longer period of time. Our nearest approaches to the study of writing tool grip have been the studies of Ziviani (1982) and of Sassoon (1986). Ziviani has based her research on the early work on prehension by Rosenbloom and Horton, and Sassoon has taken eclectic analysis by observing the grip of pupils at work. Ziviani describes her work at length in Chapter 3 in this book.

Occasionally, teachers of physical education, physiotherapists and occupational therapists take an interest in the writing task and a few have devised exercises for the development of physical aspects such as hand function and shoulder stability. This more global approach to the pupil's development of handwriting skill is to be

7

welcomed. It discourages each professional from viewing the child only from his own viewpoint or from looking at a specific skill such as letter formation in isolation. However, as with other aspects of practice, we should search for the validity of recommendations through the monitoring of individuals and their progress, and through applied research models, which by their complementary strengths can teach us more about how pupils with difficulties can be helped. In general, decisions that are not made on the basis of research evidence should remain questions to be examined and not statements on which firm recommendations about teaching can be made.

REFERENCES

Alston, J. (1985) 'The handwriting of seven to nine year olds.' *British Journal of Special Education, 12* (2).

Briggs, D. (1980) 'A Study of the influence of handwriting upon grades using examination scripts.' *Educational Review, 32* (2).

Bullock, A. (ed.) (1975) *A Language for Life*. HMSO, London.

Burnhill, P., Hartley, J., Fraser, S., Young, M. (1975) 'Writing lines: an exploratory study'. *Programmed Learning and Educational Technology, 12* (2).

Czerniewska, P. (1985) *National Writing Project*. School Curriculum Development Committee, London.

Department of Education and Science (1978) *Primary Education in England*. HMSO, London.

Department of Education and Science (1984) *English from 5 to 16: Curriculum Matters 1*. HMSO, London.

Department of Education and Science (1986) *English from 5 to 16: The Responses to Curriculum Matters 1*. HMSO, London.

Rubin, N. and Henderson, S. (1982) 'Two sides of the same coin: variation in teaching methods and failure to learn to write.' *British Journal of Special Education, 9* (4).

Sassoon, R. (1986) 'An analysis of children's penholds,' in Kao, H.S.R., van Galen, G.P., Hoosain, R. (eds.), *Graphonomics: Contemporary Research in Handwriting*. North Holland Press, Amsterdam.

White, J. Assessment of Performance Unit, Department of Education and Science, (1986) *The Assessment of Writing: Pupils Aged 11 and 15*. NFER — Nelson, Windsor, Berkshire.

Ziviani, J. (1982) 'Children's prehension — while writing'. *British Journal of Occupational Therapy, 45* (9).

2

Beginning to Write: The Development of Grapho-Motor Skills

Over the years, or even the centuries, psychologists and paediatricians have reported norms of development and have recorded performance of graphic items that can be observed in an objective 'yes' or 'no' manner. For example, 'Can he copy a circle of diameter two inches? Will the end product be recognisable as a clear circle?' Several of these milestone items will be reported in this chapter. However, the intention is to report the qualitative changes in behaviour that might seem to have bearing on the development of writing and its associated skills. Bedford and Alston (1987) give an example of this qualitative approach when they refer not only to whether the child has a leading hand but also whether he is able to use the two hands for bilateral tasks. For this purpose, the child uses a leading hand and a helping hand. Handwriting is such a bilateral task, as observation of tool hold, paper arrangement and body position for the left-to-right writing sequence will reveal to the perceptive observer.

The normative information referred to here is a composite from writers (Griffiths 1970, Illingworth 1975, Sheridan 1975) who have reported since the time of Arnold Gesell. Small changes in the rate at which children develop have been recorded in recent years (Hanson, Aldridge Smith and Hume 1985) and an attempt to note those changes is made. The reason for paying close attention to the norms of development for writing and its prerequisite skills, however, is simply so that underlying skills and general order of development can be noted. Precise recording of the emergence of specific skills seems much less important than general trends and the evidence that the child is mature enough to cope with the writing task. Gesell himself draws attention to the general maturity of children's adaptive behaviour and the manner in which they are able

9

to organise themselves when they need to imitate and accommodate to different aspects of the expectations from the general environment. The reader's attention is drawn to the qualitative changes in the development of fine motor tasks, the relationship between unilateral and bilateral hand performance, and the relation of all performances to the child's understanding and management of the body as a whole. More recent work on normative information about the development of hand function and completion of writing- and drawing-associated tasks is presented. However, the reader should note that much of the recent work owes its origins to the understanding afforded by the work of Gesell and his colleagues earlier this century.

STAGES OF DEVELOPMENT IN THE YOUNG CHILD

28 weeks

Gesell (1954) states that, at that period, ocular adjustments are more advanced than manual adjustments. The child may perceive a string or even a pellet but be unable to touch it precisely or procure it.

40 weeks

The index finger and thumb show specialised extension and are able to probe and pluck. The pad of the thumb can oppose the pad of the index finger. Evidence of hand preference may appear.

One year

Fine prehension is quite deft and precise and voluntary release are in their early stages. He may begin to show that he is learning to use one hand so that he can reach further. Here there is evidence of the competing skills of one-handed or two-handed employment for task completion. The able child resolves the problem by learning to use one or two hands as appropriate. For the less able child, however, the resolution is not so easy. In later years, some of our children discard the 'helping' hand in writing with the associated consequences of insecure paper positioning and bad posture that often accompanies the problem.

Three years

The child likes to use crayons and is interested in the finer manipulation of play material. In spontaneous and imitative drawing, he shows an increased capacity to inhibit and delimit movements. His strokes are better defined, less diffuse and less repetitive. He has increased coordination in the vertical plane, i.e. within his own central body axis. He cannot deal with the diagonal for folding paper or imitative drawing. Gesell writes, 'Nature has not yet matured the prerequisite neuro-motor girders for oblique movement.'

Four years

He can take a fine pointed instrument, like a knitting needle or pencil, and thrust it into an appropriate-sized hole. Gesell claims that handedness seems well developed for some tasks at this stage and that, for the right handed, copying a circle will be well circumscribed and usually executed in a clockwise direction. In the manipulation of fine objects such as a pellet, however, it is claimed that handedness is much less developed and dominant.

Five years

He combines reaching and placing an object in one continuous movement. Neuro-motor development is advancing and this is reflected in his good facility in executing vertical, horizontal and to a lesser extent oblique strokes so long as the oblique stroke stands alone. The composition of a figure from oblique strokes is not within the reach of the average five-year-old but he is well able to copy a square and, as he moves towards his sixth birthday, a simple triangle. At this stage, he keeps better time to music than previously. This evidence of increasing awareness of rhythm may well have implications for the teaching of writing.

Six years

He tends to be only slightly superior to the five-year-old in steadiness of arm but the superiority of five- and six-year-olds to the average four-year-old is usually marked. Children with long fingers

11

seem to enjoy prehensile advantages over short-fingered children and show greater dexterity and speed of manipulation. Six-year-olds may show a gradual decrease in the size of writing with age. This evident maturity is probably due to the cutting out of superfluous movements as well as to the maturity of function in the prehensile grasp. He will be learning to vary the muscular tensions and releases for the task in hand; development and maturity will now, in school, be aided by the regular practice in manipulation that the normal infant classroom is likely to offer.

Seven years

He is competent in gross motor and eye/hand co-ordination skills and is able to do the following: run at various speeds; skip a little, using a small skipping rope; hop three hops on one foot with the foot raised; tie his shoe laces with a two-looped bow; draw a recognisable diamond in imitation; and write the figures 0–9 correctly.

The debate amongst those concerned with the teaching of handwriting continues to raise the question of whether print or cursive script should be employed from the early stages of teaching the child to write. The observation that the average seven-year-old can copy a diamond reminds us that around 50 per cent of seven-year-olds find imitation of the diagonal line in configuration difficult to execute. Is there a suggestion that the diagonal join in cursive writing is so short that it cannot really be considered to be a diagonal line (as reference to Kellogg's spontaneous scribbles might indicate), or are we overlooking the fact that to expect children to do cursive writing from an early stage may be to make an unrealistic expectation for some children?

Taylor (1985) basing her observations on the norms presented in Sheridan's (1975) text, suggests that a child who has difficulty in copying the triangle or diamond is also likely to have difficulty in executing the diagonal lines in the letters *k, v, w, x, y* and *z.*

RELEASE

The development of 'release' in hand function deserves special mention. Psychological aspects and observations receive attention here. The occupational therapist's viewpoint is given by Ziviani in Chapter 3.

Release seems more complex and certainly more difficult than 'hold' or 'lift' for the young child. Up to one year, the child can usually release an item only by pressing it against a resisting surface. At one year of age he has become proficient at 'dropping', a much less precise action. When the young child places a shape in a form board or a block on a tower of blocks, he tends to push, sometimes toppling that which he intends to build. The difficulties are created because, for release, different relationships are required between the extensor and contracting muscles of the arm and hand, from those of grasp. Timing of the releasing act may also create problems and this may be observed when the child begins to throw a ball, i.e. he releases too early or too late for the ball to be directed accurately towards the target he intends.

In the early stages of building a tower from bricks, he may have difficulty in the following actions: (a) placing the item (brick) flatly, (b) releasing the fingers simultaneously, and (c) withdrawing the hand in order to clear the construction without toppling it. In the early stages of lacing his shoes, he may unintentionally withdraw the lace because the release mechanisms of his hand function remain immature.

The child who can adopt the finer movement and inhibition to tie his shoe laces and can learn to hold the top brick of a pile with light and fine prehension has many skills that can be brought to the task of writing. He can then be taught to consider the writing tool, paper and writing surface in relation to the following: (a) his own position and proximity and angle to them, (b) his own view of the task and how he himself can vary that position and view, and (c) the need to vary the mechanisms of grasp and release for the variable movements essential to the writing task.

EARLY GRAPHIC PERFORMANCE

Several writers have referred to the development of early graphic skill and to the psychology of children's drawings. Helga Eng's report (1954) of her niece Margaret was an early comprehensive study, and, although it referred to only one very able child, was an objective study from which much can be learned. Kellogg (1969) presented her analysis of approximately a million drawings completed by young children from a variety of economic and social backgrounds and from world-wide geographical locations, her own analysis of the drawings resulted from 20 years of study. The texts of Di Leo (1971) and Goodnow (1977) are much less useful for our current purpose.

Helga Eng observed Margaret and recorded her progress with considerable precision. Her model is presented with that of Kellogg to provide a framework through which the reader might observe graphic development in young pre-writing children. Eng shows how a definite 'wavy scribble' is repeated and perfected in the early stages of pencil-and-paper activity. She shows how, although the scribble seems to change little, the line becomes firmer and surer. The early wavy scribble indicates use of the elbow and shoulder for the purpose and offers little evidence of variable movement in the hand and fingers. The change from wavy scribble came fairly suddenly, and the change was towards well-defined circles. Round and oval scribbling in dense mass became the norm for a while and lasted for a period of around two months. Variegated scribble began a new phase, two months later in Margaret's case, and consisted of straight lines, angles, crosses, zig zag lines and loops, forming a tangle of lines. There followed a period when all these elements became 'loosened up' but remained part of the general drawing repertoire. All the described elements remained part of the repertoire for some time, each being used in isolated scribbling or as practice for the representational drawing, which began with 'Mama'. Kellogg, discussing Eng's writing, states that whilst Eng believed that all children wish to pictorialise and therefore tended to see 'a man', for example, in a child's drawings, Kellogg herself might describe the same drawing as perhaps a '. . . cross diagram and a few scribbles'.

Di Leo (1971) refers to the early graphic practices of children as 'kinaesthetic drawing' and shows that the children he studied followed similar sequences to those inherent in Margaret's development. He refers to the children's employment of horizontal, vertical and circular scribble, presented in different degrees of firmness and orientation. Although his work is much less detailed than that of Eng, his reference to the importance of kinaesthetic drawing undoubtedly has implications for the children who seem less skilled than average in the graphic tasks when they reach school. The basic scribbling patterns presented by both Eng and Di Leo are similar to those that might be advocated as prewriting exericises for those for whom writing seems a very tense and laboured task.

Kellogg developed a general thesis from the extensive examination and analysis of her vast collection of children's art. She referred to 20 basic scribbles (see Figure 2.1), noting that some are single

Figure 2.1: Kellogg's 20 basic scribbles

Scribble 1	• ◥	Dot
Scribble 2	|	Single vertical line
Scribble 3	—	Single horizontal line
Scribble 4	\ /	Single diagonal line
Scribble 5	⌒	Single curved line
Scribble 6	⋀⋀⋀	Multiple vertical line
Scribble 7	≋	Multiple horizontal line
Scribble 8	⫽	Multiple diagonal line
Scribble 9	⌒	Multiple curved line
Scribble 10	⌁	Roving open line
Scribble 11	⌁	Roving enclosing line
Scribble 12	⌇	Zigzag or waving line
Scribble 13	ℓ	Single loop line
Scribble 14	ℓℓℓ	Multiple loop line
Scribble 15	◎	Spiral line
Scribble 16	◉	Multiple-line overlaid circle
Scribble 17	◐	Multiple-line circumference circle
Scribble 18	◠◠◠	Circular line spread out
Scribble 19	⬭	Single crossed circle
Scribble 20	◯	Imperfect circle

and some are multiple lines. She states, 'Whether the single or the multiple scribbles are the first ones to be made by the child I do not know . . . I do know that both the single and the multiple lines are made at age two and that they are used later for the purpose of art.' She refers to the 'motor pleasure' of scribble but also draws attention to the visual element, noting that either the motor or the visual element might at any stage be the primary or predominant one. Her claim is that the 20 scribbles, or their combinations and variations,

Figure 2.2: Kellogg's 17 placement patterns

PLACEMENT PATTERNS

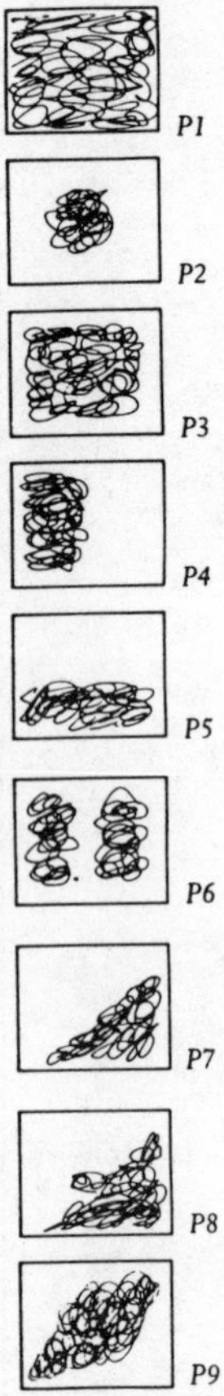

P1. Over-all. The entire paper is covered, and there may or may not be emphasis of corner or edge markings.

P2. Centered. The scribblings are centered on the paper, and they may be large or small.

P3. Spaced border. The scribblings are not necessarily centered, but there is an absence of lines along the perimeter.

P4. Vertical half. The scribblings are confined to one vertical half of the paper.

P5. Horizontal half. The scribblings are confined to one horizontal half of the paper.

P6. Two-sided balance. The scribblings are placed on one vertical or horizontal section of the paper to balance scribbles on the other side, with space between.

P7. Diagonal half. The scribblings are confined to one diagonal half of the paper.

P8. Extended diagonal half. The scribblings spill over somewhat beyond the diagonal half.

P9. Diagonal axis. The scribblings are evenly distributed on a diagonal axis so that two corners are filled and two are left empty.

Author's sketches

16

P10. Two-thirds division. The scribblings are confined to about two-thirds of the paper, or the markings on two-thirds are distinctly separated from those on the other third, or they have different characteristics of line or color.

P10

P11. Quarter page. The scribblings are confined to a quarter of the paper.

P11

P12. One-corner fan. The scribblings flare out from one corner over the center, leaving the other three corners empty.

P12

P13. Two-corner arch. The scribblings cover one of the wide edges of the page and much of the page itself, but leave two corners empty, and so the total markings give a half-circle or arch effect.

P13

P14. Three-corner arc. The scribblings leave only one corner of the paper unmarked.

P14

P15. Two-corner pyramid. The scribblings cover one of the narrow edges of the paper and converge toward the center of the edge opposite, leaving two corners empty and making a pyramidal shape.

P15

P16. Across the paper. The scribblings go from one edge to the edge opposite.

P16

P17. Base-line fan. The scribblings flare up from one edge and move toward one or both of the adjoining edges.

P17

comprise all the marks that are made by spontaneous movement with or without the control of the eyes. Vision enables the child to observe scribble and to perceive elements within it that suggest Gestalt or modifications that he might make through further drawing. She describes how the child often places one scribble over another, changing direction frequently, probably to prevent muscle fatigue, the change in direction of the scribble usually causing changes in its form.

In her analysis, Kellogg also refers to 'placement pattern' (Figure 2.2), indicating 17 positions that show the relation between drawing and the paper on which it is performed. The identification of a placement pattern is dependent on a well-defined perimeter or 'frame'; Kellogg noted that scribbles do not require eye control whilst placement patterns so obviously do. She states, 'Scribbles can occur whether or not the eye is guiding the hand. Placement patterns require both seeing and the eye's guidance of the hand.' Her three placement patterns, 'spaced border', 'horizontal half', and 'across the paper', seem particularly relevant to our discussion of handwriting. In observation of children's use and management of paper, she concluded that, in general, they prefer to place the paper so that one of the longer edges is towards them and the paper as they work upon it is wider rather than higher.

Many persons practising in the field of art are interested in handwriting and may have studied the art of calligraphy. It is suggested, however, that the links between children's spontaneous and controlled drawings and handwriting development remain tentative. If we consider the competence of children as it can be seen in spontaneous scribble or the more contrived imitation, then simple diagonal scribble, for example, is a very different task from the 'copying of a diamond' expected from the average seven-year-old. As Kellogg's theory implies, it is the extent of the eye's guidance of the hand that differentiates the two. For the teacher concerned with the writing development of young children, study of the texts to which we refer might offer further insights for her assessment and diagnosis. While reference to Kellogg's classification of scribbles and placement patterns is recommended, the teacher's milestone checklist may also be of value.

A TEACHERS' MILESTONE CHECKLIST

Wavy scribble

Circular scribble

Variegated scribble

Looser variegated scribble or combines

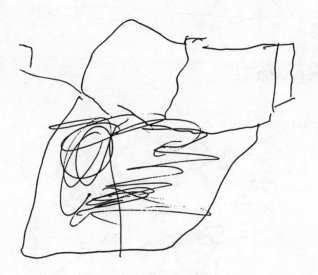

Representational drawings or aggregates

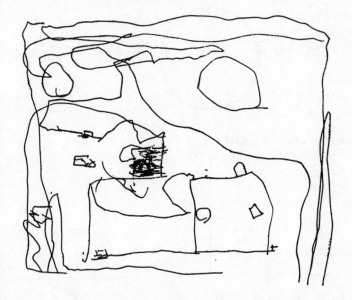

Imitating vertical line (2 years)

Imitating horizontal line (2.5 years)

21

Imitating circle (3 years)

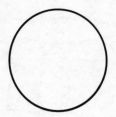

Imitating cross (4 years)

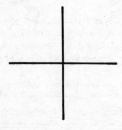

Imitating square (5 years)

Imitating triangle (5.5 years)

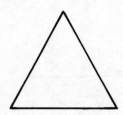

Imitating diamond (7 years)

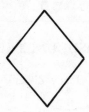

REFERENCES

Bedford, S. and Alston, J. (1987) *Helping Clumsy Children with Hand-writing: A Multidisciplinary Viewpoint*. National Council for Special Education, Stratford upon Avon.

Di Leo, J.H. (1971) *Young Children and their Drawings*. Constable, London.

Eng, H. (1954) *The Psychology of Children's Drawings*. Routledge and Kegan Paul, London.

Gesell, A. (1954) *The First Five Years of Life*. Methuen, London.

Goodnow, J. (1977) *Children's Drawing*. Open Books, London.

Griffiths, R. (1970) *The Abilities of Young Children*. Child Development Research Centre, London.

Hanson, R., Aldridge Smith, J. and Hume, W. (1985) 'Achievement of infants on items of the Griffiths scales: 1980 compared with 1950.' *Child Care, Health and Development, 11*, 91–104.

Illingworth, R.S. (1975) *The Development of the Infant and Young Child: Normal and Abnormal*, 6th edn. Churchill Livingstone, Edinburgh.

Kellogg, R. (1969) *Analyzing Children's Art*. Mayfield Publishing, Palo Alto, California.

Sheridan, M.D. (1975) *From Birth to Five Years: Children's Developmental Progress*. NFER–Nelson, Bucks.

Taylor, J. (1985) 'The sequence and structure of handwriting competence.' *British Journal of Occupational Therapy, 48* (7).

3

Pencil Grasp and Manipulation

Jenny Ziviani

A complex and perceptual motor skill such as handwriting is dependent upon the maturation of the individual's sensory-motor abilities along with appropriate instruction and guidance. While the manipulation of the handwriting implement is the most visible aspect of handwriting, it remains only one component of this intricate skill; it is, however, usually the first thing to receive attention when a child shows signs of writing difficulties, yet knowledge of the impact of different types of pencil grasps on handwriting speed and legibility remains limited. More to the point, inferential conclusions that handwriting problems are a result of an unusual pencil grasp may in some cases mask a more fundamental problem. The execution of writing, in the closed loop paradigm (Sovik 1974) is dependent upon the following: sensory reception and perception (particularly visual, tactile and kinaesthetic); motor planning and execution; and finally feedback on the basis of performance. Further, it is influenced by the child's behavioural and cognitive predisposition, as well as the quality of instruction received. Obviously, the cause of dysfunction could involve any of these factors, or more likely a combination thereof. It is the aim of this present discussion, however, to elaborate upon just one aspect of handwriting — the development and utilisation of grasp.

The manipulation of a writing implement is one of the most complex of man's prehensile skills, the foundations of which are established during infancy. At this time the child progresses from a state of being controlled by primitive reflex movement to becoming capable of highly precise grasp and release activities. This process and the resulting grasp patterns are the initial focus of this chapter. More detailed attention is then accorded the emergence of the dynamic tripod grip — the one most commonly employed for

24

writing. Its development and variations are examined for evidence of their influence on handwriting performance. Finally the interaction of grip and type of writing implement is discussed along with some practical suggestions for evaluating the contribution of pencil posture to the child's overall writing performance.

MATURATION OF GRASP

The early work of Gesell, Halverson, Thompson, Ilg, Castner, Ames and Amatruda (1940), Halverson (1931), Napier (1956) and Twitchell (1965) underpins our understanding of grasp and manipulation. While authors of developmental assessments (Bayley 1969; Frankenburg, Dodds, Fandal, Kazuk and Cohrs 1975; Knoblock, Stevens and Malone 1980) place age expectations on the various stages of grasp progression, it is probably more appropriate, in this context, to look at the transitions themselves. This makes it easier to determine which component of the developing grasp is adversely influencing or delaying progress to the next, more advanced stage. Therefore while this section traces the emergence of various grasp patterns from reflexive to voluntary control it is intended merely as a framework upon which to evaluate performance rather than a categorisation into which performance must be placed. Chronologically mature children may still demonstrate aspects of a less mature grasp that may be dysfunctional. In order to help these children, the transition into a more mature grasp needs to be understood.

Primitive reflexes

Successful voluntary prehension and object manipulation are dependent upon the adequate integration or inhibition of primitive reflexes. Primitive reflexes refer to posture or movement patterns that are elicited in response to specific stimuli. These stimuli may be gravitational, proprioceptive, tactile or auditory. The purpose of primitive movements is related to early functions such as feeding, protection and orientation to the environment (Gilfoyle, Grady and Moore 1981). Control of these reflexes is usually accomplished by 6 months of age. While there are many reflexes and variations reported in the literature (Holt 1977), it is, for our purposes, only necessary to concentrate on those that influence upper limb and eye-hand co-ordination.

At birth the infant's hand is usually fisted, and an object placed in it is held by a reflexive grasp without any voluntary prehension. Twitchell (1970) maintained that this fisting could not be isolated from the total flexion pattern of the upper extremity that is called the traction response. At this time, hand closure is accompanied by visual fixation, which is thought to be a necessary adjunct to visual motor co-ordination and subsequent visually guided movements. The palmar grasp is easily demonstrated in the neonate but fades rapidly and is seldom seen after 4 or 5 months of age. Similarly, as objects are reflexly grasped they are also quickly dropped as the avoiding response is elicited by stimulation of the finger tips causing fingers to open and abduct. These early reflex patterns provide movement experiences for which the child would otherwise not be motorically ready and lay the basis for more mature behaviour.

In a supine position, a child of 2 months is not able to bring hands to the midline. This is due mainly to the persistence of the tonic labyrinthine reflex, which causes increased extensor tone and shoulder retraction when the child is lying on his back (Fiorentino 1981). Bringing the hands to midline and finger play are important pre-requisites for developing bilateral and eye-hand co-ordination.

By 3 months, sustained regard of clasped hands at midline and bilateral activity are emerging (Erhardt 1974). Gradually the traction response subsides so the hand is no longer fisted during swiping. The grasp reflex is developing and isolated grasping of the hand without total upper extremity flexion pattern occurs. At about 5 months the traction response becomes integrated, allowing the hand to open during reaching and fix around objects using a radial-palmar grasp.

Visually directed reaching is well developed by 6 months, but its foundations are also reflexive in nature. The asymmetrical tonic neck reflex seems to play an important role in visuo-motor development. The stimulus that initiates the reflex consists of sideways turning of the head (passively or actively). The response consists of increased flexion in the arm on the occipital side and increased extension of the arm on the face side. The reflex is most evident between 2 and 4 months of age, the same time at which visual fixation on nearby objects is developing. Hence a vital link is formed between reaching and visual fixation.

Having commented upon the importance of inhibition of early reflex patterns it is necessary to point out that they do not disappear but persist in a controlled fashion throughout life. They may reappear either in stressful situations or following cerebral damage. Therefore, in children with varying degrees of impairment of the central nervous system, the influence of these primitive reflexes needs to be considered in the evaluation of prehension. It could also be argued that if a child is presented with a task for which he is not motorically ready it too could be regarded as a stressful situation. Such stress in turn will mean that more effort needs to be directed towards controlling postural reactions and thereby detracts from concentration on skill development. This points to the importance of assessing readiness for skill training on the basis of ability rather than chronological status.

Voluntary control of reach, grasp and release

Visually directed reaching or conscious control of the hand and fingers occurs from 5 months of age. However, because the infant's grasp and release patterns are not well developed at this age, movements are inefficient. Halverson (1931) described actions of under- and over-reaching along with a circuitous approach as indicative of this immaturity. It is not until between 8 and 10 months, when thumb and index finger opposition emerges, that the infant can accurately pick up objects of progressively smaller size.

Voluntary control of visually directed reach, grasp and release goes through various stages of refinement before its presentation in mature form. For example visual control of arm and hand movements is founded in the initial engaging of fingers and hands in midline. The time devoted to this behaviour by the infant is indicative of its important role. It is followed at about 5 months by fast backward swipes at objects within the visual field and grasp range, which usually are unsuccessful. It is not until 7 months (Halverson 1931) that the infant visually monitors the total movement, thus facilitating greater accuracy. From this time the process undergoes increasing refinement, which is monitored through a fairly predictable series of well-defined grasp-and-release actions. These will be elaborated upon in the subsequent section on grasp profile.

The infant's ability to voluntarily release objects does not appear until approximately 40 weeks of age, when the successful placement of an object on a surface is possible. Prior to this objects are dropped or released only because of the influence of the avoidance response (3–24 weeks), or objects being pulled out of one hand by the other (approximately 28 weeks).

27

Once able to grasp and release objects, the infant is ready to interact actively with objects in the immediate environment and refine proficiency. Simultaneously he is also learning the basics of tool use, among which drawing and handwriting will later become an important focus. Such learning involves experiencing the weight, force and size of objects (Mounond and Bower 1975), and accordingly adjusting grasp responses. Specifically in writing, which has been described as a complex serial task (Laszlo and Bairstow 1984), the child needs to 'control the force exerted by the fingers on the writing instrument and its pressure on the paper. He must be able to programme movements within strictly prescribed spatial limits, while maintaining the necessary force, and must aim at movements programmed with acceptable velocity. Thus spatial, temporal and force programming must be controlled throughout the performance of task.'

Also important is the increasingly selective nature of movements (Erhardt 1982). Involved is the inhibition of movements in those parts of the body that may be unnecessary or even disruptive to the performance of a task. For example, trunk and shoulder stabilisation is important to enable the elbow, wrist and fingers to make the necessary movement adjustments for writing. This can only really come about when the child is able to break down the total postural patterns so indicative of the primitive reflex phase. The important concept of stabilisation before mobilisation has its basis here. Having described grasp and release maturation, I shall now expand on the type of grasp profiles that emerge.

Grasp profile

Grasp refers to the ability to pick up an object with hands and fingers. It is contrasted with manipulation, which refers to the way in which objects are handled for a particular purpose or task. The grasp used for acquiring an object is dictated by both the object's configuration and the skill level of the person. By 12 months the infant has made substantial progress towards achieving the basic movement patterns needed for fine motor skills and refinement ensues from interaction with a wide variety of implements. The major stages leading to the dynamic tripod grasp (used for writing) are summarised in Figure 3.1 and are based on the work of Castner (1932), Cliffs (1979), Erhardt (1982) and Halverson (1931). It can be seen from this profile that while the hand is initially used as a means of trapping an object against a surface, before long it can independently encapsulate objects. This comes about with the development of thumb/finger opposition and culminates in the ability to perform very fine pincer grasps. The control of a pencil within such a grasp is intrinsic to the dynamic tripod grasp.

DYNAMIC TRIPOD GRASP

The development of pencil grasp in children starts with a crude palmar grasp at around 12 months and usually culminates in the dynamic tripod grasp at around 4.5 years (Rosenbloom and Horton 1971). The latter can be observed even earlier if sufficient practice is undertaken, as reported by Saida and Miyashita (1979) with a sample of Japanese children. The early introduction of chopsticks, which necessitate similar grasp patterns as pencil grip, is apparently facilitative. Similar early training in related tasks was observed in Chinese children (Sassoon 1986), who were observed to demonstrate few difficulties in producing complex Chinese characters. Whether their facility with writing is related to early fine motor experiences or the delayed introduction of writing instruction until the child has better motor readiness remains unclear. One simply recalls the suggestion of Laszlo and Bairstow (1984) that some children are not kinaesthetically mature enough to master the complexities of writing until approximately 6 years of age.

Evolution of the dynamic tripod grasp

The dynamic tripod grasp is most commonly used for writing. It involves resting the writing implement on the distal phalanx of the middle finger and controlling it between the pad of the thumb and the index finger — the hand being held in slight supination (Figure 3.2). Writing is accomplished by the action of intrinsic finger movements in co-ordination with the stabilisation of the trunk and shoulder, as well as with appropriate fixation and release at the elbow and wrist joints. It becomes obvious, therefore, that hand and finger movements are only the result of a far more complex motor sequence.

While different authors may vary in their terminology, the evolution of the dynamic tripod grip generally follows the sequence depicted in Figure 3.2. The child progresses from pronate to a more

Figure 3.1: Grasp profile (approximate ages only)

Primitive squeeze grasp
(20–24 weeks)

This is the first voluntary grasp, when object is trapped by flexed fingers against the palm and pushed against other hand or body

Palmar grasp
(24–28 weeks)

Fingers are clasped around the object, trapping it against the palm. There is no thumb opposition and object cannot usually be lifted off a surface.

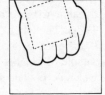

Radial palmar grasp
(28–32 weeks)

Object is still held against palm by flexed fingers but first stages of thumb opposition are used.

Superior palmar grasp
(32 weeks)

Thumb is actively opposed to the index finger and the fingers are actively used to press the object against the thumb and palm.

30

Radial digital grasp
(36 weeks)

Fingers now operate independently to the palm of the hand. Objects are also generally picked up by the fingers on the radial (thumb) side of the hand.

Inferior pincer grasp
(40 weeks)

First true fingertip grasp. Object held in first three, or sometimes four digits, with thumb actively opposing fingers. At this stage hand still needs to rest on a supporting surface.

Superior forefinger grasp
(44–60 weeks)

The wrist is extended as the object is picked up. In the latter stages does not require to place hand on supporting surface

Source: Based on Castner (1932), Cliffs (1979), Erhardt (1982) and Halverson (1931).

31

Figure 3.2: Evolution of dynamic tripod grasp

Palmar grasp
(approx. 1–1.5 years)

Crayon held in fisted hand. Arm moves as a unit.

Digital pronate
(approx. 2–3 years)

Pencil held with fingers. Wrist pronated and slightly ulnar deviated. Forearm moves as a unit.

Static tripod
(approx. 3.5–4 years)

Pencil held proximally in crude approximation of thumb, index and middle fingers. Hand moves as a unit.

Dynamic tripod
(approx. 4.5–6 years)

Pencil held with precise opposition of distal phalanges of thumb, index and middle fingers. Ring and little fingers flexed to form a stable arch. Exhibits fine localised movements of Proximal interphalangal joints.

Source: Adapted from Rosenbloom and Horton (1971) and Erhardt (1982).

supinated hold as well as diminishing surface contact with the writing implement. This is accompanied by more isolated movements (fine finger movements) instead of total arm pattern.

Variations in tripod grasp

While the ideal dynamic tripod grasp (as depicted in Figure 3.2) is espoused in most books on handwriting, numerous variations exist. They have often been linked with poor handwriting in groups of disabled children such as those with learning disabilities (Page and MacAuslan 1978) and spina bifida (Anderson 1976). However, the extent to which atypical pencil grip is the prime cause of poor handwriting remains uncertain since there is also considerable grip variation in non-handicapped populations (Ziviani 1983). Variation was found to evolve around the following: (a) the number of fingers resting on the pencil shaft, (b) the degree of forearm supination/pronation, (c) presence of thumb and finger/s pad to pad opposition, and (d) degree of index finger flexion. When these characteristics were further considered for their impact on writing speed and legibility amongst a sample of 218 children attending regular schools, there was no statistical significance among even the most abnormal patterns (Ziviani and Elkins 1986). This finding has also been supported by Sassoon, Nimmo-Smith and Wing (1986). It is therefore reasonable to suggest that while there may be a greater representation of atypical patterns of dynamic tripod posture among poor writers, it is not, on its own, a predictor of poor writing. Nevertheless, it may be that some grips are more facilitative than others. The presence of writer's cramp may signify a dysfunctional grip that is placing undue strain on specific muscle groups. More study is required to help identify the precise nature of such grips. Further, their utility in situations of varying stress, i.e. examinations, or over prolonged periods of writing needs to be addressed.

Not all 'good' writers hold their pencils in the standard way (Graham and Miller 1980). Some authors (Callewaert 1963) have even suggested that an alternative method, whereby the writing instrument is placed between the middle and index fingers, is better designed to reduce pressure and thereby minimise fatigue. Subsequent research found this grip to result in acceptable levels of speed and legibility.

Another variation, the so-called inverted hand posture (hand held above the writing line with pencil tip pointing towards the bottom of the page) has received considerable academic attention since its proposed link with cerebral specialisation by Levy and Reid in 1976. While lively debate has followed this initial work (Levy 1982; Weber and Bradshaw 1981) the point here is not so much the link with cerebral organisation but the presence of such a variation at all. Though more prevalent in left-handed writers (Shanon 1978) this pattern is also present in right-handed writers. Possibly left-handed writers are more prone to demonstrating atypical pencil grasps in an attempt to obtain a better view of their writing. The normal left-to-right progression is better suited to the right hander. Guiard and Millerat (1984) also suggest that left-handed writers usually begin by writing using a non-inverted posture. They point to the need to provide paper stability by resting the right hand below the pencil point as forcing an inverted posture to occur.

One outstanding component between grasp and writing is the instrument used, and brief reference to this topic is made in appropriate sections of this book. However, little research has been conducted on the subject and it is useful here to examine how implements can influence the grasp adopted.

MANIPULATION OF WRITING IMPLEMENTS

Distinction is drawn here between the grasp of a writing implement and its manipulation. The basis of this differentiation is function; while an implement may be picked up in one way depending on its size and shape, its utilisation may vary according to the demands of the task in question.

Writing implements

Some work has been done to examine the influence of implements on the quality of writing (Krzesni 1971). Little has been said, however, about whether or not various implements predispose changes in pencil posture. There are now an enormous number and variety of writing implements on the market, including fountain, felt-tip and ball-point pens. They all have different qualities, which can be influential in writing. First is the ease with which the implement can produce a mark. This can affect the pressure with which the pen is held. If a line can be produced with minimal effort regardless of the angle of the pen, then the writer is less likely to require constant readjustment of grasp. The new felt-tip pens offer this flexibility and should not be withheld from children if they facilitate writing. The main factor to stress here is individuality. With the vast array of pens available it is only reasonable to select one that produces the most comfortable and functional grip. By so doing it can also help to reduce unnecessary problems of muscle cramping and poorly controlled writing.

The second aspect of writing implements is the size and structure of the barrel. It has long been a practice to introduce children to writing by means of thick-barrel pencils. This is thought to best suit their level of motor ability, i.e. gross rather than fine motor control. However, while this practice may be sound for gaining experience in the control of a pencil it does not lay the foundations for the exact nature of handwriting, which necessitates finger action. Knowledge of how fine finger movements can be used to control letter formation is the basis of learning handwriting. It is probably advisable therefore to discourage any prosthetic features such as triangular moulds or built-up shafts when trying to either teach or remediate dysfunctional grips. If such features are employed then they should be only viewed as temporary.

The exterior of the barrel can also vary from being shiny and slippery to being sculptured and more resistant. It is probably only after children have gained confidence in the control of their writing implement that they can accommodate the extra control needed with the former. Introduction to more demanding writing implements too early may result in compensatory grip. A rule is that, when learning to write, children should not have their attention diverted from the task by unnecessary concentration on the implement being used. If the implement is held in a tight, awkward fashion, experimentation with other implements is probably advisable while at the same time simplifying the writing demands.

Grip evaluation: practical considerations

In the early years of writing instruction grasp immaturity may be seen in the following ways: excessive forearm pronation, lack of isolated finger movements, or the necessity to utilise three or even four fingers on the pencil shaft in order to achieve control.

While immature grasp may not cause difficulties in the early years of schooling, it may become noticeable as education requirements become more demanding. Such children may be indicating that they have not had adequate motor training as a pre-requisite to learning handwriting. Further, they run the risk of becoming 'dysfunctional writers' in later years when called upon to write at greater speeds.

Early manipulative experience is essential as a basis on which to develop adequate control of writing implements. To this extent, pre-school and kindergarten teachers have a fundamental role in determining the adequacy with which children approach the task of writing. As mentioned, children need to experiment with implements of differing size and weights as a basis for general tool use. After all, a pencil is just like any other tool. Just as children learn to thread beads or use a hammer, so they will learn to manipulate a writing implement.

There is a wide range of activities available to children in the pre-writing years that will encourage better pencil hold. While drawing and painting seem obvious choices, the use of building blocks, play-dough and threading all help develop isolated finger movements, kinaesthetic memory and basic upper-limb muscle tone. Without this preparation children cannot be expected to progress onto the motorically more demanding aspects of learning pencil control.

When considering the pencil grasp and manipulation of the 'dysfunctional writer' the focus should be upon the child and his level of ability — not on an arbitrary model of performance. Individual instruction and remedial assistance is widely recommended (Stott, Moyes and Henderson, 1986) and the objective of instruction must always remain paramount. Within an educational context, a teacher's objective is that children attain a level of writing performance that is both fast and legible in order to facilitate educational progress. Aspiration to calligraphic excellence is beyond the scope of most curricula, which are struggling to find adequate time to cover basic requirements.

Therefore, pencil grasp, being only one component of hand-writing performance, may require attention when it: (a) results in muscular tension and fatigue to the extent that the writer and writing are suffering, or (b) influences the proficiency by which writing is accomplished by impeding either letter formation or writing speed. Both these conditions are readily recognisable by teachers and need to be addressed in order to implement appropriate remedial assistance. Unfortunately, in many cases by the time they are identified motor learning has been established and re-learning needs to occur. The following points are offered by way of a practical guide when dealing with 'dysfunctional writers' exhibiting poor grasp and

36

manipulation skills.

(1) Does the child demonstrate the adequate postural and upper limb muscle tone to support the development of pencil grasp and manipulation? The child with low muscle tone may demonstrate a slouched posture when sitting, along with inadequate isolated movements. Further he may need to use more than the first three fingers to control the pencil. In the author's experience such children also show excessive joint mobility, which can be demonstrated in finger hyperextension. Assistance here needs to increase muscle tone in both upper limbs and trunk. Therapists can advise on the appropriate use of activities to help improve muscle tone. They may include compression (weight bearing) through the upper limbs, i.e. wheelbarrow races, or traction, i.e. suspending on monkey bars.

(2) The ability to perform isolated fine finger movements may also influence the pencil grasp adopted by children. When such isolated control is not evident children tend towards a more fisted grasp. There is less likelihood of thumb-index finger pad-to-pad opposition in these cases. The writing implement may be held closer to the palm and movements are primarily generated at the wrist and metacarpophalangeal joints of the hand. A prerequisite for good isolated finger movement is experience with a range of activities demanding fine manipulative control. If children have difficulty it is useful to repeat such activities. Similarly the teacher or therapist can manually guide the child's fingers by placing her/his hand over that of the child. This can provide a kinaesthetic model for the movements required.

(3) Finally concern is warranted when children show signs of developing a grip — such as the inverted hand posture described earlier — that places the hand at an anatomical disadvantage. This grip requires the muscles that flex the wrist and fingers to function at both joints concurrently. Since muscle action is more efficient if muscles are only required to function at one joint, the demands of this position mean that function will be impaired. In the case of the inverted hand posture the major action is occurring at the wrist, so making finger flexion, which is so important for the formation of letters, more difficult. This is known as active insufficiency (Soderberg 1986). This grasp may also result in more muscular fatigue as the hand remains in a state of static contraction.

In the cases mentioned above and in all conditions where pencil grasp is causing concern, the earlier intervention takes place the better. Once children have developed a motor trace for a movement it is very difficult to modify without a lot of conscious effort.

REFERENCES

Anderson, E.M. (1976) 'Handwriting and spina bifida.' *Special Education: Forward Trends, 3* (2), 17–20.

Bayley, N. (1969) *Manual for the Bayley Scales of Infant Development.* The Psychological Corporation, New York.

Callewaert, H. (1963) 'For easy and legible handwriting.' In Herrick, V. (Ed) *New Horizons for Research in Handwriting.* University of Wisconsin Press, Madison.

Castner, B.M. (1932) 'The development of fine prehension in infancy.' *Genetic Psychology Monographs, 12,* 105–91.

Cliffs, S. (1979) *The Development of Reach and Grasp.* Guynes Printing, Texas.

Erhardt, R.P. (1974) 'Sequential levels in development of prehension.' *American Journal of Occupational Therapy, 28,* 592–6.

Erhardt, R.P. (1982) *Developmental Hand Dysfunction.* Ramsco, Maryland.

Fiorentino, M. (1981) *A Basis for Sensori-motor Development.* Continuing Education Programs of America, Minneapolis.

Frankenburg, W.F., Dodds, J.B., Fandal, A.W., Kazuk, E., Cohrs, M. (1975) *Denver Developmental Screening Test.* Ladoca, Colorado.

Gesell, A., Halverson, H.M., Thompson, H., Ilg, F.L., Castner, B.M., Ames, L.B., Amatruda, C.S. (1940) *The First Five Years of Life.* Harper and Brothers, New York.

Gilfoyle, E.M., Grady, A.P., Moore, J.C. (1981) *Children Adapt.* Slack, New Jersey.

Graham, S., Miller, L. (1980) Handwriting research and practice: a unified approach. *Focus on Exceptional Children, 13* (2), 1–16.

Guiard, Y., Millerat, F. (1984) 'Writing postures in left handers: inverters are handcrossers.' *Neuropsychologia, 22* (4), 535–8.

Halverson, H.M. (1931) 'An experimental study of prehension in infants by means of systematic cinema records.' *Genetic Psychology Monographs, 10,* 107–286.

Holt, K.S. (1977) *Developmental Paediatrics.* Butterworth, London.

Knoblock, H., Stevens, F., Malone, A.F. (1980) *Manual of Developmental Diagnosis.* Harper and Row, New York.

Krzesni, J.S. (1971) 'Effect of different writing tools and paper on performance of the third grader.' *Elementary English, 47,* 821–4.

Laszlo, J.I., Bairstow, P.J. (1984) 'Handwriting: difficulties and possible solutions.' *School Psychology International, 5,* 207–13.

Levy, J., Reid, M. (1976) 'Variations in writing posture and cerebral organisation.' *Science, 194* (4262), 337–9.

Levy, J. (1982) 'Handwriting posture and cerebral organisation: how are they related?' *Psychological Bulletin, 91,* 589–608.

Mounond, P., Bower, T.G.R., (1975) 'Conservation of weight in infants.' *Cognition, 3,* 29–40.

Napier, J.R. (1956) 'The prehensile movements of the human hand.' *Journal of Bone and Joint Surgery, 38B,* 902–13.

Page, S., MacAuslan, A. (1978) 'Poor handwriting and pencil hold of learning disabled children.' *British Journal of Occupational Therapy,* *41*, 282–3.

Rosenbloom, L., Horton, M.E. (1971) 'The maturation of fine motor skills in children: manipulation of a pencil in young children aged 2 to 6 years old.' *Journal of Human Movement Studies, 5*, 104–13.

Saida, Y. and Miyashita, M. (1979) 'Development of fine motor skill in children: manipulation of a pencil in young children aged 2 to 6 years old.' *Journal of Human Movement Studies, 5*, 104–13.

Sassoon, R. (1986) 'A handwriting for life.' *Child Language Teaching and Therapy, 2*, 2–30.

Sassoon, R., Nimmo-Smith, I. and Wing, A.M. (1986) 'An analysis of children's penholds.' In Kao, H.S.R., van Galen, G.P. and Hoosain, R. (eds) *Graphonomics: Contemporary Research in Handwriting*. North Holland Press, Amsterdam.

Shanon, B. (1978) 'Writing positions in Americans and Israelis.' *Neuropsychologia, 16*, 587–91.

Soderberg, G.L. (1986) *Kinesiology: Application to Pathological Motion*. Williams and Wilkins, Baltimore.

Sovik, N. (1974) *Developmental Cybernetics of Handwriting and Graphic Behaviour*. Norwegian Research Council for Science and Humanities, Universitetsforlaget.

Stott, D.H., Moyes, F.A., Henderson, S.E. (1986) *Diagnosis and Remediation of Handwriting Problems*. Brook Educational, Ontario.

Twitchell, T.E. (1970) 'Reflex mechanisms and the development of prehension.' In Connolly, K.J. (ed) *Mechanisms of Motor Skill Development*. Academic Press, London.

Weber, A.M., Bradshaw, J.L. (1981) 'Levy and Reid's neurobiological model in relation to writing hand posture: an evaluation.' *Psychological Bulletin, 90* (1), 74–88.

Ziviani, J. (1983) Qualitative changes in dynamic tripod grip between seven and 14 years of age. *Developmental Medicine and Child Neurology, 25*, 778–82.

Ziviani, J., Elkins, J. (1986) 'Effect of pencil grip on handwriting speed and legibility.' *Educational Review, 38*, 3.

4

Graphic Development in the Early Years at School

Drawing tasks and those approximating to writing patterns and writing are usually many faceted in our infant classrooms. The teacher's attempt to encourage the child to express himself and develop in the least restrictive environment usually entails free experience with paints, crayons and similar media. There may also be a variety of tools for the experience of writing patterns and writing. We show at other points in this text that prescriptive decisions about writing tools for the handwriting task seem inappropriate, and we certainly encourage the teacher to be discriminating in the selection of writing tools for purchase and in deciding which writing tool might suit each child at each stage of his or her writing development.

Traditionally, we have considered the 'draw a person', and the wealth of data and the centrality of the 'person' concept to child development encourages us to continue this discussion. The simple concepts of 'usual' and 'unusual' rather than 'normal' and 'abnormal' will be employed, principally to avoid the value judgements that may provoke inappropriate conclusions about those children who may be slightly out of step with what can be expected but might, through general maturation or teacher help, go on to mature graphically in the usual manner.

The normal 'draw a man' has been well documented (Goodenough 1926, Goodenough and Harris 1950, Harris 1963). Kellogg (1969) adds a qualitative dimension when she states, 'Humans are not drawn from life, nor are they crude, immature stumbling efforts in art. They represent an advanced stage of the child's evolving mental capacity to create complex Gestalts.' She also supports the generally held view that ability to draw humans correlates with general intellectual maturity, the child who can draw humans in

40

great variety surely possessing sufficient ability to learn to read. Her statements imply that those who draw humans in variety and do not read need that further diagnosis that will uncover the reasons for their lack of literacy. In our current task of assessing association between drawing and writing, we have little precedent in the work of authoritative writers or researchers.

We choose here to give examples of 'draw a man' from a number of children selected as in need of extra help at infant level. The drawings were completed in response to a request that they should draw themselves. However, it becomes obvious when working with children in the five- or six-year-old age range that they do not refer to any person in the same room who might be observed but tend to draw from 'within themselves', i.e. an internalised concept of what they think 'a person' should look like; in this case, themselves. This is a later stage of representation than that inferred by Kellogg when she states, 'I find it difficult to convince adults that the child's early pictorials are not mainly based on observations of objects and persons in the child's environment.' Figures 4.1 to 4.6 show a variety of examples of 'draw a person', each of which is accompanied by comments about how the drawings might offer some information about the child's graphic development or about indicators that might alert the teacher to a need for further perusal or investigation. Although, in preceding discussion, child art theory has been considered, ensuing reference is made simply to graphic performance in children who have difficulty in accommodating to the writing requirements of school.

Andrew is a normal six-year-old who draws the human figure well, has a concept of five for finger formation, has the relative sizes of different parts of the human figure well presented, and offers evidence of motor control appropriate to his age. He writes his name well, but has not yet developed the ability to form letters of appropriate relative size. In this instance, human figure drawing and writing ability correlate well.

Paul, who is five and a half, shows his good motor control through ability to draw accurate vertical and horizontal lines and to colour in the shapes with considerable accuracy. His formation of circles for eyes and head also indicates that he can pay attention to letter shapes but the writing of his name shows that relative size of letters still eludes him.

Neil shows great inconsistency in his 'draw a man' and also in the letter formation for his own name. On his best figure, the eyes have eyeballs, the nose is a precise circle and the teeth are evenly

Figure 4.1: Andrew

Figure 4.2: Paul

presented. The body is not well formed and the legs are inconsistent, giving indication of abnormality of self concept. Certainly, for this little boy, 'draw a man' and letter formation for his name have inconsistencies that have elements in common.

Figure 4.3: Neil

Shaun is an eight year old from a limited or restricted background, and in general performance he seems to be in the lower ranges of ability. The drawing is certainly immature and there is some evidence of weak body awareness and organisation. There may be a slight tremor in the pencil strokes and the pencil-to-paper pressure is variable. The variability in pencil stroke and in relative letter size is apparent.

Raymond, at the age of five, drew his figure upside down on each of several occasions. His figure was also inverted when he drew on the blackboard placed vertical to his own upright body. Raymond was extremely immature, a little uncertain on his feet for a five year old, and immature in speech or articulation and in language. He could not write his name but made attempts at all the figures presented. Again, we have close correlation between 'draw a man' and other graphic skills.

43

Figure 4.4: Shaun

Shaun

Figure 4.5a: Raymond

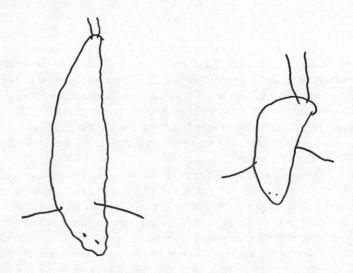

Figure 4.5b: Raymond's shape copying

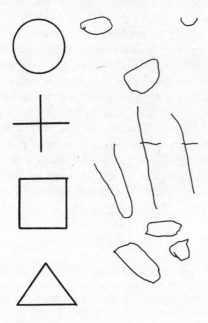

Figure 4.6: Jason

My self

I blue eies and Blond
hair and I lik mooglin
and I lick playin

45

Jason's lack of sensory-motor organisation is apparent in his disorganised 'draw a man' and in his writing. There is some evidence that when he lifts his pencil after finishing a letter, he is unsure of where to place the pencil to begin the next. At seven years of age, he is struggling to write as other children do in his class.

Bill Michael (1985) suggests that ability to draw a person should be an indicator of whether the child is ready to begin writing. He states '. . . unless the child is able to draw a clear head which relates to legs and arms there is little point in teaching writing, until the child has matured.' Taylor, however, has taught several children to write who, for some time, showed poor body concept in their drawings. Firm recommendations again seem inappropriate, and the association between 'draw a person' or other graphic skills and writing performance is worthy of further research.

REFERENCES

Goodenough, F.L. (1926) *Measurement of Intelligence by Drawings*. Harcourt, Brace and World, New York.

Goodenough, F.L. and Harris, D.B. (1950) Studies in the psychology of children's drawings. *Psychological Bulletin, 47*.

Harris, D.B. (1963) *Children's Drawings as Measures of Intellectual Maturity*. Harcourt, Brace, Jovanovich, New York.

Kellogg, R. (1969) *Analyzing Children's Art*. Mayfield Publishing, Palo Alto, California.

Michael, Bill (1985) *Letterforms*. Jordanhill College of Education, Glasgow.

5

Earlier Developments and Current Models

It is not intended that an extensive history of handwriting should be written in this context, and particular selection will be adopted in the interest of brevity. Our awareness has been considerably heightened by the writings of Prue Wallis Myers, who has so kindly made her wealth of experience available to us.

Handwriting has evolved from influences that occurred long before the Greek and Roman civilisations, and they in turn affected written forms of communication. The Romans, for example, made changes to a Greek script and, by the introduction of the wax tablet and stylus, made it possible to erase and to change so that writing might be utilised for a wider range of purposes. In Saxon and medieval times, the scribes were largely associated with the established church. The 'small' letters, i.e. miniscule, seem to have been influenced by an Englishman, Alcuin of York. Alcuin was an Anglo-Saxon who became Abbot of St Martin's of Tour (France) between 796 and 804. This was the period of development for the Carolingian Miniscule, from which the rounded 'cursive' hand that we know today developed. Charlemagne, king of the area that is now France and Germany, took both advice and writing instruction from Alcuin, and by ordering the revision of Church books in the year 789, established the status of handwriting in Western Europe.

Copperplate handwriting, a cursive, sloping, looped style, was evident in our church schools when Her Majesty's Inspectors began to visit them in 1839. It was taken into the curricula of the elmentary board schools, when they were established by the Education Act of 1870. One might observe that copperplate writing seems a somewhat sophisticated form for the young child, and changes were likely to occur as perceptive teachers observed their children writing. Jackson (1981) indicates by his illustrations that by 1906, children could be seen copying printed letters and employing slates for this practice. We shall refer to the italic hand, which preceded copperplate writing, when reference is made to the more recent advocates of the italic hand, i.e. members of the modern Society for Italic Handwriting, which was established by Alfred Fairbank in 1952.

Figure 5.1: Copperplate writing

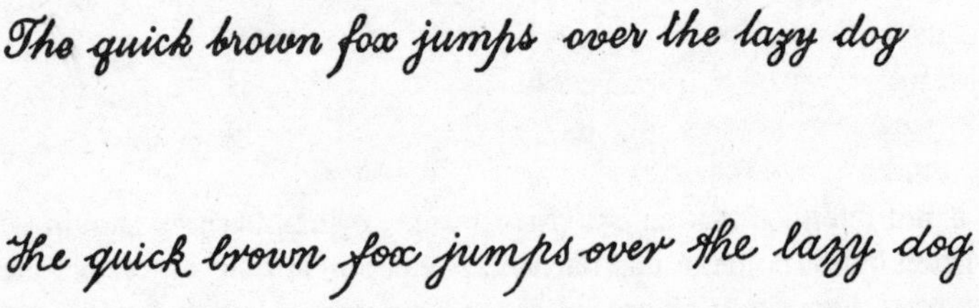

The quick brown fox jumps over the lazy dog

The quick brown fox jumps over the lazy dog

For its effect on current models, we must refer to the work of Edward Johnston (see Wallis Myers 1983) who, at the request of the London County Council, had reviewed 30 or so existing copybooks, and assessed their suitability for use with pupils in school. In fact, he rejected all that he examined and recommended that children should be first taught a skeletal letter form, which could be elaborated later by employing a broad square-nibbed pen, which would allow the writer to make thick and thin strokes. He suggested that teachers, in demonstration, should use the writing tool that the children would themselves be expected to employ. Johnson may have been somewhat misunderstood, perhaps too much emphasis was placed on his recommendation of skeletal form, and the Print Script was initiated. The Board of Education pamphlet 'Print-script' was published in 1922. Letters were to consist of straight lines, circles, and parts of circles; in its poorest form, its influences are observable as the 'ball-and-stick' print script, which can still be observed in some schools today. The promoters of print script claimed that it was closer to the print of children's reading books and, in consequence, easier to read and produce. Wallis Myers indicates that Johnston did not wish to be thought responsible for the introduction of print script because he had not been associated with the experimental work. However, Bevan (1985) suggests that his views may have been misinterpreted, and this could also be a reason why he preferred not to be associated with its introduction to schools. Child (1985) refers to a statement from Johnston, and

quotes 'I should not wish it to be thought that I was directly responsible for the form of print script characters . . . My impression is that
they are rather formless skeletons of roman l.c. It is difficult to give
and preserve form in letter skeletons except by skill and knowledge.'
Regardless of origin, the influence of print script remains in the
initial teaching of handwriting in the majority of schools in the
United Kingdom today and, in the views of some authorities on
children's handwriting, is responsible for many of the handwriting
difficulties that we observe. At the time of its growth in popularity,
print script was introduced in the United States of America by
Marjorie Wise (Fairbank 1970; Barbe, Lucas and Wasylyk 1984).
It became known as 'manuscript' and has retained its popularity as
a model for beginner writers.

Robin Tanner retained elements of the simple, rounded script, but
also looked for his inspiration to eleventh century Carolingian script,
revived by Edward Johnston. The broad-nibbed pen allowed him to
advocate what seemed to be a joined and elaborated lettering form.
An important contribution seems to be his view that pupils might be
helped to develop a cursive hand, based on traditional writing, for
general use, but also a more formal book hand in which the letters,
both lower case and capital, could be more finely finished. His
contribution to the Ministry of Education's *Handbook on Primary
Education*, published in 1959, draws attention to the errors of
introducing print script in the initial stages of writing, and refers to
the need to learn to write all over again, when the joined and cursive
form is introduced.

Figure 5.2: Robin Tanner's rounded joined script

The quick brown fox jumps over the lazy dog

Probably the most enduring modern handwriting model was
introduced by Marion Richardson. Bevan describes Richardson's
general theories on the development of young children as being
regarded as revolutionary during the 1920s and 1930s, and notes that
her publication *Writing and Writing Patterns* has endured for at least
a fifty-year period, being still in use in some schools. The influence
of the 'Civil Service Script', i.e. cursive, looped and forward
sloping, though somewhat less so than copperplate, was in the
schools, and Marion Richardson observed the children at work on
that model. She noted that little children found the looped style with

the required thick and thin strokes physically difficult to achieve. Print script was also beginning to have its influence and her observation of children employing that model led her to observe their rather staccato movements and principally to note that print script did not lead naturally to a cursive hand. The writing tool could be an added difficulty, and after advocating the use of the broad nib for her earlier Dudley Writing Cards, she later in her career suggested that young children should begin their writing patterns using chalks, thick soft pencils and crayons. The staccato movements were to be discouraged by providing younger children with large sheets of paper and encouraging them to incorporate 'rhythm and swing' in their writing and writing pattern activities. She selected six basic patterns as being those natural to the movements of the child, advocating that the patterns should be practised before, during and after the writing script had been mastered.

Figure 5.3: The Marion Richardson letter forms

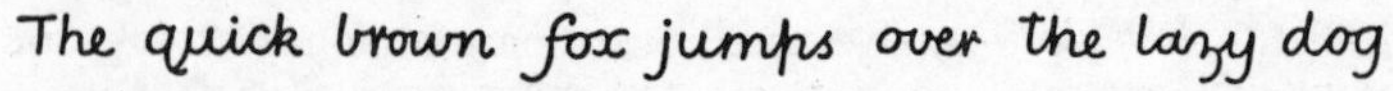

The quick brown fox jumps over the lazy dog

Marion Richardson intended her writing scheme to be employed flexibly by teachers, so that a basic form could be established from which the pupil could progress to an individualised written style. However, its critics have noted that many of the pupils retain the rather immature rounded hand long after their school days, which may be the result of the way in which the scheme is followed in school and rigidly perpetuated long after it is needed by individual pupils, i.e. when they have established a model that could be varied for their individual writing purposes. An important aspect of the scheme was that the letters taught were to be employed throughout the pupil's writing development, avoiding the change to joined script, and the difficulties that might be encountered in the process. However, Wallis Myers draws our attention to one incorrect element in Richardson's scheme, but one that influences the manner in which the pupil's running hand develops. She describes the scheme as being a hybrid in which some letter forms were poor adaptations of the roman alphabet. The letters are linked with a wide curve which '. . . the scribe avoids in the cursive hand. He knows to compress his letters and to steepen his ligatures at speed so that the tops of letter shapes — from which legibility comes — are preserved' (Wallis Myers 1983). The scheme is also described, by Wallis

Myers, as encouraging an inappropriate use of the thumb to create the broader letter-linking curve. Our attention is also drawn to Richardson's influence on the rather sprawling English 'hand' which contrasts so strongly with the sloping handwriting of those taught in schools on the Continent or in the USA. Regardless of the weaknesses of this model, however, it has many characteristics to commend it and there is some evidence (Stanton 1986) that, in a speed-writing situation, letters written in the Marion Richardson manner deteriorate less than those of several other modern handwriting schemes.

Richardson suggested, during discussion about how children might progress on her own scheme, that around the ages of 11 and 12 years some might like to try italic writing. Richardson's emphasis of pattern making has influenced most modern handwriting schemes, including those whose major influence has been from the italic hand.

An oval letter model was introduced in the Beacon Writing Scheme, and is described by Wallis Myers as '. . . a great improvement on the ball and stick letters . . .'. However, an overriding problem that pupils encounter when letter joining is introduced remains, i.e. where does the letter end and the join begin, or, more important, how does the printed or drawn shape become a fluent cursive written style.

Figure 5.4: The Beacon writing scheme

The quick brown fox jumps over the lazy dog

Alfred Fairbank (1970) offers information on the introduction and growth of italic handwriting in the United Kingdom. He describes how William Morris, the 19th century poet and craftsman, purchased a number of Italian sixteenth-century writing books, including Ugo da Carpi's version of Arrighi's 'La Operina'. Morris studied Arrighi's model and then made his own version of the italic hand. Fairbank refers us to many of the conventions of italic script, and his chapter, 'The Italic Hand of Today', is a useful introduction for the reader who has developed an interest in handwriting through contact with pupils in the classroom and may be unaware of the conventions of the italic script. He informs us, for example, of the following:

The learner must hold the pen so that the thinnest stroke the pen makes runs up to the right at an angle of 45 degrees (but not less) to the writing line.
The italic letters are not so wide as roman or print script letters and their proportions are not related to the square or the circle. The letter 'o' is elliptical.
The simplest letters . . . end with a narrow bend (not a point) and the stroke upwards stops as soon as it becomes a hairline.

In 1970, he predicted a growth in popularity of the italic script, claiming it as traditional, sensible and pleasing.

Tom Gourdie's simple modern hand is based on the Italic style. In his text *The Sheaffer Handwriting and Lettering Book* (1981), referring first to the roman hand, he describes italic as being the first completely integrated style to emerge after fifteen-hundred years or so. He describes it as a purely natural style, based on the natural scribble of the hand and including only those ligatures that can be made naturally. He writes:

Italic Writing is a most practical hand for it comprises between a totally joined and a totally unjoined script. It takes into consideration the limit of the movement of the hand — to about three letters or so. Joins or breaks, therefore, occur only where expedient.

He refers to the room for variation in the practice of the italic style. His own modification, the simple modern hand is, he claims, especially devised for those who wish to write with a modified italic hand, using a ball-point pen or other modern writing instrument. A few principles form the basis of what he prescribes:

(a) the basic alphabet emerges from the simplest scribble pattern of the hand,
(b) only three of the 26 letters of the alphabet require two strokes, all the rest being single stroke letters,
(c) unnecessary loops are avoided and
(d) pen lifts occur only where expedient.

Gourdie recognises the calligraphers' convention when he suggests that capital letters should be only three-quarters as tall as the ascenders of small letters.

Figure 5.5: The simple modern hand

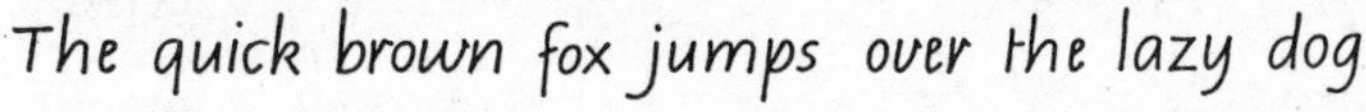

The quick brown fox jumps over the lazy dog

Christopher Jarman's basic modern hand has many of the elements advocated by Gourdie and is based upon a number of principles from the Italic style. In stage one of his writing scheme (1979), he elects to place exit ligatures on *l* and *t*, and his letters are oval and sloping slightly forward from the vertical. Ligatures or hooks are added at stage two, prior to joining. Joins are advocated only as appropriate for ease of word construction, with the letters *b, g, j, p, s* and *y*, without joins to the letters that follow them. He states the following principles as being of importance for legibility and a fluent hand:

(a) letters start and finish in the correct places,
(b) similar letters should be of even height,
(c) downstrokes should be parallel.

Figure 5.6: Jarman's Basic Modern Hand

The quick brown fox jumps over the lazy dog

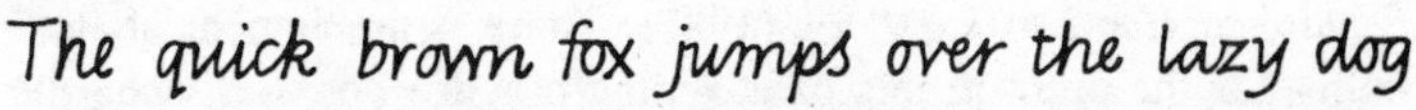

The dyslexia movement, e.g. The Dyslexia Institute, in Britain, advocate the use of cursive writing as a basis for their multi-sensory programme. This general principle was, of course, the rule of copperplate writing and the Civil Service round hand. Many children with specific reading, writing and spelling difficulties have considerable spatial and directionality difficulties. When they lift the writing tool from the paper, they may be uncertain of where it should be placed when they begin the next letter or word. In order to assist such chidlren, a constant is developed, i.e. that all letters begin on the line, and develop into the conventional letter movement from that point. Although it could be considered that there are some redundant movements with such an approach, some of the children we are discussing are extremely handicapped and, for them, the approach is often helpful.

Tom Barnard, supported by the Educational Services Department of Platignum, has talked to large numbers of teachers, across a wide geographical area of the United Kingdom. His script shows a number of influences from both Marion Richardson and italic

53

Figure 5.7: Structured cursive writing (Hickey, unpublished data; Chasty and Phillips)

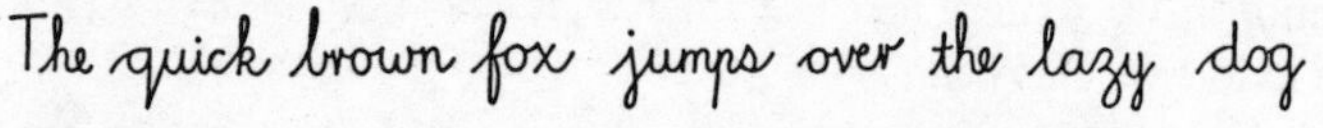

The quick brown fox jumps over the lazy dog

models. He presents writing patterns largely based on those of Marion Richardson and the initial letters that he advocates are also similar to, though somewhat 'squarer' than hers. He then moves the pupil to a slightly forward sloping script. Entry and exit strokes are attached to all letters that will, as the pupil progresses, comfortably join, and he draws the pupils attention to some of the commonly accepted principles:

(a) Try to keep all the down stokes level with a slight slope to the right,
(b) Make the rounded letters egg shaped,
(c) Keep the different parts of the letters in their correct spaces,
(d) Notice how the letters start and end.

One of his publications of the 1980s is aptly entitled *The Old Fashioned Handwriting Book* (1981). There is an element of flexibility for the pupil in this handwriting practice booklet, when the alternatives of pointed or rounded entries into letters such as *m* and *n*, and the options of open or closed *b* and *p* are presented.

Figure 5.8: Tom Barnard's model

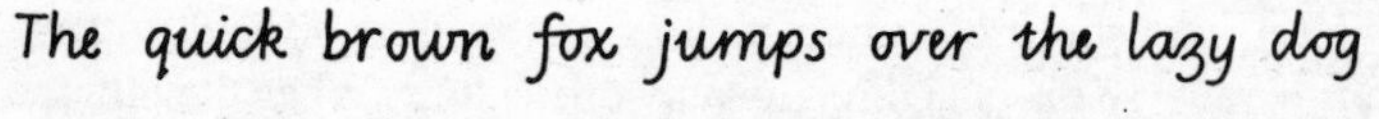

The quick brown fox jumps over the lazy dog

New Nelson Handwriting (Smith and Inglis 1984) has its early stages based on print script. Its authors offer little information about how its principles might have been based in handwriting traditions, and the emphasis of attention is upon letter direction rather than body movement, balance or posture. For the joining of letters, our attention is drawn to the importance of the 'swing pattern' as the important element of most joins or ligatures. This is in contrast to the insistence on the 45° join advocated by those who support use of the italic hand.

The authors offer little research evidence or authoritative statement in support of many of their recommendations. Advice is offered about paper position, lined or unlined paper, and the special needs of left handers, for example. All have received considerable attention from writers and researchers in recent years but there is little evidence that conclusions from research evidence were noted when the scheme was constructed.

In favour of the 1984 Nelson scheme, it can be said that its model is based upon the first Nelson scheme, published in 1961, and the publishers claim considerable consultation with schools when the earlier scheme was in use. The five 'rules for joining' are clearly stated, i.e. so that the rules can refer to the letters that have been grouped according to starting and finishing points. The authors acknowledge the individuality of pupils' development in handwriting skill and encourage the teacher to manage the programme of pupils from early print script through to the introduction of 'shaded' writing, by use of the straight-edged or 'broad nib', and then to encourage individual style. The comprehensive nature of the scheme and its promotion by an experienced publisher has ensured its wide adoption by schools in the United Kingdom.

Figure 5.9: New Nelson handwriting

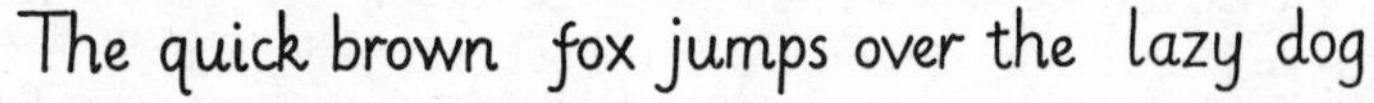

The quick brown fox jumps over the lazy dog

DEVELOPMENTS IN THE USA

Gourdie (1981) writes, 'There is no difficulty in recognising writing emanating from the United States,' claiming that the Spencerian system of the 19th century has had its influence through Palmer and Zaner Bloser type teaching. However, informal discussion with teachers from Illinois suggests that '. . . different states, even different school districts, have different programs . . .' and leads us to conclude that the Spencerian influence may be less evident than in former years.

The Palmer handwriting model, with its emphasis on use of the whole arm for looped cursive writing, is still central to the hand-writing curriculum in some schools. Readers should refer to atten-tion given to the Palmer model in the reference to New Zealand research (Chapter 13) and can consider its characteristics in the context of handwriting development in the two geographical areas.

Zaner-Bloser handwriting is also popular in the USA. Referring particularly to the manuscript alphabet, its advocates (Barbe *et al.*

1984) state: 'The Zaner-Bloser alphabet is the most widely used and accepted alphabet in the United States.' In their 1984 text they trace the historical development of writing style, review the research relating to efficiency through speed and legibility, and weigh the evidence, before presenting the model they advocate. The reader is then informed that:

> The manuscipt alphabet students learn in the classroom today is similar to the style used by ancient Romans. The letters that decorate the rooms predating the birth of Christ could be identified by students who have learned manuscipt.
>
> The ease of acquisition, legibility, and the fact that the letters resemble the type used in most readers are just a few reasons why manuscript is so popular in schools today.

We are informed that the six basic strokes — horizontal, vertical, backward circle, forward circle, slant right and slant left — form the building blocks of manuscript writing and that competence in formation of the basic strokes is essential before letter formation is taught. The script has considerable resemblance to the 'ball and stick' approach and as we are offered the information that 'The vertical stroke is always made from top to bottom, except in the upper case letter U, which contains a push-up stroke,' we can conclude that d is also intended to be formed beginning at the top of the ascender. The authors' claim that the entire alphabet is made up using the basic six 'building blocks' indicates how this model contrasts with those that emphasise the rhythmic aspect and continuity of movement in writing.

Detailed information for handwriting instruction is presented, with recommendations for consideration such as 'Horizontal strokes are best made with good arm movements. The stroke should never be made using only finger movement.' A valuable aspect of what these writers recommend is the claim that the six basic strokes are also the criteria for evaluation and that this, because of its simplicity, assists accurate self evaluation.

Although a case for continuing manuscript writing in the later years in school is presented at different points of this text, the writers recognise the demands for a cursive script from pupils, teachers and parents. They advocate a forward sloping, looped, joined style, with considerable flourishes or redundant forms on capital letters. (Readers should note that the Faas checklist, referred to in Chapter 9, has its items based on the Zaner-Bloser cursive model.) The authors emphasise the importance of developing rhythm and fluency for those who wish to master cursive writing skill and note that illegible cursive writing can sometimes lead to irredeemable errors in communication. The movements, slant curve, undercurve, downcurve and overcurve are emphasised as important for competent cursive writing. The student writer is advised that as each letter form is mastered, more speed can be applied. He is warned, however, that speed should not exceed that at which legibility can be maintained and that 'Writing eighty letters per minute is praiseworthy only when the letters are correctly formed.'

Publicity for *D'Nealian Handwriting* (Thurber 1987) includes comments on pupils' responses to the scheme from teachers across the USA. Supportive views are presented, for example, from Texas, Georgia, Michigan, New York, California and Minnesota, i.e. areas widely geographically representative of the USA. A history of hand-writing is presented in the publisher's publicity and reference is made to a wide range of research. The publishers, Scott, Foresman, then conclude that 'D'Nealian Handwriting represents a return to practical, sensible handwriting by offering a new manuscript alphabet featuring a unique continuous stroke and simple joining strokes which make transition to cursive easy.' They see the strength of the script as lying in its emphasis upon the modern need for attention to movement and also in the aspects that reflect a return to the best centuries of traditional cursive penmanship.

Donald Thurber is the initiator of D'Nealian script and makes the following statements about its emphases:

(a) most letters are formed with one continuous stroke, so that rhythm, an essential ingredient in cursive writing, is built in from the beginning;
(b) manuscript letters are slanted, as cursive letters are;
(c) the manuscript that has been learned is not unlearned but, rather, built upon.

In common with other cursive beginner scripts, curved exit strokes are attached to all letters except *b, f, g, j, o, p, r, s, v, w, y* and *z*. Once letter form is established, most manuscript letters become cursive by addition of simple joining strokes. With both beginner and cursive scripts, capital-letter formation is delayed until formation of the lower case letters is well established. The cursive capital forms of *a, m* and *n* are enlarged editions of their lower-case counterparts. It is difficult to see, then, why the capital manuscript forms of *A, M* and *N* are introduced as beginner capital letters. However, this seems to be a small inconsistency in an otherwise consistent handwriting scheme. The flexibility of this scheme is emphasised when Thurber states 'There is no one right time to begin cursive . . . Those children who aren't ready for cursive by the end of the first grade should stay with manuscript until it is mastered.'

Individuality in handwriting is emphasised throughout the scheme, so that whilst attention is paid to letter form, slant, size, spacing and rhythm, it is realised that, other than in the letter form itself, each individual may bring his own characteristics to the writing task. When attention is paid to slant, for example, 'normal' slant is described as being 15° to 20° to the right. However, Thurber accepts that forward or backward slant may be characteristic of the writer; only variable or inconsistent slant is the one to be avoided. In general, the claim is made that, 'If teachers look for consistent slant, size and spacing in children's writing, legibility will develop.'

Thurber makes statements with which some readers will disagree. When referring to grip, he writes, 'There's little that can be done about grip . . . the teacher will not be able to change it much.' He does correctly state, however, that '. . . there is no firm research that establishes what "proper" grip is.' However, he also advocates that left handers who twist or hook the hand should also be left alone. Readers will note that the research by Guiard and Millerat (Chapter 8) leads us to suggest that with correct posture and paper position in the early writing stages, it may be possible to prevent the development of the hooked grip on the writing tool. Those concerned with teaching handwriting are now becoming more aware that aspects of the writing task depend on a complexity of circumstances and that grip and writing slope, for example, can be influenced by writing posture, paper position, degree of shoulder stability and degree of tone or tension in the muscles of the arm and hand.

REFERENCES

Barbe, W.B., Lucas, V.H, Wasylyk, T.M. (1984) *Handwriting: Basic Skills for Effective Communication*. Zaner-Bloser, Columbus, Ohio.

Barnard, T. (1979) *Handwriting Activities* (Books 1 and 2). Ward Lock, London.

Barnard, T. (1981) *The Old Fashioned Hand-Writing Book*. Ward Lock, London.

Bevan, C. (1985) Belles letters: Marion Richardson. *Times Educational*

Supplement, 31st May.

Chasty, H. and Phillips, M. (1981) *Structured Cursive Writing*. Ann Arbor, Michigan.

Child, H. (Ed.) (1985) *The Calligrapher's Handbook*. Black, London

Fairbank, A. (1970) *The Story of Handwriting*. Faber and Faber, London.

Gourdie, T. (1981) *The Sheaffer Handwriting and Lettering Book*. Sheaffer Pen, Textron.

Jackson, P. (1981) *The Story of Writing*. Studio Vista/Parker Pen Co.

Jarman, C. (1977) 'A helping hand for slow learners.' *Special Education: Forward Trends, 4* (4).

Smith, P. and Inglis, A. (1984) *New Nelson Handwriting*. Nelson, Walton-on-Thames, Surrey.

Stanton, D. (1986) 'An examination of the relative importance of speed and legibility in the handwriting of eleven-year-old children.' Unpublished dissertation, Crewe and Alsager College of Higher Education.

Thurber, D.N. (1987) *D'Nealian Handwriting*, Second Edition. Scott, Foresman, Glenview, Illinois.

Wallis Myers, P. (1983) 'Handwriting in English education.' *Visible Language*, *XVII* (4).

6

Causes of Poor Handwriting

Handwriting problems may have their origin intrinsic to the child, i.e. they may be caused by the child's physical characteristics or problems, or they may be caused by external factors such as poor teaching methods or the provision of inappropriate equipment or furniture. The different causal or associated aspects may not be easily discerned by the casual observer but some attempt to alert the teacher, parent or the child himself to possible problem areas or pitfalls is attempted here. Examples of the drawing and handwriting samples of children experiencing particular difficulties are presented to illustrate the discussion. Some suggestions for possible teaching procedures are offered.

Rebecca at the age of six, shows how she can draw with precision, yet her writing is poorly spaced and often illegible (Figure 6.1). The teaching of correct movements for letter formation and a clear indication that each letter has a relationship to other letters and to the writing base line would help her to resolve her problems. Instruction on the grouping of letters according to the common movement patterns would help her to place *b* and *d* in different letter movement groups and reduce the considerable confusion that she shows in her writing. Rebecca seems to have received inadequate teaching for the early stages of her writing development.

Marie aged nine, has been given lines. Her problem seems to be that she cannot place her letters upon them and that, in general, she has difficulty in forming shapes and letters in the manner in which she intends (Figure 6.2). At the beginning of each line of writing, she tends to place her letters more closely to the base line than she is able as she progresses along it. In her first line of writing, she is also able to begin at the beginning of the line but is less able to do so as the script progresses. These two observations and her own

Figure 6.1: Rebecca's drawing and writing

discussion about her problems indicate that she is well aware of what she intends to do but is often unable to achieve the motor performance intended. At the time of completing the writing, her reading age is in the region of seven and a half years, which leads us to suggest that if she has perceptual problems, they are not so severe that they impede her reading greatly. Because she has severe problems in carrying out intended drawing and writings tasks, her concentration is being diverted from the writing content and for that reason it is difficult to help her reach her full reading and writing potential. Observation of the incorrect manner in which many of her letters are formed shows that she needs precise instruction in this area. An extra guideline to help her to limit the lower case 'x' height sections of her letters would help her to improve her work. Although typewriters should rarely be introduced early in a child's education, Marie might benefit from the use of one, especially when she reaches secondary school. Word processing, now available in many primary schools, gives added benefit.

Andrew is eight years of age and, in this piece of writing, gives us much information about his friend (Figure 6.3). Apart from being in need of instruction about breaking his script into sentences, he needs help with classifying his letters according to size. In Andrew's script, r, t, h and i are of similar height and show no difference between 'x' height letters and those with ascenders. A containing line for 'x' height letters would help him to differentiate the letter groups for size, and additional instruction would help him to pay attention to the spaces between words. Andrew's s is unnecessarily

61

Figure 6.2: Marie's writing

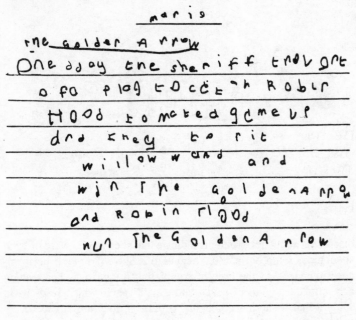

tall and shows the common fault of children who have difficulty in recognising that *s* is the only 'x' height letter that requires a change in direction within the 'x' height. Instruction that *s* begins in the same place as *c* but that it is first important to make a tiny *c* before changing direction usually helps them to resolve this problem. Andrew will eventually need help in differentiating between lower case and capital letters in the general script. However, there is a limit to the amount of information that can be absorbed by each pupil within a specific period of time. Teaching objectives, for children with a number of difficulties, should be placed in order of priority, and introduced as each child is able to deal with them, i.e. when objectives given greater priority in the teaching programme have been mastered.

Paul, at the age of nine, had writing that deviated badly from the baseline and his spelling was poor (Figure 6.4). By drawing a retaining line in his ordinary exercise books, to show him where the 'x' height letters should reach, he quickly improved his writing, spaced his words more appropriately, and even improved his spelling.

Figure 6.3: Andrew writes about his friend

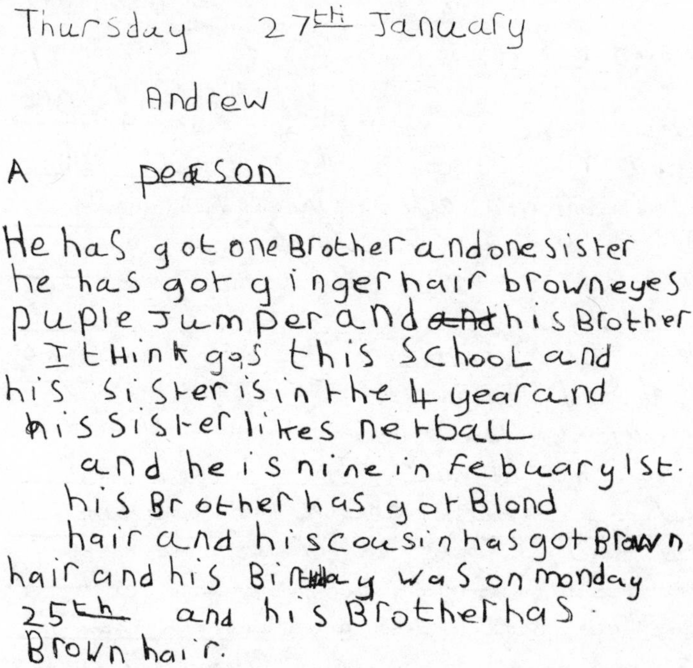
Thursday 27th January

Andrew

A person

He has got one Brother and one sister he has got ginger hair brown eyes puple Jumper and and his Brother I think gos this School and his sister is in the 4 year and his sister likes netball and he is nine in febuary 1st. his Brother has got Blond hair and his cousin has got Brown hair and his Birthday was on monday 25th and his Brother has Brown hair.

Figure 6.4: Paul, aged nine, has writing and spelling difficulties

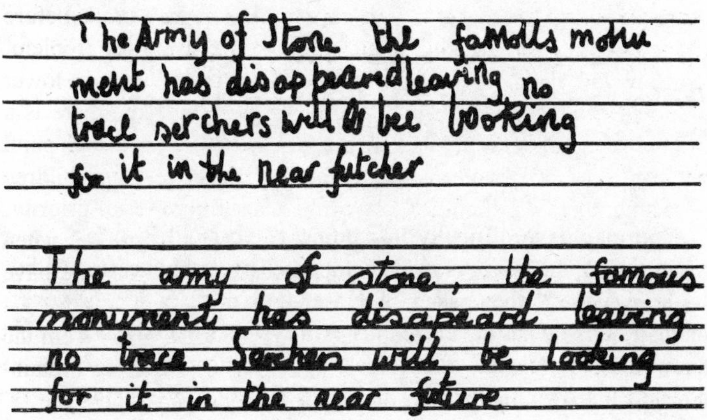
The Army of Stone the famolls monu ment has disappeared leaving no trace serchers will be looking for it in the near futcher

The army of stone, the famous monument has disapeard leaving no trace. Serchers will be looking for it in the near future

Figure 6.5: Peter's writing

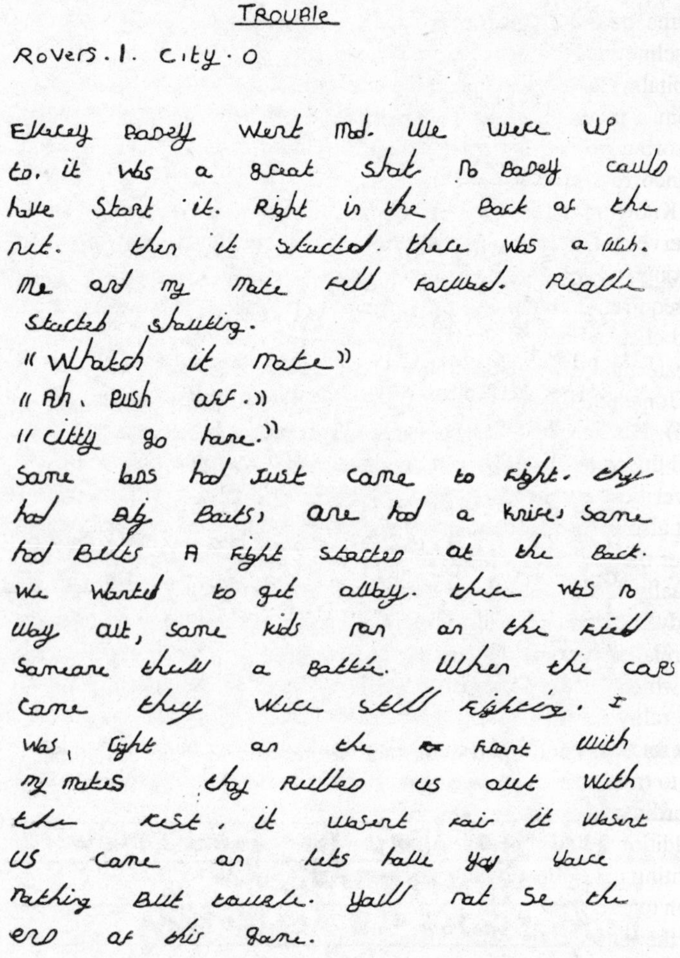

TROUBle

RoVers . 1 . City . 0

Elkcey Bovey went Mod. We were up to. it vas a great stat ro Bovey could have Start it. Right in the Back of the net. then it stacked. there vas a ruh. Me and my mate fell faulted. Really stacked shauting.

"Whatch it mate"

"Ah. push off."

"citty go hane."

Same boos had rust came to fight. they had big Bouts; one had a knife same had Belts A fight stacked at the Back. We wanted to get allby. there was ro way out. same kids ran on the rield Sameone threw a Bottle. When the cars came they were still fighting. I was, fight on the front with my mates they rulled us out with the rest. it wasent rair it wasent us came an lets talk you have nothing But touble. youll rat se the erd of this game.

You may have difficulty in reading 13-year-old Peter's writing (Figure 6.5); the teachers in his comprehensive school certainly did. 'Is he dyslexic?' they asked. A closer look at his work, however, indicates that he has developed his own system of cursive script. He knew that his friends did 'joined up' writing and was eager to develop his own. However, he seems to have missed instruction about cursive writing in school. It is not clear whether he was absent during instruction or whether he attended a primary school where cursive writing was not taught. A closer look at the script shows that he has developed his own joining system and when in doubt returns to the baseline, moves his pen along it and then leads from the baseline into the next letter. His *o*s appear like *a*s, his *d*s are often capitals, and all *p*s stand on the line. The piece written here is copied from a textbook and indicates that he can read or to some extent absorb a printed text, hold the information in mind, and then copy it incorrectly.

Knowing that the writing is difficult to read, how can the teacher intervene? Precise observation of Peter's difficulties, if necessary through use of a handwriting checklist (e.g. Alston and Taylor 1984) is required. Principally, the formation of each letter has to be taught and checked before the specific letter entry and exit strokes, which create ligatures for cursive writing, can be attempted.

Jonathan, at the age of six, has directionality problems (Figure 6.6). His general ability is in the considerably above average range and this is reflected in his conversation and attempts at writing. The severity of his directionality problems is reflected in his free writing but also in his presentation of the dictated sentence 'The bad dog ran after the red bus'. The child with directionality problems in writing usually has a weak awareness of sidedness in relation to his own body, has not internalised verbal labels for the placement of items in relation to the body, and is unsure of how to refer to the directions in which his own body or those of others turn. Body awareness and laterality normally form the basis of directionality for writing. It is not uncommon for children below the age of seven to reverse letters or to transpose them in words. However, Jonathan's problems seem inordinate for his good level of ability and general performance. Additional help in the form of a green cross on the left side of the writing page and a red circle on the right, might help. Early progression to cursive writing often reduces difficulties and verbal rehearsal of the letter movement patterns will often assist children who have problems.

Although the writing samples presented in this section show problems emanating from different areas of handwriting development and teaching, they have in common the fact that at some stage of the teaching process, the child's own development of handwriting skill has been lacking. The problems indicated as we peruse the samples are:

Figure 6.6: Jonathan has letter and line directionality problems

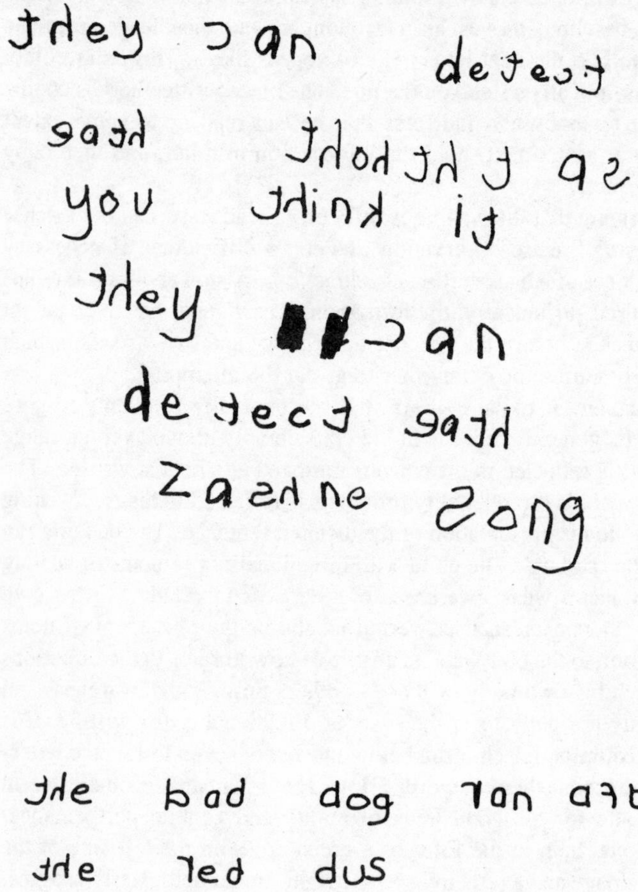

(1) poor letter formation,
(2) uncertainty of the direction each letter should take as it is formed,
(3) poor motor accuracy or inability to form letters as intended,
(4) poor motor accuracy or inability to place letters on the line,
(5) an inability to relate letters to each other in terms of size and grouping,
(6) irregular spacing between letters,
(7) lack of knowledge of how letters should be joined to each other,
(8) lack of spacing or irregular spacing between words.

The listed problems refer principally to the mechanical motor task of handwriting. However, it is important to realise that attention to basic handwriting skills, both for the early stages of handwriting development and during changes in demands throughout school life, is essential if the complex skill of writing for general purposes is to develop.

REFERENCE

Alston, J., Taylor, J. (1984) *Handwriting Checklist*. Learning Development Aids, Wisbech, Cambridgeshire.

7

Paper for Writing: Research and Recommendations

J. George Pasternicki

PAPER SIZE, POSITION AND COLOUR

The choice of lined or unlined paper has tended to be the predominant issue in discussion about writing paper selection in recent years. However, although the selection of lined or unlined paper for children's writing will be discussed at some length, there are, of course, several other characteristics that are worthy of attention. Some practitioners now advocate, contrary to more traditional practice, that the greater length of each sheet for writing should be placed horizontal to the child's view rather than vertical. Lancaster (1986) advocates this particular policy for the early stages of writing in the primary school, Richards (1980) publishes horizontally lined file paper of a ten-by-eight inch dimension in her 'Attack' phonic reading and writing scheme, and Alston (1985) advocates paper of short vertical dimension for short-statured physically handicapped children. Reasons for advocating that paper for writing should be placed with its greater length horizontal are primarily to encourage the left-to-right direction of both eye movement and writing but also so that young and short-statured children can reach easily to the top of the paper. However, some children may have limited reach in the horizontal dimension, and the perceptive teacher will also take this characteristic into account.

Taylor, in 1979, developed her writing practice booklet in A5 size, but with the longer dimension vertical, so that it could be placed in a position that would allow the writing hand to be in an optimum position on the paper for as long a period as possible while the child is writing. She observed that many children begin to write at the top of the page, gradually working down the page, without changing the position of paper or booklet on the writing surface.

68

When this occurs, the hand and arm move nearer to the body and the elbow is no longer supported on the writing surface. These children do not appear to have learnt that it is better to move the paper up so that the arm can retain its well-supported position, and the manageable size of Taylor's booklet, giving a facility for moving its position, is intended to assist them.

Irlen (1983) refers to the existence of a specific visual dysfunction, 'scotopic sensitivity', which occurs when the image has been focused on the retina. It affects those who are excessively sensitive to light and is particularly apparent in fluorescent lighting. She suggests that glossy paper should be avoided and that it can be beneficial to present reading material on coloured paper, suggesting that blue, green, pink, buff and yellow are appropriate for the purpose. The work has, at present, been extended principally to reading. However, its application to the paper on which pupils write is apparent and is worthy of attention as a subject for research.

It is also apparent to most sophisticated writers that paper quality and finish affect the quality of writing. Certainly those responsible for partially sighted children concern themselves with degree of matt or shiny finish, the complementary aspect of lighting, and the manner in which light is directed towards the paper.

LINED OR UNLINED PAPER?

Teachers of handwriting remain undecided about whether lined or unlined paper should be used when teaching the skill to beginner writers. Jarman (1979) points out that the debate about paper type has prevailed for more than 400 years. The issue in question relates to two opposing views: the first maintains that unlined paper takes account of the beginner writer's lack of fine muscular co-ordination, the second considers that lined paper assists in the acquisition of a well-aligned script that is of an acceptable size.

The supporters of unlined paper consider its use is essential with beginner writers as it compensates for the younger child's poor fine motor control and it also assists in encouraging the child to move the larger arm muscles rather than just the fingers, and this helps to reduce fatigue. Further to this, there are educators who feel that the presence of lines on paper actually inhibits the beginner writer because the size of his writing needs to be predetermined and this may lead to an undesirable and unnatural conformity of script.

Advocates of lined paper view it as an essential in assisting the pupil to learn to write in a straight line, in a script that is of an acceptable size and so that he can be taught the relative position of each letter to other letters. Lines are then seen as having three purposes; they are direction indicators, height controllers or boundaries, and assist with relative letter positioning but can leave the child free to decide on the size of his writing. Once established, many believe that these conventions also leave the child free to write in a productive and creative manner.

The support that each of these views receives from the literature is now examined.

Support for unlined paper

Most of the support for using this paper type with beginner writers is found in textbooks concerned with teaching the subject. It is the view of Gordon and Mock (1960) that the use of lined paper for handwriting is '. . . not only uninspiring, but by its drab monotony it is conducive to corresponding characteristics in handwriting'.

Inglis and Connell (1964) consider that it is '. . . general practice in infant rooms to use blank paper for all forms of writing exercises, as it enables the child to write freely and rhythmically letters of a size in keeping with his stage of neuromuscular development'. The authors have strong feelings about the use of lined paper, in particular multiple lines, when they state '. . . there is some evidence to show that . . . writing by multiple line rulings hinders the development of the ability to appreciate and write letters of the correct relative size'.

Inglis and Connell consider that the advantages of using unlined paper outweigh those of using lined paper and state, in support of their view: 'Not only does its [unlined paper's] use facilitate the development of correct size and spacing of letters and words, but children using it find pleasure and satisfaction in their work. They welcome the emancipation from the restriction of lines and the freedom to set out their work according to their own tastes and abilities.' Unfortunately, Inglis and Connell present neither the source of their evidence nor the method by which they determined children's 'pleasure and satisfaction' in their own work.

The Bullock Committee (Department of Education and Science 1975) supported the widespread use of unlined paper in schools in no uncertain terms by stating that '. . . the paper on which children are to write should always be unlined and of sufficient size to be unrestricting'. In the opinion of Smith (1977), lines may act as more of a hindrance to pupils learning to write as they impose a set of restrictions to the writing. Smith feels that some pupils have difficulty in regulating the size of their letters to conform to the spacing between the lines. In his opinion: 'Given plain paper and a sensibly tolerant teacher most children can obtain satisfaction from their early attempts at writing print-script.'

Jarman (1979) agrees with the use of unlined paper by young children when allowing them to practice writing as he feels that they can only '. . . concentrate upon one aim at a time . . .' and the aim, in his opinion should be '. . . forming the letters with the correct hand movements initially . . .' Graves (1983) considers that unlined paper helps the beginner writer to '. . . learn space . . .'

Support for lined paper

Presland (1971) feels that lined paper can be used advantageously with young pupils as it can help them to place different letters in the correct relationships to each other vertically. Jarman (1979) does lend some support for the use of lined paper and feels that for children below the age of seven years, the lines should be at least 15 mm apart in order to prevent cramping of writing. He feels that it is not the line upon which the writing rests that causes problems in handwriting development, but the line above the writing.

In an early study comparing the effects of paper type on the handwriting of young children, Burnhill, Hartley, Fraser and Young (1975) showed that six- and seven-year-old pupils improved the legibility of their story writing when using lined paper rather than unlined paper. Teachers of the children who participated in the study felt that the overall structure of the pupils' work had improved with use of lined paper. For a number of these teachers, the improvements in legibility were so impressive that they changed classroom policy to include use of lined paper by their pupils.

A later study by Burnhill, Hartley and Davies (1980) examined the effect that use of lined paper has on the creativity and legibility of young pupils' writing. In this study 56 children with a mean age of 7.2 years were required to write two stories (the titles were provided). One story was written on one type of paper, the second story was written on the other type of paper. The resulting stories were photocopied so that the blue/green feint lines were obliterated and were then judged for legibility by ten undergraduate certificate of education students. The results were supportive of the earlier study; 75 per cent of stories written on lined paper were rated more legible, 5 per cent were rated as more legible when written on unlined paper, and for 20 per cent it was considered that use of lined or unlined paper made no difference. The results also indicated that for most measures of creativity, there was no significant difference between the use of either lined or unlined paper.

The effects of lined and unlined paper on the writing ability of young children have been further examined by Lindsay and McLennan (1983). In their study, 101 children at four age levels within the primary school (mean ages, 6.2 years, 7.2 years, 8.4 years, 9.2 years) were required to write two pieces of free writing. The titles were provided. Half of the children wrote their first story on lined paper, with the second story being written on unlined paper; the remaining half completed these arrangements in the opposite order. The resulting stories were all photocopied so that evidence of lines was removed from the paper. Five experienced educationalists were asked to rate each story for both creativity and legibility. Legibility ratings consisted of deciding which of the two pieces of work was the more legible. Four measures of creativity were used. The results indictated that legibility shows an interaction with both paper type and also the age level of the child; stories written by the youngest age group (mean age, 6.2 years) on unlined paper were rated as the most legible. The opposite relationship held for the oldest group — their work was more legible when written on lined paper. Neither paper type was found to be superior for the seven- and eight-year-old groups, and Lindsay and McLennan consider that this age range may act as a changeover period with neither lined nor unlined paper being superior. Creativity was found to be unaffected by either paper type for each of the four age groups.

In a further study that examined the effects of paper type on the creativity and legibility of young children's writing, Pasternicki (1984) also looked at possible relationships between creativity and reading ability, and between manual co-ordination and legibility.

Eighty children at four different age levels (mean ages, 6.8 years, 8.4 years, 9.4 years, 10.2 years) wrote two pieces of free story writing; both story titles were provided. Within each age level, half the children wrote the first story on unlined paper and the second on lined paper; the other half wrote the stories in opposite order of paper type. The size of the paper types was constant (20 × 16 cm) and lines were 1 cm apart. Forty minutes was allowed for the writing of each story. The two schools in which the study was conducted used unlined paper as part of their internal policy towards writing although each school did allow individual pupils to use lined paper if they elected to do so. Once written, each story was photocopied.

To determine legibility, a panel of five examiners (four primary teachers, one psychologist) rated each story along a four-point rating scale. To determine creativity, three measures were used: examiner ratings along a four point 'creativity' scale, total number of words written in each story, and use of tenses other than the present tense in each story.

The total number of subjects were divided into two smaller mixed-age groups by using working definitions of reading ability (current reading ability of at least twelve months above and twelve months below chronological age) and manual co-ordination (a manual co-ordination score of at least twelve months above and twelve months below chronological age, as determined using the manual dexterity tasks from Stott, Moyes and Henderson 1972). The first group consisted of 28 high readers (whose reading ability was at least twelve months above their chronological age) and 21 low readers (reading ability at least twelve months below their chronological age); the second consisted of 14 highly co-ordinated pupils (whose manual co-ordination scores were at least twelve months above their chronological age) and 22 poorly co-ordinated pupils (whose manual co-ordination scores were at least twelve months below their chronological age). These four groups were used for the second part of the study.

Analysis of the results indicated that legibility was significantly affected by paper type for each of the four age groups — the stories written on lined paper were rated significantly more legible than the stories written on unlined paper. The results for each group are presented in Table 7.1.

Table 7.1: A comparison of legibility ratings and paper type

Age of subjects (years)	Mean legibility ratings		t	df	P
	Lined	Unlined			
6	12.9	10.45	4.678	19	<0.001
7	15.15	11.60	6.400	19	<0.001
8	14.25	11.30	6.03	19	<0.001
9	15.55	12.05	9.04	19	<0.001

The results relating to paper type and its effects on creativity were not so straightforward or conclusive and have been summarised elsewhere (Pasternicki 1986). The results of the high-reading-ability group were in the expected direction — their stories were rated as significantly more creative than the stories written by the low-reading-ability group.

Stories written by the highly co-ordinated group were rated more legible than stories written by the poorly co-ordinated group on both paper types, with the most significant difference occurring when lined paper was used. Results are presented in Table 7.2.

Table 7.2: Comparison between legibility ratings of two co-ordination groups for two types of paper

| Paper type | Mean legibility rating | | t | df | P |
	High co-ordination group	Poor co-ordination group			
Unlined	12.28	10.09	2.01	34	≈ 0.05
Lined	15.64	12.91	2.78	34	< 0.01

When the legibility ratings of the highly co-ordinated group's stories on unlined paper are compared with the legibility ratings of the poorly co-ordinated group's stories on lined paper, then the difference between the legibility ratings becomes negligible (Table 7.2). In fact, the trend is for the poorly co-ordinated group to have the slightly higher legibility ratings. These results are summarised in Figure 7.1.

The results presented in Table 7.2 provide strong evidence that lined paper is beneficial in improving and maintaining the legibility of handwriting. The presence of lines has been shown to aid both the child with a high level of manual co-ordination and also the child who has a poor level of manual co-ordination. In fact, lines improve the legibility of written work to such an extent that differences in the degree of manual control are greatly reduced.

AMERICAN RESEARCH AND AUSTRALIAN RESEARCH

Concurrent with research in the United Kingdom, research on line-width and its appropriateness or otherwise for young children has been conducted in the United States of America during the 1970s.

Figure 7.1: Comparison of the legibility of the high co-ordination group writing on unlined paper with the legibility of the poor co-ordination group writing on lined paper

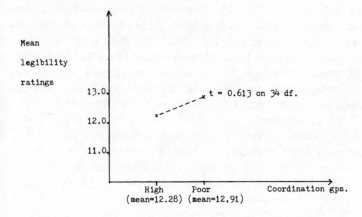

In several Australian states, applied research has led practitioners and educational advisers towards precise guidelines for the teaching of handwriting and recommendations for the use of lined paper have tended to emerge from that research. Guidelines for the teaching of handwriting in the different Australian states receive detailed attention in Chapter 13.

Halpin and Halpin (1976), at Auburn University in the USA, compared the handwriting quality of 44 kindergarten children using four different types of paper. The types used were as follows: one-inch wide writing spaces with open ends, one-inch wide writing spaces with closed ends, one-half-inch narrow writing spaces with open ends and one-half-inch narrow writing spaces with closed ends. Their handwriting samples were rated by two judges using five criteria (uniformity of slant, uniformity of alignment, quality of line or stroke, letter formation, and spacing between letters and words). After handwriting lessons using the different paper types, four matched groups of children showed no differential effects that could be associated with the paper employed. The authors concluded that their study gave no justification for requiring beginner writers to use paper that is different from the type that they will use as adults, i.e. that with narrower lines and with open ends.

Leung, Treblas, Hill and Cooper (1979), at Ohio State University, compared the accuracy of handwriting on 3.4-cm spaced paper and 1.6-cm spaced paper of 71 suburban and 62 inner-city first-grade pupils. Pupils were randomly assigned to two experimental groups and were required to copy ten model lower case manuscript letters on to the given writing paper. These writing samples were assessed by three trained examiners using plastic evaluative overlays. Results from the study suggest that pupils from suburban and inner-city schools wrote better when large-spaced paper was used, and that pupils from suburban schools wrote better than their inner-city counterparts regardless of the line spacing used.

Leung and her co-authors feel that their results do justify the continued use of large-spaced lined paper for first-grade students. They consider that the discrepancy between their results and those of Halpin and Halpin may be due to the differences in age range of subjects in the trials and to differences in the levels of motor co-ordination between kindergarten and first-grade children.

Further American research support for the use of 3.4-cm spaced paper by younger writers was provided by Hill, Gladden and Porter (1982), when they examined the manuscript letter-strokes made by second- and third-grade pupils when large-spaced and normal-spaced writing paper were used. The results from this study indicate that second graders made significantly more correct letter strokes when using the large-spaced paper, whereas the third graders showed no difference in their performance on either normal or large-spaced paper. Hill and fellow workers conclude that, in their opinion, the transition from large- to normal-spaced paper may be appropriate during the second grade period.

RESEARCH IMPLICATIONS, CONCLUSIONS AND RECOMMENDATIONS

Research findings provide strong evidence that, for the majority of children, use of lined paper facilitates more legible handwriting than unlined paper. Such findings are contrary to previously held opinions that stressed the advisability of using unlined paper when teaching handwriting. Findings based on research rather than conjecture need to be disseminated, as some primary schools use unlined paper throughout the pupil age range and infant departments use it almost exclusively with beginner writers.

Writers making recommendations from an authoritative viewpoint (Sassoon 1983, Jarman 1979, Pickard and Alston 1985) refer to priorities for teaching handwriting as legibility, speed and freedom for the development of a personal hand. The first aim, legibility, implies that the writing will be easy to read, with letters and words evenly written and evenly spaced; current research shows that such aspects are encouraged by the use of lined paper. It is suggested then that the beginner writer should be introduced to lined paper at the earliest opportunity, i.e. when beginning to learn the writing skill. Many pupils have haphazard acquaintance with lined paper in the primary school years and have to wait for transfer to secondary education before encountering lined paper in a wide-spread manner. By this time, speed becomes more important than in the primary school years, with secondary expectations being that pupils should write legibly, in a straight line, with correctly formed and appropriately spaced letters and words. In many ways, the pupil who enters secondary school with a less than legible script soon finds himself further disadvantaged. He is likely to find that:

His lack of accuracy and legibility will also affect the speed with which he can write, as well as being further affected when he tries to write at speed. Such a child, who found himself somewhat of a failure at writing when in the primary school, soon finds that the secondary school offers no quick solution to his problems — in fact in many ways, his already poor handwriting is again presented in a further negative light.

(Pasternicki 1986)

It is not difficult to envisage why such a pupil who sees his hand-writing as a 'constant visual reminder of inadequacy . . .' (Sassoon 1983) soon begins to lose interest in those subjects that demand a speedy, accurately written hand.

What of the pupils themselves? Do they have any preference for using one type of paper as opposed to another? In a study to examine subjective and objective methods of assessing children's hand-writing, using children in the final month of their primary careers, Toft (1985) asked 108 pupils aged 10.8 to 11.7 years, what kind of paper they would like to use. Of the sample, 69.4 per cent chose lined paper, 12 per cent chose unlined paper, 10.2 per cent chose unlined paper with paper that had bold guidelines showing through to the paper on which they were writing, and 8.4 per cent were undecided about their choice. It is clear from these results that the majority of primary aged pupils would like to use lined paper even though, in some schools, they are generally expected to use unlined paper.

Children in infant and junior school classes do not come in

77

standard packages. The normal range of intellectual and motor performance is, for each class, likely to range across three or four normal years of development. Taylor, from her day to day work with children experiencing difficulties, suggests that they can be assisted by the introduction of one constant, 'the baseline for writing'. However, beyond this assertion, flexibility with guidance for each pupil is what we recommend. The tentative conclusions, examined in this chapter, make way for further research on the many aspects of paper type and its advisability or otherwise for the development of children's writing.

We suggest that:

(a) The beginner writer can be shown how to form his letters through correct letter movements on plain and, if necessary, large paper.

(b) Concurrent with instruction on letter formation through correct movement, he is shown that the letter being formed sits on or has a relationship to a writing baseline.

(c) Teachers should note that pupils will, at some stage, be expected to learn appropriate labels by which the parts of letters, ascenders, descenders and midline letters, can be differentiated. The terms will be more easily understood if at least a base line is employed.

(d) Teachers through the primary age range have access to a wide range of plain and lined paper formats.

(e) Each teacher is encouraged to develop a perceptive eye to observe whether each pupil might be assisted by an introduction to a particular paper type or a change from the writing paper currently in use.

(f) For some pupils, a baseline may be adequate for their needs. Others may require more visual cues and may be assisted if additional lines are introduced. A baseline may be heavy, drawn with a fluorescent pen or, for older pupils, simply be evident from a heavily lined paper underlay. Additional lines to indicate the limits of 'x height' letters, or of letter ascenders or descenders, can be helpful for some pupils.

(g) Teachers should observe the sources of lighting in the classroom, and ensure that, as far as possible, no pupil is casting a shadow on his own writing surface.

REFERENCES

Alston, J. (1985) 'Brittle bones: a handicap with special occupational therapy needs.' *British Journal of Occupational Therapy, 48,* 103–5.

Burnhill, P., Hartley, J., Fraser, S. and Young, N. (1975) 'Writing lines: an exploratory study.' *Programmed Learning and Educational Technology, 11,* 84–7.

Burnhill, P., Hartley, J., and Davies, L. (1980) 'Lined paper, legibility and creativity.' in Hartley, J., *The Psychology of Written Communication.* Kogan Page, London.

Department of Education and Science (1975) A Language for Life (The Bullock Report). HMSO, London.

Gordon, V.E.C. and Mock, R. (1960) *Twentieth Century Handwriting.* Methuen, London.

Graves, D.H. (1983) *Writing: Teachers and Children at Work.* Heinemann, London.

Halpin, G. and Halpin, G. (1976) 'Special paper for beginning handwriting: an unjustified practice.' *Journal of Educational Research, 69,* 267–9.

Hill, D.S., Gladden, M.A., and Porter, J.T. (1982) 'Variables affecting transition from wide-spaced to normal-spaced paper for manuscript handwriting.' *Journal of Educational Research, 76,* 50–3.

Inglis, A. and Connell, A. (1964) *The Teaching of Handwriting.* Nelson, Sunbury-on-Thames.

Irlen, I. (1983) *Successful Treatment of Learning Disabilities.* Paper given at Ninety-First Annual Convention of American Psychological Association.

Jarman, C. (1979) *The Development of Handwriting Skills.* Blackwell, Oxford.

Lancaster, J. (1986) *A Handwriting Programme for the Primary School.* Paper given at Handwriting Interest Group Study Day, University of Manchester.

Leung, E.K., Treblas, P., Hill, D.S., Cooper, J.D. (1979) 'Space, size and accuracy of first grade students' manuscript writing.' *Journal of Educational Research, 73,* 79–81.

Lindsay, G.A. and McLennan, D. (1983) 'Lined paper: its effects on the legibility and creativity of young children's writing.' *British Journal of Educational Psychology, 53,* 364–8.

Pasternicki, J.G. (1984) 'Lined paper: its effects on legibility and creativity of young children's writing.' Unpublished M.A. thesis, University of Nottingham.

Pasternicki, J.G. (1986) 'Teaching handwriting: the resolution of an issue.' *Support for Learning, 1* (1), 37–41.

Pickard, P. and Alston, J. (1985) *Helping Secondary School Pupils with Handwriting: Current Research, Identification and Assessment, Guidance.* LDA, Wisbech.

Presland, J.L. (1971) 'A psychologist's approach to backwardness in handwriting.' *Remedial Education, 6,* 26–33.

Richards, J. (1980) *Attack.* Portland Blend System, Mansfield, Nottinghamshire.

Sassoon, R. (1983) *The Practical Guide to Children's Handwriting*. Thames and Hudson, London.

Smith, P. (1977) *Developing Handwriting*. MacMillan, Basingstoke.

Stott, D.H., Moyes, F.A., and Henderson S.E. (1972) *Test of Motor Impairment*. Brook Educational, Guelph, Ontario.

Taylor, J. (1979) *Writing is for reading*, Book 1. 14 Dora Road, London SW19 7HH.

Toft, C. (1985) 'Subjective and objective methods of assessing handwriting in 11-year-old children.' Unpublished dissertation, University of Nottingham.

8

Left- and Right-Handed Writers

WHY ARE SOME PEOPLE LEFT-HANDED?

The human body is a complex structure and the variety and complexity of what the human being can do should impress us all. Handedness is the outward sign that a composite of human functions can be brought together to give the individual a competent tool for the completion of a wide variety of tasks. It is established that the left cerebral hemisphere controls the right side of the body and that the right cerebral hemisphere controls the left side of the body. Neurologists generally accept that, for most of us, language processing is conducted in the left hemisphere of the brain, it is co-ordinated with the motor area for hand function also in that hemisphere, and the individual performs the written task with the right hand.

Because there are considerably fewer left-handed than right-handed writers in the community, we assume that left-handed writers are at least different from the population in general. Certainly our instructions for the writing task are constructed with the right-handed writer in mind and this, in itself, can lead to possible pitfalls for left-handed writers.

There are probably at least two groups of left-handed writers. The members of one left-handed group seem to come from families that have a greater-than-average incidence of left-handers amongst their members. We do not know whether members of this group have particular characteristics that make them distinguishable from other left-handed writers. Those concerned with teaching pupils affected by developmental dyslexia or specific written language difficulties, however, suggest that they have a more-than-usual proportion of such children in their groups. Other left-handed writers may have developed use of the left hand because the mechanism that would normally have made them right-handed has been 'changed'. It is well recognised (Penfield and Roberts 1959) that if, for one reason or another, an area of the cortex does not develop in the conventional manner then another area of the cortex will take over its function. Sometimes, in those who might otherwise be right-handed and have hand-motor function located in the left cerebral hemisphere, hand function may be moved to the right hemisphere so that greater control is located in the left hand. The language areas, however, may remain in the left cortex, creating, however slight, a difference in the language-hand function co-ordinating mechanism. Springer (1985) draws attention to several attempts to find differences between the two groups of left-handers to which we have referred. She states that '. . . the bulk of the evidence . . . supports the idea that left-handers with left-handed relatives differ from those without' but notes that there is no conclusive evidence of how the groups differ.

Gordon (1986) reviewing neurological evidence and behavioural research relating to familial or acquired left-handedness, suggests that those not genetically intended to be left-handed can probably be identified by their inordinately weaker right hand i.e. one which has led to adoption of the left hand by an otherwise right-handed person.

Because writing is a complex task that has to be learned and because the conventions of teaching tend to favour the right-handed writer, left-handed writers may, in general, be predisposed to greater difficulties than their right-handed counterparts. Figure 8.1 shows the left cerebral hemisphere in which language and hand function, as well as areas that support them, are located for the population in general. It shows areas important for vision, auditory processing, language comprehension (Wernicke's area), language production (Broca's area) and the sensory and motor areas normally associated with the right hand. It is likely that, for all left-handed writers, the neurological structures essential for completion of the writing task are not so well located and co-ordinated. The human nervous system is extremely complex and it is unlikely that any human being has a nervous system that is developed completely according to plan. So long as there are sufficient well-developed aspects of the human structure, small differences are likely to have little effect upon the manner in which we operate. Left-handers who show no problems in the skills they are taught, probably fall into this category of normally skilled human beings. In some left-handed writers the differences between them and their right-handed colleagues may be greater than for even the general population of

Figure 8.1: The left cerebral hemisphere. Areas important for different cerebral functions are identified: a, vision; b, auditory processing; c, language comprehension (Wernicke's area); d, language production (Broca's area); e, sensory-hand area; f, motor-hand area.

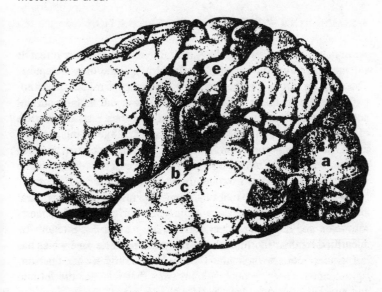

left-handers. For these individuals in particular, a policy for left-handed writers is essential.

WHAT IS THE INCIDENCE OF LEFT HANDEDNESS?

Enstrom, in 1962, examined handedness in 92,656 children in the USA and concluded that 12.5 per cent of boys and 9.7 per cent of girls were left-handed writers. A New Zealand study (1980) of 3738 11- to 12-year-old pupils showed the incidence of left-handed writers to be 13 per cent of boys and 11 per cent of girls. A study of 1094 Manchester six-year-olds, conducted in 1980 by Smart, Jeffrey and Richards, showed also the incidence of left-handed writers in the children's parents and grandparents, the increasing incidence with each generation being 6.2 per cent, 10.6 per cent and 17.5 per cent. The considerable increase of incidence in the six-year-olds probably reflects two factors. The grandparents were probably discouraged from being left-handed by their teachers and parents and some of the six-year-olds may not yet truly have their handedness resolved. However, teachers and parents are, in general, much more tolerant of left-handed writers and it is likely that a significant increase in incidence exists.

WRITING TOOL POSTURE AND PAPER POSITION

As in many areas of handwriting study, there has been little research relating to writing tool or grip. We tend to assume that an appropriate grip for left- and right-handers is when the barrel of the writing tool is held principally between the first finger and thumb with the pads of those digits opposed; the writing tool then rests on the side of the middle finger. Observers of secondary age pupils tend to agree that a large proportion have unconventional tool grip and that selection of writing tool is also often inappropriate. With the poor quality ball-point pen so frequently employed, the writer's control is often reduced, and the tool runs away with the writer as he writes. Uncontrolled and less precise movement leads to poorer line in letter formation and if writing is less legible than normal it is likely to be even further affected. In order to see the writing as he writes, the left-hander needs to hold the writing tool a little higher than the right-handed writer, probably 3 cm from the point for the former and around 2 cm or a little less for the latter.

Writing tool barrels are made in various shapes and sizes and there is need for further research on the desirability of those that are offered. Ziviani examined tracing accuracy when three groups of eight-year-olds used pencils of different diameters and when they used triangular pencil grips. She concluded that pencil shape and size had no influence on the children's ability to perform the simple motor task but that a more mature pencil posture was adopted by those children using the thicker pencil and those equipped with an 'Easy-grip'. Alston conducted trials with eight-year-olds who had equal amounts of writing practice with triangular and more conventional six-sided pencils. She concluded that, at the age of the children examined, pencil shape did not influence pencil grip and that, when the children were asked to select a pencil, they selected that which most suited their established writing tool hold. Researchers have not addressed themselves to the special needs of left-handers or to whether the adaptation of left- or right-handers to particular writing tools differ. Clearly, there is a need for applied researchers who will address themselves to these areas of handwriting study.

Whatever the neurological differences between left- and right-handed writers might be, both groups are required to write in the conventional left to right across the page direction. The right-handed writer can, if body and paper are suitably positioned, move writing hand from the body midline in an away from the body direction. We relatively rarely see the right-hander who has true postural problems. Sometimes, however, teachers exacerbate postural problems by insisting that the paper is placed squarely in front of the writer with its lower edge parallel with the edge of the writing surface. Compared with the right-handed writer, the left-hander has to write in the much less natural direction of left to right and, unless given instruction to do otherwise, across his own body midline. Left-handed writers then, as the writing arm moves, may have it cramped into the side of the body. Authoritative statements about paper position have been numerous and as subsequent research has shown, often erroneous. Research, in which large numbers of writers are observed, is more likely to give guidelines about how successful left-handers cope with the writing task.

Enstrom conducted research in 1962 in which he examined paper position in 1103 school attenders. It was an extensive piece of research in which he grouped and regrouped the pupils' different techniques of coping with their left-handed writing tasks. Criteria for classification were:

(a) quality of writing product,
(b) rate of writing,
(c) ability to produce neat smear-free papers,
(d) healthful body posture and considerations.

He concluded that not only is it helpful for the left-hander to turn his paper in the clockwise direction but that certain degrees of turn are more efficient than others. He gives information about the paper positions of pupils, indicating which positions proved to be more efficient than others. Figure 8.2 shows positions used by Enstrom's subjects in decreasing order of efficiency.

Enstrom also noted that a sizable number of his subjects adopted the hooked writing-tool position. For these subjects, he was also able to identify parameters adopted by the writers in whom the position was established. Figure 8.3 shows the hooked writing posture from which Enstrom concluded that, in its most efficient use, the writer turns the wrist on edge enough to permit maximum flexing, and the paper is turned leftward as for right-handed placement. Numerous pitfalls associated with this posture were noted by

85

Figure 8.2: Left-handed pupils' paper positions in decreasing order of efficiency

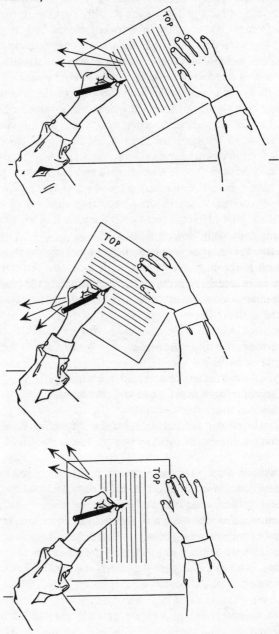

Figure 8.3: Left-handed hooked writing posture (Enstrom)

Enstrom, who concluded that writing techniques in which the hand is below the line are best and that they should be taught at the beginning stages of writing.

In more recent research, Guiard and Millerat (1984) attempted to differentiate neurological from postural strategies relating to left-handed writers. They were searching for differences between left-handers who adopted a conventional writing tool hold from those who adopted an inverted hand posture, i.e. a hooked writing position. They assesssed their 51 adult subjects for the following:

(a) degree of handedness, including strength of grip;
(b) familial history of sinistrality;
(c) asymmetry in the ability to flex single fingers and pairs of fingers within the two hands.

The writing postures of their subjects were also photographed at a predetermined point in the copying of a standard text.

No consistent relationship between the neurological data and writing position was observed, and it was concluded that laterality and other neurological factors were unlikely to have determined either inverted-hand or below-the-line posture. Analysis of photographs, however, led to some interesting findings. The subjects could be shown to fall into two groups:

(1) 13 subjects who rotated the top page to the left and were inverters;

87

(2) 34 subjects who rotated the top of the page to the right and were non-inverters.

It was also observed that on average, the page was slanted 15° to the left by inverters and 32° to the right by non-inverters.

The forearms of inverters were almost at right angles to the paper's vertical edge and those of non-inverters were nearly parallel to the paper's vertical edge. There was no overlap between the forearm positions of the two populations. The vertical positioning of the non-writing hand was also different for the two groups. To non-inverters, the position of the right support hand did not seem important. For most of the inverters, however, the right hand was placed just below the line of writing in a strikingly stereotyped manner. In these inverters, the right hand was usually nearer to the left of the page than the pencil tip. These writers cross their hands as the writing proceeds. As part of this research, it was observed that left handers usually begin to write in a below the line position. It is then suggested that there is difficulty in keeping the paper stationary because the writing tool is inclined to push the paper away from the writer. In order to avoid this situation, the supporting hand holds the paper on the left and below the point of the pencil. In order to proceed, the forearm then has to be placed horizontal rather than vertical to the page and the act of writing then requires a counter clockwise rotation of the sheet of paper. With this position established, the inverter's hand and writing tool then pull along the paper surface as the right hander's does and the paper is also held stationary.

The research suggests that if teachers are aware that inverted hand posture is a postural strategy and that it develops as the pupil progresses through school, then its development can probably be avoided.

WRITING PRESSURE

Clark (1974) and other authors have suggested that left-handers tend to grip the barrel of the writing tool more tightly than right-handers. The pressure of grip can only be monitored with fairly sophisticated equipment and there is no research to support the views expressed. Herrick and Otto, in their 1961 research, showed that for a majority of subjects, those who grip the barrel tightly will also press the writing point heavily on the paper and, similarly, those who hold the barrel lightly will make light contact between pencil and paper. (They do not identify the writing hand of their 56 subjects.) There are, however, some exceptions to this general rule. It is likely that, on the whole, if point-to-paper pressure is reduced then barrel grip will also be reduced, i.e. a general reduction in pressure of hand and instrument. Just talking about pressure might help and so might interleaving of carbon paper to discourage hard and distinct copies. Relaxation of the hand and fingers can also have a part to play.

WRITING SPEED

Some writers have suggested that writing speed is reduced for left-handed writers and over the longer periods of writing tasks this suggestion is not yet supported or denied. Over a short period of two or three minutes, however, there is little evidence for significantly lower writing speeds amongst left-handed writers. The New Zealand study (1980) showed that, over a three-minute period, right-handers wrote on average 79 letters per minute and left-handers wrote 73 letters per minute. Sex differences showed a higher discrepancy than that for handedness, with girls writing 84 letters per minute and boys writing 72. The three-minute trial gives little evidence about what would occur if left- and right-handers were compared over a longer period so that fatigue or other factors could be introduced to the writing situation.

The following suggestions for the early stages of the left-hander's writing should help teachers to advise their pupils appropriately:

(a)   the paper is placed to the left of the body midline,
(b)   the paper is tilted approximately 32° to the right,
(c)   the paper is supported by the right hand,
(d)   the writing tool is held in a below the line positon,
(e)   the writing tool is held sufficiently far from the point to enable the writer to see what he is writing,
(f)   the writing tool allows smooth movement across the paper.

REFERENCES

Alston, J. and Taylor, J. (1984) *The Handwriting File: Diagnosis and Remediation of Handwriting Difficulties*. LDA, Wisbech.
Alston, J. (1986) 'The effects of pencil barrel shape and pupil barrel

preference on hold or grip in 8-year-old pupils.' *British Journal of Occupational Therapy, 49* (2).

Clark, M.M. (1974) *Teaching Left Handed Children*. University of London Press, London.

Enstrom, E.A. (1962) 'The relative efficiency of various approaches to writing with the left-hand.' *Journal of Educational Research, 55* (10).

Franks, J.E., Davis, T.R. and Totty, R.N. (1983) *The Discrimination of Left and Right Handed Writing*. Home Office Forensic Science Laboratory, Birmingham.

Gordon, N. (1986) 'Left-handedness and learning.' *Developmental Medicine and Child Neurology, 28* (5).

Guiard, Y. and Millerat, F. (1984) 'Writing posture in left handers: inverters are handcrossers.' *Neuropsychologia, 22* (4).

Herrick, V.E. and Otto, W. (1961) 'Presssure on point and barrel of a writing instrument.' *Journal of Experimental Education, 30* (2).

New Zealand Department of Education (1985) *Teaching Handwriting*. Wellington, New Zealand.

New Zealand Department of Education (1980) *A Study of the Handwriting of Form 1 Pupils in New Zealand Intermediate Schools*. Wellington, New Zealand.

Penfield, W. and Roberts, L. (1959) *Speech and Brain Mechanisms*. Princeton University Press, Princeton.

Smart, J.L., Jeffery, C. and Richards, B. (1980) 'A retrospective study of the relationship between birth history and handedness at six years.' *Early Human Development, 4* (1).

Springer, S. and Deutsch, G. (1985) *Left Brain, Right Brain*. Freeman, New York.

Ziviani, (1981) 'Effects of pencil shape and size on motor accuracy and pencil posture of 8-year-old children.' Department of Occupational Therapy, University of Queensland.

9

Assessment Scales and Checklists

Early work in handwriting assessment took the form of handwriting scales, constructed so that there were standard models with which scripts for identification or assessment could be compared. A range of script models allowed one, by comparison, to judge quality or progress of subject or pupil. Thorndike's scales (1910), were constructed from research employing 1,000 scripts from children and adult women and from decisions made by 30 to 40 judges. Script judgement criterion at that stage was 'general merit' and is generally thought to have referred also to 'artistic and pleasing appearance'. Ayres (1912–1915) referred to 'legibility' and assessed it by the time required for a judge to read a written passage. To produce the written passage, the writer was instructed to copy the text until he was familiar with it and then, with a copy of the text available, to write it at his 'usual writing speed'. Freeman (1915) introduced the passage incorporating all letters of the alphabet, 'the quick brown fox jumps over the lazy dog'. The writer was instructed to completely memorise the text, and in the manner 'usual for writing well' to write for a two-minute period. Norms for words per minute were available from Freeman's research. Groff (1961) instructed subjects to read and memorise a text and presented writing speed norms of letters per minute, based on time taken to write the memorised text. Ziviani added her own Brisbane Australian norms in the early 1980s for comparison with those of Ayres and Groff. The New Zealand Department of Education commissioned an extensive study of first form intermediate pupils in 1981. The New Zealand research was replicated by Pickard in 1984, so that letters per minute for 11- to 12-year-olds, using two different texts, are available. Legibility and speed are examined separately in the New Zealand and Pickard studies.

Herrick and Erlebacher (in Herrick 1963) recognising the complexity of handwriting and its component skills, rejected the idea of a single scale with one sample for each quality level. Writers were, by this time, referring to handwriting size, slant and alignment and simple criteria such as 'general merit' or even 'legibility' were thought to be somewhat imprecise. However, it seems that few problems were resolved, as the master list of six-hundred scaled samples, resulting from Herrick and Erlebacher's extensive research and refinements, provided a reference model for researchers rather than a working model for either research or practical application. Fischer (1964) identified five handwriting factors, drawing particular attention to the importance of size and slant. Askov, Otto and Askov (1970), in their review of handwriting research, predicted directions that future research might take and stated '. . . perhaps scales should be built on information obtained from factor analysis of handwriting characteristics'. Progress in the 1980s, reported in ensuing sections, will show how development in checklist construction and in component skill assessment and measurement have followed that prediction.

Checklists of varying degrees of complexity and relevance have existed for some time. It seems that the complexity of handwriting's component tasks, the numerous handwriting models, and the inability of authoritative writers to agree on the desirability of any one model in preference to another, have all presented obstacles to the development of checklists that are both manageable and valid. Faas included a 97-item checklist in his 1980 publication which, by its size alone, seemed unmanageable. However, his inclusion of the rather ornate Zaner-Bloser Cursive capitals in the checklist items, and the lack of clarity or discreteness of the items was likely to be a further reason why the checklist did not receive immediate approval.

The Handwriting Checklist (Alston and Taylor 1981) was first published in 1981. Its construction was based on handwriting skills referred to in recent research, but item selection was also influenced by discussion with teachers on in-service courses who were concerned about pupils experiencing handwriting difficulties in their classrooms. A relative simplicity has been retained so that it can be used as a classroom tool, and some areas of difficulty can be identified from a sample of writing without the presence of the pupil. The aim of the checklist is that it should enable the teacher to identify precise problems experienced by each pupil, in a systematic manner. At some point, it is essential to monitor the pupil during the writing process so that all items on the record sheet can be completed accurately. No scoring is suggested as the checklist is intended as a diagnostic tool.

Section one of the checklist refers to essential or pre-requisite skills such as writing tool hold, writing posture, paper position and variation in writing pressure. Section two is concerned with both the language for letter identification and with letter form and movement. Letters are presented in groups that have similar letter movements rather than in alphabetical order. By identifying groups of letters that have movements in common, those causing problems in any one group may be highlighted. Within the third section, basic patterns essential to competent letter formation are presented. Pupils may be asked to complete the patterns so that basic movement pattern difficulties may be identified. The final section relates to presentation and draws the teacher's or therapist's attention to the importance of consistent letter size and slant, spacing between letters and words, size of writing and the importance of being able to align writing correctly or write on the lines provided. There is a space for teaching objectives, intending that corrective teaching items should be placed in order of priority and dealt with in that order. The practitioner is advised to retain writing samples from each pupil, so that progress can be monitored. This section could form a valuable basis for discussion between teacher and pupil. Progress in writing, like other literacy skills, is more likely to improve if the pupil is prepared, under direction, to accept responsibility for his own progress.

Standardisation of the handwriting checklist was completed in 1982 on the twenty items that could be completed from writing samples and without the pupil's presence. Samples for the standardisation were selected from 17 schools representative of Chesire and, by certain implications, England and Wales. The coefficients for inter-marker and mark-remark reliability were highly significant, indicating that the checklist is a reliable tool for assessment. Checklist validity was examined by comparing checklist marking with teacher subjective assessment of handwriting quality. It was noted that the reliability and validity coefficients resulting from checklist standardisation compared well with similar statistical data presented with tests of reading, spelling and mathematics, and published at approximately the same time.

The Handwriting File (1984) was designed to complement the checklist. Each item on the checklist is numbered and has a corresponding section in the file. File sections refer to relevant research evidence or authoritative assertions. Guidelines indicate how identified difficulties might be overcome. Teachers' reference sheets give information about letter and number formation, writing patterns, writing guidelines and common letter combinations.

Diagnosis and Remediation of Handwriting Problems (DRHP; Stott, Moyes and Henderson) was published in 1985. The complete kit consists of a manual, diagnositic record form, group record form, student's specimen writing card and a standard writing sheet on which the child should complete a writing sample for observation.

The authors state that the kit is intended as a systematic means of identifying faults, for use in clinical assessment and for research. It is considered to be most useful for children who have completed two years in writing but may also be used for brain-injured adults who have lost the ability to write. Faults in the writing of normal adults, it is claimed, are quite different from those of children and scrutiny, using the DRHP would not be helpful. In general, the kit is intended for the analysis of difficulties, to identify the fault group from which the difficulties might arise, and to identify the origin of the problems. The following four types of fault receive particular attention:

(1) Concept, which includes incorrect use of letter forms and improper joining of letters. These difficulties may arise from poor teaching or from the pupil's inability to benefit from the teaching when it occurred.
(2) Spacing, which may be inappropriate between letters or between words. The suggestion is that the child may be ignorant of the convention of letter grouping, may have a perceptual disability or merely have his eyes too close to the paper.
(3) Control, which detracts from writing appearance. These faults are further classified into:
    (a) Inconsistency of slant
    (b) Inconsistency of letter size
    (c) Poor word alignment
    (d) Random letter distortion
    (e) Tremor
(4) Writing position, referring to posture, physical disadvantage such as poor motor control or laterality, or faulty ways of addressing the task.

The scoring system is determined by the purpose for which the test might be employed. Although methods of scoring are presented, and are quantified according to degree of deviance from that which is normal or desirable, it is not intended that the scores should be summed to give an over-all score. The quantification is made available for research purposes, where quantitative measures allow one to evaluate more objectively. Quantitative measures, utilised through transparent diagnostic templates, are applied to writing slant and alignment or deviation from the writing base line. Other quantitative scoring is based on measurement of word spacing but dependent on the scorer's accuracy and decision when making numerical awards.

A standard sheet, presenting a picture story sequence from which the child is asked to write his own story, is of use for classroom monitoring and identification of those children who differ from the general performance norm. Observations about how the pupil performs the task can be noted. This follows the pattern of Stott's long-standing interest in learning style and how children apply themselves to the task in hand.

Precise instructions are given for scorer training. The authors recognise that few teachers will have the time to use this diagnostic tool in full for each student who may have handwriting difficulties and state that, for the teacher the '. . . important thing is to acquire the type of perception that will enable him or her to recognize the particular faults in any student's handwriting which should be corrected.'

Ascender/descender, word alignment, and spacing measurement criteria were submitted to scoring reliability studies and, in the authors' words '. . . gave very modest reliability levels'. They assert, however, that the reliability coefficients achieved do not give the complete picture of the DRHP. The decision to publish was based on the need to make available this existing experimental instrument.

A booklet entitled *Handwriting and Spelling* can be obtained from Barbara Maines, who is an Educational Psychologist for the County of Avon. In the booklet, she describes research in which she examined the handwriting of first-year pupils in four comprehensive schools, noting that the pupils in those schools were drawn from 42 primary schools. In her specified writing task, when requested to write '. . . as neatly and quickly . . .' as they were able, 40.8 per cent of 11- to 12-year-olds used print script, 22.4 per cent used mixed style with some joins, and 36.8 per cent showed evidence of established cursive handwriting. The lack of stability and sophistication of handwriting skills in secondary school pupils was noted.

Developing from the survey, and as part of her interest in hand-writing policy, guidelines for record keeping were constructed, drawing the attention of teachers to twelve areas of development that might have bearing on handwriting skill. Six items then draw attention of the practitioner to ways in which the development of skills, essential to the development of small components of written language, can be examined and monitored. Barbara Maines states the following:

When the teaching of writing begins it is important to look at learning of letter formation at various different stages, and to establish that learning has actually occurred at each level. For each letter or letter string learned, can the child:
1. finger trace, starting in the right place, with a fluent movement?
2. pencil trace, as above, with correct pencil grip?
3. produce the letter correctly when a model is shown?
4. produce the letter correctly when a model is shown and removed?
5. produce the letter correctly when the letter name or sound is given?
6. still do it two weeks later?
In this way each stage of the acquisition of writing can be monitored as the child progresses through the scheme at his/her own pace.

A more comprehensive record form, linking handwriting with letter strings, draws attention to the important relationship between writing and spelling. A useful sequence, ranging from ability to trace or copy a simple vertical stroke to the construction of complex letter strings such as 'ound', is presented.

The booklet includes a short critique of handwriting models. Spelling techniques from the work of Peters and Cripps are mentioned in context appropriate to discussion on the development of handwriting skills.

REFERENCES

Alston, J. and Taylor, J. (1981) *Handwriting Checklist*. LDA, Wisbech.
Alston, J. and Taylor, J. (1984) *The Handwriting File: Diagnosis and Remediation of Handwriting Difficulties*. LDA, Wisbech.

Askov, E.N., Otto, W. and Askov, W.A. (1970) 'A decade of research in handwriting: progress and prospect.' *Journal of Educational Research, 64* (3).

Ayres, L.P. (1912, 1915) 'A scale for measuring the quality of handwriting of school children.' Russell Sage Foundation Division of Educational Bulletins, no. 113, New York.

Faas, L.A. (1980) *Children with Learning Problems: A Handbook for Teachers.* Houghton Mifflin, Boston.

Fischer, Gerhard (1964) 'Zur Faktoriellen Struktur der Handschrift' (Factorial Structure of Handwriting). *Zeitschrift fur Experimentelle und Angewandte Psychologie, 11*: 254–80.

Freeman, F.N. (1915) 'An analytical scale for judging handwriting.' *Elementary School Journal, 15*, 432–41.

Groff, P.J. (1969) 'New speeds in handwriting.' In Otto, W., Koenke, K. (Eds) *Remedial Teaching: Research and Comment.* Houghton Mifflin, Boston.

Herrick, V.E. (1963) *New Horizons for Research in Handwriting.* University of Wisconsin Press, Madison.

Maines, B. (1985) 'Handwriting and Spelling.' South House, Yatesbury, Nr Calne, SN11 8YE.

Peck, M., Askov, E.N. and Fairchild, S.H. (1980) 'Another decade of research in handwriting: progress and prospect in the 1970s.' *Journal of Educational Research, 69*, 283–97.

Pickard, P., Alston, J. (1985) Helping Secondary School Pupils with Handwriting: Current Research, Identification and Assessment, Guidance. LDA, Wisbech.

Stott, D.H., Moyes, F.A. and Henderson, S.E. (1985) *Diagnosis and Remediation of Handwriting Problems.* Brook Educational, Guelph, Ontario.

Thorndike, E.L. (1910) 'Handwriting.' *Teachers College Record, 11*, 83–175.

Ziviani, J., Elkins, J. (1984) 'An Evaluation of Handwriting Performance.' *Educational Review, 36* (3).

10

The Sequence and Structure of Handwriting Skills

Writing is a complex activity requiring the integration of verbal, perceptual and motor skills. For writing to be a useful means of expression, the writer must have learned both the structure of written language and the mechanics of forming the appropriate marks on paper. In this chapter the mechanics of handwriting will be examined.

Handwriting is a basic skill in which a complicated pattern of movement is required in order to form a mark into a letter shape. Once a movement pattern has been firmly established it is resistant to change. Teachers must therefore observe each pupil regularly when he begins to write, to ensure that he learns and develops good writing habits. As a pupil moves up through the school, each successive teacher must continue to monitor his progress to ensure that he develops a personal handwriting that is fast, fluent and legible.

Before a child starts school, he may have enjoyed experimenting with paints, crayons and pencils. He may, for example, have written his name on greetings cards to various members of the family. He may have learned to write using capital letters but he may know nothing else about letters. Some children may know the names of the letters, others the sounds, some may know both, others may be able to write several small letters of the alphabet. Therefore, when the child starts school, it is important for the teacher to observe each pupil individually to ascertain his existing strengths and weaknesses so that she can offer a handwriting programme to match his needs.

Before considering the assessment of handwriting skills, the teacher has first to decide whether she considers handwriting as an integral part of written expression or as a separate skill closely linked to the reading and writing processes. During recent decades there seems to have been a movement away from the formal teaching of handwriting *per se*, towards integrating the teaching of hand-writing with the teaching and development of literacy skill in general. Using the latter approach, in the initial stages the teacher writes what the child dictates and the child then copies what the teacher has written. By learning handwriting in this manner the child can commence a letter at any position and move his pencil in any direction. Consequently he may not develop an awareness of the constancy of letter shape that the use of directionally correct movements in writing would reinforce. For many children this may not be of great import as they will pick up the correct movement patterns irrespective of the teaching method, but for a small number of pupils, learning handwriting in this manner may allow them to establish incorrect movement patterns that will resist modification later. A more formal approach, emphasising the letter shape and mastery of the correct, fluent, rhythmical movements required to create that shape, enables a child to master the basic skill.

Sassoon (1983) states that the crucial time for letter form instruction is the '. . . moment a child reaches a formal teaching situation'. Michael (1985) suggests that while the pupil is mastering correct letter formation he should not be involved with formal writing activity but should be encouraged to communicate through draw-ings. The pupil should learn to pay attention to detail and learn to record this detail on his pictures. In addition, pictures should not be drawn in isolation but should form a story sequence so that the pupil can be introduced to the concept of structured writing. Michael (1984) states that writing should give children the power to select, shape, reorganise and understand experiences. Should the teacher wish to link reading to the child's drawing, then cards on which individual words are written can be provided by the teacher and selected by the child to indicate the subject of the picture. Word cards for sentence construction are utilised by Mackay, Thompson and Schaub (1973) in *Breakthrough to Literacy*.

Figure 10.1 illustrates the broader aspects of the processes involved in mastering the basic skill of handwriting. Failure to learn may be due to a breakdown in any one or more of the processes. These aspects are now examined in more detail.

THE TASK

The pupil has to master the formation of twenty-six small and capital letters, simple punctuation and the numerals 0 to 9. (The basic signs

Figure 10.1: The processes involved in mastering handwriting skills

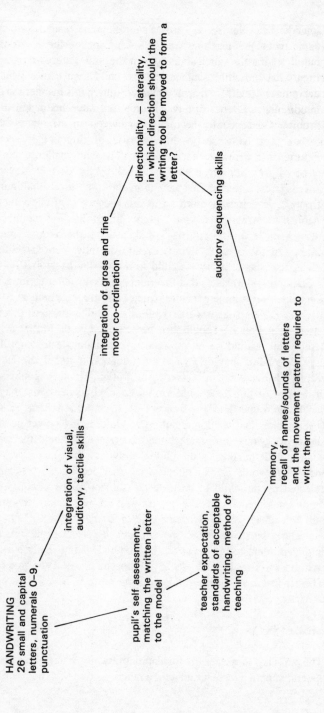

HANDWRITING
26 small and capital letters, numerals 0–9, punctuation

integration of visual, auditory, tactile skills

integration of gross and fine motor co-ordination

directionality — laterality, in which direction should the writing tool be moved to form a letter?

auditory sequencing skills

memory, recall of names/sounds of letters and the movement pattern required to write them

pupil's self assessment, matching the written letter to the model

teacher expectation, standards of acceptable handwriting, method of teaching for addition, subtraction, multiplication and divison will also need to be included when the need arises.) Letters may be grouped in families based on their common movement patterns as shown in Figure 10.2. If the pupil is made aware of the similarities in the movement pattern and direction of some of the letters within a family, the learning load will be reduced and indeed some of the problems of reversals, rotations and inversions may be avoided.

Figure 10.2: Patterns found in letters

The round pattern found in the letters *a, c, d, g, o, s, e, f, g*

The hump patterns found in the letters *r, n, m, h, b, p*

The straight line and cup patterns found in the letters *l, i, t, u, y, j, g, w*

The zig-zag patterns found in the letters *v, w, k, x, z, y*

The groups are as follows:

(1) *c, a, d, g, o, s, f, e, q*
(2) *i, l, t*
(3) *u, y, j,* (w)
(4) *r, n, m, h, b, p,* (k)
(5) *v, w,* (y)
(6) *k, x, z*

As *w y* and *k* can be written in either of two ways they can be put into alternative groups.

To assist the child to visualise the dominant pattern in each group, the group may be given a further linguistic label, e.g. the letters *r, n, m, h, b, p* may be called 'hump letters'.

If letters that end on the base line, *a, d, h, i, l, m, n, t, u,* are taught with exit strokes (ligatures) from a very early stage, progression from an unjoined to a semi-cursive script can take place smoothly.

Capital letters appear to be easier to master because the shapes of most of them are based on circles, parts of circles and straight lines and may be made with a number of separate strokes. This may be related to the fact that children between the age of three and four years are generally able to draw a circle and a cross. Many young children learn to write using capital letters and the older pupil with poor handwriting, often uses capital letters inappropriately in his written work.

INTEGRATION OF VISUAL, AUDITORY AND TACTILE SKILLS

As our knowledge of how visual, auditory and tactile skills are involved in the complex activity of handwriting is limited, it is difficult to find tests that usefully define the precise areas of deficit which might be related to poor handwriting. However, there appear to be three areas of potential weakness. The first is a weakness in visual perception skills that contributes to faulty production of letter shapes. Quin and MacAuslan (1981) state that '. . . if there is faulty visual perception of the shapes required, then there will be faulty production of those shapes, however intact the rest of the nervous and muscular systems between brain and ball point'. The second is inadequate motor skill to form the letter. As the child learns to write a letter he is developing an internalised model for that letter. A child with difficulties in hand-eye co-ordination will need very precise instructions to ensure that a clear image of each letter is firmly established. The third is weakness in auditory perception that contributes to incorrect verbal labelling of the letter shapes. Children may be expected to learn the names and sounds of letters, but for the child with auditory perceptual problems, the recollection of an arbitrary set of names or sounds may prove difficult. Incorrect verbal labelling of the letter by the child, can add to his confusion.

INTEGRATION OF GROSS AND FINE MOTOR CO-ORDINATION

Children with gross and fine motor co-ordination problems are given a variety of labels; for example, they may be referred to as perceptually or minimally handicapped, clumsy, experiencing learning difficulties or dyspraxic. Bedford and Alston (1987) aptly describe these children as 'lacking in grace' and state the following:

> 'Fine and gross motor skills share common bases, some of which are as follows:
> (1) Normal postural tone provides a stable postural background to our movements.
> (2) The body can be appropriately aligned in space.
> (3) The pupil has normal balance reactions . . .
> (4) The head, body and limbs can be moved in the desired direction, at the right time and at the right speed.
> (5) The pupil is aware of the parts of his body and has intact sensory feedback mechanisms so that existing movements are monitored.
> (6) Effort is directed only where it is required.
> (7) There is an ability to isolate and make movements only in the parts necessary for the task. Unnecessary movements, which could occur in other parts of the body or limb are inhibited.'

They list activities that will enable the teacher to identify the pupil's area of weakness and offers some exercises that can be used to help the child to master the postures and movements he finds difficult. Exercises such as these could be included in a well-structured physical education programme. McKinlay (1982) writes as follows:

> '. . . if there were a broader knowledge and acceptance of what is normal within child development and a greater tolerance of children with motor delay in our competitive society, together with a more sophisticated acceptance of a responsibility to find solutions within schools for those pupils who are clumsy, their predicament would be easier'.

A degree of fine motor control is required for tool hold. It is not known to what extent tool hold might be related to legibility or fluency. Nevertheless, when using any tool there is an optimum method of holding it that is more effective than others, e.g. if a

103

hammer is held near the head it is harder to bang in the nail. Therefore it is important when learning handwriting that the functional tripod grip should be mastered from the beginning. Unfortunately a child often starts school with an awkward grip already firmly established and resistant to change.

The shape of each letter is produced by the fine movement of the fingers while the horizontal movement across the page is produced by movement at the wrist and forearm. Lack of fine finger movement must inhibit correct letter formation and in that situation the child may be using his wrist and/or his arm muscles inappropriately in order to shape letters. Fatigue and pain may result when he is required to write for long periods.

Increasingly, physiotherapists and occupational therapists are being asked to help children with problems such as these. Although a child is likely to benefit from help directed towards improving his gross and fine motor co-ordination, he is also likely to require precise instructions when letter formation is being taught.

LATERALITY/DIRECTIONALITY

Laterality is not only an awareness of left and right, it is the internalisation of this knowledge. It enables us to orientate ourselves in the world about us. When laterality is not well established this seems to give rise to directional confusion. Many pairs of letters are very similar, the only difference being the direction in which they are orientated; *b/d, p/q* are frequently reversed, while *d/p, b/q, m/w, f/t* are rotated or inverted. It is generally considered (Chapman, Lewis and Wedell 1970) that such confusions are common until about the age of seven. If the letters are taught in families, some of the confusion is eliminated. For example, *b* and *d* commence at different places and have different movement patterns. The letter *b* starts 'at the top' with a vertical line and then 'humps over' like an *h*, whereas the *d* starts 'like a *c*' with a round anti-clockwise movement.

SEQUENCING SKILLS

So many of the things we do we take for granted, without appreciating that complex sequences of skills are involved. Consider, for example, learning to ride a bicycle or to swim; a complex sequence of movement has to be perfected in order for success to be achieved.

Once mastered, the movement becomes automatic and it is then possible to concentrate on perfecting the skill. In the handwriting context, writing a letter appears simple but the sequence of movements to produce each letter varies. For example, the movements required to write the letter *w* are quite different from those required for the letter *e*. This has implications for the pupil with difficulty in motor co-ordination because planning a sequence of movements is, for him, an area of weakness and may cause problems when he has to recall the sequence of movements required for correct formation of letters.

'Digit span' is a test often administered as part of a battery of psychological tests. The subject is asked to repeat a series of numerals first forwards and then backwards, with the number of digits to be repeated being gradually increased. A low score may indicate a difficulty in auditory memory, i.e. difficulty in memorising and organising information received through the ears. A pupil with weak auditory perceptual and memory skills may find auditory sequential tasks such as learning the days of the week, the months of the year and multiplication tables difficult. This has implications both for the pupil with poor handwriting and for his teacher. The pupil may not remember the series of verbal instructions for a given letter, which may mean that the teacher will have to break down her instructions into small enough steps to ensure that the pupil remembers and can repeat them before he makes any mark on the paper. Haskell (1977), reviewing a number of research projects, suggests that the majority of studies indicated that the mental rehearsal of a movement pattern improves performance by two or three times compared with performance without rehearsal.

MEMORY

The expression 'it is on the tip of my tongue' is familiar to most of us. A child in the early stages of learning to write seems to experience a similar problem when he says that he cannot remember what a letter looks like. If, however, he is given a verbal clue, the letter may be recalled instantly. Visual, auditory, motor and sequential skills, laterality and directionality all constitute part of the memory bank necessary for letter formation. For each letter, there has to be an internal model, a memory trace that can be automatically recalled. These traces will be extended into letter strings as the pupil learns to write words and to compose meaningful sentences.

Many people consider that there should be a positive link between the teaching of handwriting and spelling (Peters and Cripps, 1983, Maines, 1985, Michael 1985, Taylor 1979). This can be achieved by incorporating familiar letter strings or words into handwriting practice, once individual letters have been mastered.

TEACHER EXPECTATION

As the teacher's own writing may influence her pupils' attitude to handwriting, she needs to consider what model she uses when she is writing on the blackboard, writing work sheets for use by the pupils or writing comments on the pupils' work. She also needs to consider whether the teaching of handwriting is to be part of her curriculum; for example, if she writes on a particular pupil's work, 'Handwriting needs to be improved' is she prepared to offer follow-up instructions on ways in which his handwriting performance might be improved?

As handwriting is an acquired skill that, even when the basic mechanics have been established, continues to develop as a pupil matures, space should be provided in the curriculum for each pupil to continue handwriting practice, just as one would expect to practise any other physical skill.

SELF ASSESSMENT

The pupil must learn from the beginning to match what he writes with the model in use; this is the beginning of critical awareness. This ability to be self critical needs to be nurtured so that a pupil can continue to monitor and be responsible for his own handwriting performance.

REFERENCES

Bedford, S. and Alston, J. (1987) 'Helping clumsy children with hand-writing: a multidisciplinary viewpoint.' NCSE, Stratford upon Avon.

Chapman, L.J., Lewis, A. and Wedell, K. (1970) 'A note on reversals in the writing of eight-year-old children.' *Remedial Education, 51* (2).

Haskell, S., Barrett, E. and Taylor, H. (1977) *The Education of Motor and Neurologically Handicapped Children*. Croom Helm, London.

Mackay, D., Thompson, B. and Schaub, P. (1973) *Breakthrough to Literacy*. Longman, London.

Maines, B. (1985) 'Handwriting and spelling.' South House, Yatesbury, Nr. Calne SN11 8YE.

McKinlay, I. (1982) 'Clumsy children'. *Concern, 45*, 15–20. National Children's Bureau, London.

Michael, B. (1984) 'Foundations of writing'. *Child Education*, January.

Michael, B. (1985) 'Foundations of writing'. *Child Education*, May.

Michael, B. (1985) *Letterforms*. Jordanhill College of Education, Glasgow.

Peters, M.L. and Cripps, C. (1983) *Catchwords*. Harcourt, Brace, Jovanovich, London.

Pickard, P. and Alston, J. (1985) *Helping Secondary School Pupils with Handwriting: Current Research, Identification and Assessment, Guidance*. LDA, Wisbech.

Quin, V. and MacAuslan, A. (1981) *Reading and Spelling Difficulties*. Unibooks, Hodder and Stoughton, London.

Sassoon, R. (1983) *The Practical Guide to Children's Handwriting*. Thames and Hudson, London.

Taylor, J. (1979) 'Writing is for reading.' Available from 14 Dora Road, London SW19 7HH.

11

The Assessment and Teaching of Handwriting Skills

Our understanding of the intellectual and perceptual components of the handwriting process are still very rudimentary, although researchers are constantly increasing our knowledge. In this chapter techniques for assessment, initial teaching and remediation, found successful with children experiencing writing difficulties, will be described.

INITIAL ASSESSMENT OF HANDWRITING ABILITY

Assessment is a '. . . process of collecting and organizing the relevant information about a client,' Chia (1984). An assessor must ensure that the information collected is both relevant and necessary. Some fairly complex tools of assessment are available. *Diagnosis and Remediation of Handwriting Problems* (Stott, Moyes and Henderson 1985), for example, will give fairly precise measurement but takes time to administer and is more appropriate in the research context. For a busy class teacher the use of a checklist, such as the *Handwriting Checklist* (Alston and Taylor 1984), on which specific information about each pupil's handwriting can be recorded, may be more directly useful for planning a suitable handwriting programme tailored to individual need.

Before any formal assessment takes place it is necessary to consider briefly the tools of the trade. The table and chair should be the correct height for a pupil. His forearms should rest comfortably on the table, his thighs and feet should be parallel with the floor. He should not be working in his own light. Paper and use of lines has been discussed in Chapter 7.

The diameter of the writing tool barrel most suitable in the early stages of learning to write continues to be an area of debate. If a variety of pencils is available, each pupil can select the one that suits him best. When an additional grip is used on the pencil it is necessary to confirm that the correct tool hold is, in fact, being achieved. At what age or stage of writing development a change from using a pencil to using a pen should be made, and which type of pen should be selected, remain unanswered questions. The type of pencil lead affects the quality of writing. Pencil hardness is indicated by letters and numbers; H is hard and B is soft. The average pencil is HB and is the type usually recommended for normal writing purposes. H tends to be too hard for general use. If a child has a tendency to exert too much pressure, the use of a softer lead can sometimes help. It may be necessary to advise parents of these facts so that the child can be supplied with a suitable writing tool. Provision of a pencil sharpener and good quality eraser encourages the pupil to keep his pencil sharp and to erase mistakes neatly.

Figure 11.1 shows a framework indicating, in detail, the principal processes involved in learning to write. Any handwriting assessment must allow the teacher or therapist to identify areas of breakdown from among those processes. It is recommended that the problem areas identified should be recorded on a checklist.

In the first stage of assessment the global aspects of a child's development must be considered. It is necessary to do the following:

1) Check that vision and hearing are normal. If there is any doubt about a pupil's vision and hearing then appropriate referrals to specialists should be made.
2) Check whether there were any delays in developmental milestones, e.g. delayed walking, delayed speaking.
3) Check whether the pupil is having any difficulties with gross motor activities.
4) Check whether there are any current speech difficulties.
5) Check whether the pupil has had sufficient prewriting experiences, e.g. manipulative play, painting, looking at books.
6) Consider the learning strategies that a pupil normally employs, as these may affect his attitude to mastering handwriting.

Problems in any of these areas may contribute to handwriting difficulties.

The second stage of assessment is to observe in detail the various facets of the handwriting process itself and to observe and record pupil performance.

109

Figure 11.1: The sequence and structure of handwriting competence

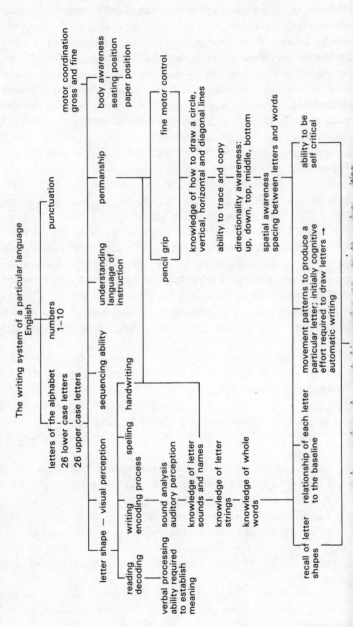

Posture and paper position

The height of the table and chair should be checked. The pupil should sit well back on the chair with his weight evenly distributed. His back should be straight with his shoulders relaxed. As he writes he should be leaning slightly forward from the hips and his non-writing hand should be placed on the paper.

The position of the paper on the table is important. It should be angled sufficiently, between 20° and 35° from a line parallel to the edge of the table, so that the pupil can see what he is writing (Figure 11.2).

Figure 11.2: Paper positions for writing

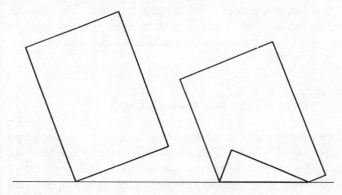

A: Approximate paper position for the right-handed writer

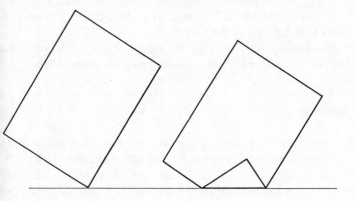

B: Approximate paper position for the left-handed writer

111

Poor posture may be an indication of poor muscle tone or poor motor co-ordination. If either seems to be the case the pupil should be offered a specific physical education programme, concentrating on the development of muscle tone or gross motor skills; alternatively the pupil may be referred to a physiotherapist.

Tool hold

The following should be recorded:

(1) The type of grip and the positions of the digits.
(2) Whether the grip is normal, tense or too loose.
(3) Whether the tool is held too near the point. When this occurs it prevents the pupil from monitoring visually what he is writing, and restricts the fine finger movement necessary for good letter formation.

Knowledge of letter sounds and names

Many pupils are confused about the sounds and names of letters. A pupil should be able to give the name or sound of each letter and be able to write each letter when the name or sound is given to him. Confusions arise because letters can be reversed, inverted or rotated. The common confusions are: *b/d* are reversed, *b/p* are inverted, *d/p* are rotated, *p/q* are reversed, *m/w* are inverted, *i/j* are reversed, *f/t* are inverted. In addition, the letters *i*, *l* and *j* are confused because the pupil fails to notice their different heights and their positions in relation to the base line.

The names and sounds of the letters *u/y*, *j/g*, *c/s* are often confused by children whose auditory reception seems weak.

Numerals

Writing numerals should be considered part of a handwriting programme. The pupil can be asked to write the numerals 1 to 10. The numerals 2, 3, 4, 5, 6, 7, and 9 are frequently reversed by children with handwriting problems. The 0 is frequently written too small, many pupils apparently being unaware that it is not the small letter *o* but a different symbol that should be the size of a capital

112

letter, as indeed should all numerals. At the appropriate stage, it is also necessary to check that the signs for addition, subtraction, multiplication and division are known and understood.

Shape copying

Figure 11.3 shows the shapes that the pupil should be asked to copy. It is important that the shapes to be copied are positioned so that they can be seen by either right- or left-handed pupils.

Figure 11.3: Shape copying test

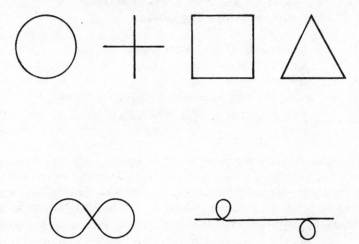

Sheridan (1975) states that a child should be able to copy a circle at three years of age, a cross at four years, a square at five years and a triangle at five-and-a-half years. Many of the letters have movements similar to those required to form a circle, a cross and a triangle. If a pupil cannot draw a circle or cross he is not ready to learn how to write letters. If he starts the circle at the bottom it is likely that he will do the same for the letter *o*. If he is unable to draw a triangle, he may find letters with diagonal lines, i.e. *k, v, w, x, z,* difficult to write.

In Figure 11.3 two additional shapes have been added to the basic shapes. In order to copy these two shapes in one flowing movement, the child has to be aware of the change in direction entailed. Pupils who have difficulty in copying these two shapes tend to have problems with mastering a cursive script.

113

Draw a person

The value of observing how a pupil draws 'a person' receives attention in Chapter 3.

Correct letter formation

A letter should begin '. . . at the right place and work in the conventional direction, that is to say, the direction which enables the letter to be formed with a continuous movement from where it can eventually be joined to the next letter' (Stott, *et al.* 1985).

The following details should be checked:

(1) Is the letter started in the correct place?
(2) Is the letter formed correctly?
(3) Are the down strokes of the letter straight?
(4) Are the round letters sufficiently rounded and closed?
(5) If joins are employed are they used appropriately?

Alignment, slant and relative height of letters

A pupil may find it difficult to keep the letters on the baseline, to have the slant of the letters consistent or to achieve the correct relative heights of letters.

Spacing between letters and words

A pupil may find it very difficult to remember to put spaces between words. He may tend to move the beginning of each successive line of writing away from the margin and he may find it impossible to write a list with each word aligned under the previous one. He may also have difficulty with setting out arithmetical calculations.

Writing rhythm

A rhythm develops as the writing of a letter becomes automatic. It is this rhythm that leads to speed and fluency. However, pupils often produce letters with small, jerky, disconnected movements, lacking

Figure 11.4: A script written at speed

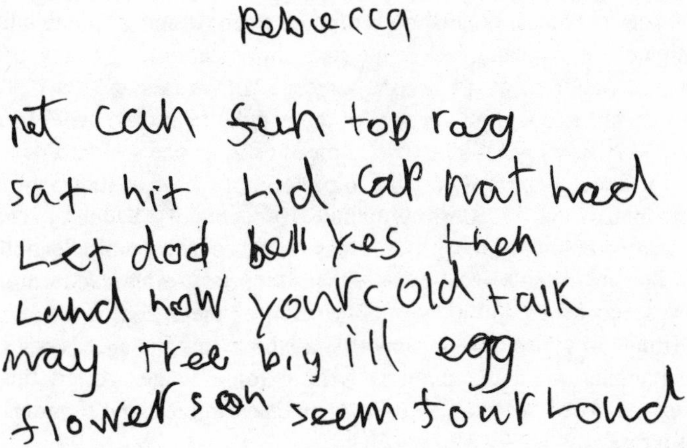

Rebecca

net cah suh top rag
sat hit Lid cap nat had
Let dod ball yes then
Land how your cold talk
may Tree biy ill egg
flower son seem tour Loud

in shape and proportion, and giving an overall appearance of untidiness. It would seem that when children are not encouraged to develop their script into a semi-joined or joined script fairly early in their school careers, print script may remain the preferred model. Pickard and Alston (1985) found that approximately half their 11- to 12-year-old sample of 149 pupils did not join letters. Figure 11.4 shows the script of a right-handed 9-year-old girl who writes at speed, but whose writing has many of the problems mentioned.

Developing fluency and speed

Legible writing is of limited value unless it can be produced with ease, fluency and speed. Once letter formation is well established the writing speed should be monitored at regular intervals. Ziviani and Elkins (1984) suggest that for a yardstick the simple phrase 'cats and dogs' should be written for two minutes and the number of letters written should be recorded. In the sample studied, the mean speed in letters written per minute varied with age as follows: 8 years, 32.8; 9 years, 34.2; 10 years, 38.4; 11 years, 46.1; 12 years, 52.1.

The girls, who wrote on average 40.05 letters per minute, wrote significantly faster than the boys, who wrote on average 35.55 letters per minute. Pickard and Alston (1985) used a slightly different approach to study the writing speed of 11-year-olds. The sentence 'The quick brown fox jumps over the lazy dog' was written

115

on the blackboard. The pupils were asked to copy this sentence, as many times as possible, for three minutes. The results showed that 68 per cent of the population scored between 61 and 103 letters per minute (i.e. a mean of 82 ± one standard deviation). The same procedure was used with a second sentence 'I love cats and dogs'; the results showed that 68 per cent of the population scored between 77 and 117 letters per minute (i.e. a mean of 97 ± one standard deviation). They concluded that the 16 per cent of the population scoring less than 61 and 77 letters per minute, respectively (i.e. one standard deviation below the mean) '. . . may be in urgent need of attention'.

It is important to establish whether the speed sample is to measure the speed of a pupil's 'normal' writing or the speed of his 'fast' writing. In either case it cannot be assumed that the speeds can be maintained when the pupil is writing for a longer period time. Regular speed tests can be used to maintain interest and to monitor progress.

Language of instruction

Although it may be inappropriate to administer a formal test, it is important to establish that the pupil really does understand the vocabulary employed when handwriting is discussed, e.g. word, letter, space, top, middle. Labels appropriate to the child's age and ability can be given to the more difficult concepts, e.g. for young children letters with descenders may be called 'letters with tails'.

Development of self criticism

A pupil needs to be encouraged to be self critical. Initially he learns to match the individual letters he writes to a prescribed model and this necessitates the development of critical awareness. As the pupil progresses, continued attention to detail such as letter formation, slant, alignment, punctuation, paragraph indentation and underlining headings all become areas that require the further development of self criticism.

Functional writing ability

Handwriting is the tool of written expression and it is important to know the extent of the pupil's functional writing ability. To evaluate writing ability, the child can be asked to write his name and to record as many words as he knows in a given time. Observing how he sets about this task may give the teacher insight into the child's learning strategies.

The older pupil can be set some free writing with a specific title, e.g. 'My favourite person or personality'. The task should be completed within a specific time. Alternatively a formal spelling test can be administered.

A pupil whose written expression is weak may need to be given specific help in expressive writing skills, in addition to the help he requires with his handwriting.

Summary

A pupil may be experiencing handwriting difficulties for a number of reasons:

(1) There are underlying physical difficulties that affect the physical and mechanical aspects of writing, e.g. posture, paper position, tool hold, letter formation and presentation.
(2) There is underlying difficuly in recalling the language of the letters, i.e. their names and sounds.
(3) There is underlying difficulty with understanding the language of instruction.

His problems may be aggravated because:

(1) There is insufficient in-depth teaching for pupils who are experiencing difficulties.
(2) There is insufficient on-going monitoring of pupils known to have handwriting difficulties.

The teacher or therapist must attempt to identify and record each pupil's areas of weakness in order to plan suitable teaching programmes.

INITIAL TEACHING TECHNIQUES

Regardless of the method employed for the teaching of handwriting, some individual instruction is usually necessary. The teaching techniques now described are based on 'one-to-one' contact between teacher and pupil, but could be adapted to suit a larger group.

Monitoring posture, paper position and tool hold

Repeating the instructions, 'Sit up' or 'Put your hand on the paper!' may have little permanent effect on a pupil's behaviour. A more positive attitude may be achieved by setting a time limit and expecting the correct posture or position to be maintained during that time. This technique is even more successful if a reward system is used.

Achieving the correct paper position relative to the edge of the table may require marking guide lines on the writing surface, e.g. masking tape can be placed in the appropriate position so that the paper for writing is then placed parallel with the tape. Instructing the pupil to place his writing arm parallel to the paper is another possible technique.

For some pupils, establishing the tripod grip is extremely difficult. The use of coloured stickers on the barrel of the writing tool to indicate the relative position of the finger and thumb may assist. If a triangular pencil grip is being used it is important that the child should be taught that part of the grip should be visible between his index finger and thumb.

Teaching letter names and sounds

It is quite common to find the older pupil with handwriting problems confused about some of the letter names and sounds. In order to prevent failure later, it is essential that letter names and sounds are mastered as early as possible. Some teachers may feel that learning sounds only is sufficient, but at some stage it is necessary to learn both names and sounds. Hornsby and Shear (1975) and Wendon (1972) are among the numerous authors who give specific techniques for learning to identify the letters. Maines (1985) reminds us that it is important 'to establish that learning has actually occurred' and that the information learned can still be recalled two weeks later.

Shape copying

The child who has difficulty with copying the shapes in Figure 11.3 will need some very specific teaching when he learns to write letters, if he is to master the correct movement pattern of letter formation. If he has found the triangle difficult he may need to work on mastering the zig zag pattern in Figure 10.2 before learning to write letters with a diagonal line.

Teaching letter formation

There are several techniques that can be usefully employed when the pupil is learning letter formation:

(1) Initially he should be encouraged to use verbal rehearsal before he writes each letter. He should state the starting position of the letter and direction in which the pencil will be moved.

(2) The pupil can trace over a letter with the index finger of his writing hand or with a suitable tool to help to reinforce the movement patterns of the letter. Letterforms (Michael 1985) contains a set of large, individual letter cards with both the starting position and changes in direction clearly indicated. A set of smaller letters is included in the pack for use when letter strings are introduced.

(3) Once he has written a letter correctly, he can be asked to write it first with his eyes uncovered and then to reproduce it with eyes covered.

(4) Letters should be taught in families. The similarities and differences should be clearly stated. This reduces the amount of new information to be learnt as each new letter is introduced.

(5) A pupil who has difficulty with copying the basic shapes should spend some time each day mastering skills designed to help him to concentrate on the acquisition of correct letter formation.

It is interesting to note that even after fluent letter formation has been achieved, a pupil may still have problems with copying shapes, indicating that specific teaching may sometimes lead to the development of only those skills specifically taught.

Memory

When the pupil has difficulty in remembering correct letter/numeral orientation, an *aide memoire* placed near him may assist. If the difficulty persists, he should be required to write those characters creating the difficulty at the top of each page of writing for his reference.

Spatial aspects of handwriting

The spatial aspects of handwriting are conventions. A pupil who has perceptual difficulties may not pick up these conventions unless he is given specific instruction and his performance is constantly monitored. Such a pupil:

(1) may not know which letters have ascenders or descenders and which are the x height letters,
(2) may be unsure of the place to commence a letter,
(3) may not place letters in the correct positions relative to the base line,
(4) may find it difficult to start each line of writing near the margin,
(5) may find it difficult to leave spaces between words,
(6) may leave uneven spaces between letters.

When difficulties occur, specific instruction appropriate to individual needs should be offered.

Punctuation

The correct use of capital letters and full stops should be introduced to the writing programme as early as possible, but instruction should be determined by the pupil's ability.

Developing speed, fluency and self assessment

Constant practice at maintaining legibility while increasing speed is essential. Once the correct movement pattern for a letter has been mastered, the pupil should be encouraged to practise it with increasing speed so that the movement becomes automatic. A stop watch can assist precise timing. The pupil is asked to write a given letter for 15 seconds. He counts the number of well-formed letters as an assessment of speed. As ill-formed letters do not contribute to his speed assessment, he begins to learn about legibility, speed and increasing fluency. He then looks again at the completed letters and ticks the 'best', so developing the concept of self assessment. Three-letter words, digraphs, blends and letter strings can also be incorporated in the programme. Practice at maintaining legibility, while increasing speed, is essential. Regular speed tests can be used to maintain interest and to monitor progress.

Progression from an unjoined to a semi-joined cursive script

Once the pupil has mastered correct letter movement patterns, he is in a position to learn how to join some of the letters. The horizontal join is the simplest to master, e.g. *oa, ow, oi, oy*. This can be followed by joins from letters ending on the base line, first joining to *x* height letters, e.g. *im, ip,* and then progressing to joining to letters with ascenders, e.g. *it, il*. The join from a letter ending on the base line to a round letter, e.g. *ca, ad,* frequently causes difficulty and specific instruction may be required.

Working with parents

All parents would benefit from specific guidelines on the school's model and methods for teaching handwriting. Guidelines for parents are produced by Hannavy (1985), Michael (1984) and the Queensland Department of Education (Boys 1984), to name a few. Guidelines could usefully include a section on how written work should be presented by older pupils.

When a pupil is experiencing handwriting difficulties, parents should be informed about the nature of the difficulties and encouraged to become involved in helping their child.

If a pupil shows any difficulty in learning to write, he should be considered 'at risk'. His performance should be regularly monitored through each educational year until writing competence has been established. Where necessary, further remedial help should be given.

121

REMEDIATION OF HANDWRITING DIFFICULTIES

If a pupil fails to master skills described earlier in this chapter, he will require further help. The problems that still persist can be a combination of the following:

(1) incorrect letter formation,
(2) reversals,
(3) incorrect use of capital letters,
(4) inconsistent height of letters,
(5) variable slant of down strokes,
(6) poor alignment,
(7) incorrect joins,
(8) incorrect spacing between letters or words,
(9) slower than normal speed,
(10) poor presentation.

There may be underlying emotional difficulty.

Discovering where the breakdown is occurring can be facilitated by collecting samples of the pupil's writing. A sample can be obtained by asking the pupil to write his name, address and the date at the top of a sheet of paper. This can be followed by a timed sample of free writing, from which additional difficulties, such as spelling problems, should be apparent. To ascertain which letters are still formed incorrectly, the teacher must watch the pupil as he writes the letters of the alphabet. Finally, a writing speed sample should be taken. Areas of difficulty can be recorded on a checklist.

Planning a remedial programme

The teacher should always observe the positive aspects of the pupil's writing and make positive comments before remedial work is begun. For example, in Figure 11.4, despite all the faults, most of the letters were started in the correct place. In Figure 11.7 the teacher could note that the height of the ascenders and descenders and the slant of the letters are regular. If the teacher acknowledges satisfactory achievement where it exists, the pupil may be more prepared to enter into discussion about his difficulties.

The next step is to ask the pupil to indicate those aspects of his handwriting that he dislikes. If he is unable to comment or finds the situation too personally threatening, the teacher should point out one of the basic rules:

all letters except *d* and *e* start at the top,
all down strokes should be straight and parallel,
the spaces between letters and words should be evenly distributed.

This may help him to identify his errors. In this way no criticism has been made by the teacher and the pupil has identified his own difficulties. A positive framework has been created in which both the teacher and the pupil can work.

The fundamentals of handwriting, such as posture, tool hold, and knowledge of letter name and sound, have been discussed in the section on initial teaching techniques and are equally applicable to the older pupil.

Many pupils seem to form letters with a minimum of fine finger movement. Naville (1985) referred to 'waking up the fingers'. Figure 11.5 shows a pupil's pencil trace before discussion about his handwriting had taken place and the traces after he had concentrated on increasing his finger movement when forming letters.

Pupils can be shown two very useful warm-up exercises to increase finger movement (Figure 11.6). For these exercises the pupil must keep his writing hand resting on the paper at all times as he makes the movement, and must concentrate on increasing the size of the circle and the length of the straight line by using only his fingers.

Figure 11.5:

A: Pupil's pencil trace before discussion

B: A pencil trace at the end of the first lesson

Figure 11.6: Two useful doodles

Once correct letter formation has been achieved it is necessary to increase speed and fluency. This can be done by carrying out the following procedure in a timed interval of 15 seconds:

(1) The letter to be practised should be written out as many times as possible in 15 seconds, with concentration on well-formed letters.
(2) Each well-formed letter should be ticked. If only one or two are ticked, then the pupil should try again, writing at a pace slow enough to allow him to produce well-formed letters.
(3) The pupil is then asked to write one or two words that contain the letter just practised. When his attention is diverted from letter formation to writing a word, old habits often creep back. If this occurs the exercise can be repeated.

Once individual letters have improved, then digraphs and blends can be introduced to the programme. The pupil should be encouraged to make up his own programme by looking at a sample of his writing and deciding which letters need to be practised. Alternatively, it may be more suitable if he is initially given a specific area to work on, e.g. horizontal joins, and for him to devise his own programme at a later date, when some progress has been made. Ideally, in the initial stages, the exercises should be practised for 5–10 minutes daily.

Concentration on a specific area of difficulty often has a spin-off effect on other aspects of the pupil's writing. Figure 11.7, shows the writing of a right-handed, 13-year-old boy (Thomas) whose script was mainly unjoined. At the end of the first teaching session he was asked to concentrate on horizontal joins; the improvement after two weeks was considerable.

124

Figure 11.7:

A: Thomas's first sample of writing

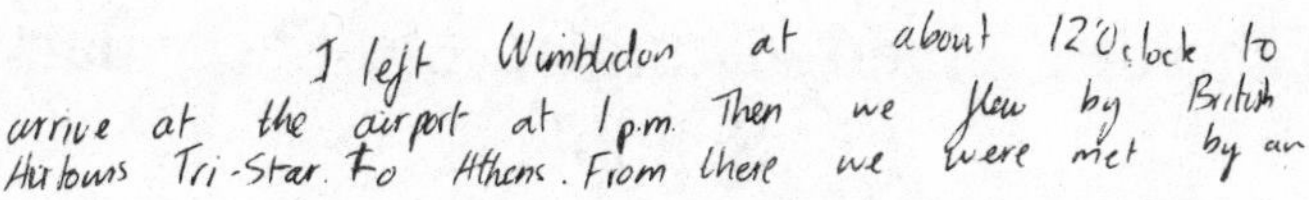

> I left Wimbledon at about 12 O'clock to arrive at the airport at 1 p.m. Then we flew by British Airways Tri-Star. To Athens. From there we were met by an

B: His writing two weeks later

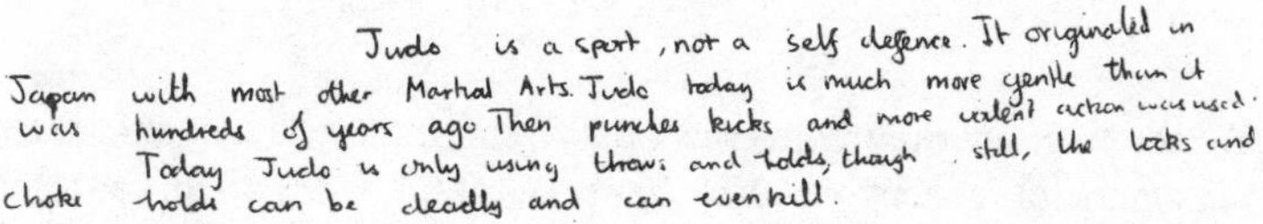

> Judo is a sport, not a self defence. It originated in Japan with most other Martial Arts. Judo today is much more gentle than it was hundreds of years ago. Then punches kicks and more violent action was used. Today Judo is only using throws and holds, though . still, the locks and choke holds can be deadly and can even kill.

REFERENCES

Alston, J. and Taylor, J. (1984) *The Handwriting File: Diagnosis and Remediation of Handwriting Difficulties*. LDA, Wisbech.

Boys, J. (1984) 'The teaching of handwriting.' Department of Education, University of Queensland.

Chia, S.H. (1984) 'Occupational therapy for children with perceptual motor disorders: a literature review'. *British Journal of Occupational Therapy*, 47, 39–42.

Hannavy, S. (1985) 'Parents helping their children with reading, writing and phonic skills.' Reading and Language Development Centre, Huntingdon.

Hornsby, B. and Shear, F. (1975) *Alpha to Omega*. Heinemann, London.

Maines, B. (1985) 'Handwriting and spelling.' South House, Yatesbury, Nr. Calne SN11 8YE.

Michael, B. (1985) *Letterforms*. Jordanhill College of Education, Glasgow.

Naville, S. (1985) 'Seminar in psychomotor therapy'. Preston District Health Authority.

Pickard, P. and Alston, J. (1985) *Helping Secondary School Pupils with Handwriting: Current Research, Identification and Assessment Guidance*. LDA, Wisbech.

Sheridan, M.D. (1975) *From Birth to Five Years: Children's Developmental Progress*. NFER–Nelson, Windsor.

Stott, D.H., Moyes, F.A. and Henderson, S.E. (1985) *Diagnosis and Remediation of Handwriting Problems*. Brook Educational, Guelph, Ontario.

Wendon, L. (1972) *Pictograms*. Pictogram Supplies, Barton, Cambs.

Ziviani, J. and Elkins, J. (1984) 'An evaluation of handwriting performance.' *Educational Review*, 36, (3).

12

Teaching Handwriting in the Secondary School

Elizabeth Whitmarsh

By the time children enter secondary school they have had at least six years of education, they have learnt to read, to decode by understanding grapheme/phoneme correspondence, phonetic and structural analysis, configuration cues, prefixes and suffixes. They are expected to comprehend what they read by following a sequence, remembering detail, skimming for information, evaluating validity and appreciating literature.

To encode, a child must have begun to cope with the decoding process, in addition to the separate skills demanded of him when writing. He needs fine motor control and visuo-motor skills and an ability to make symbolic representations of situations that can be extended to produce novel sentences through which individual experiences can be expressed. Analysing, summarising and evaluating give the writer power to manipulate time, so that it can become an extension and reflection of his own efforts to impose order on the world. It is little short of miraculous that for most children the process seems to hold no specific problems. Mistakes are made and rectified as the child progresses, the words he uses relevant to his particular background as he develops attitudes and interests that are not always part of school.

For others, the process is laborious toil, and the reasons why this might be so are too numerous to mention. A review of literature by Larry Faas (1976) reveals no less than 90 terms used to describe the characteristics of 'learning disabled children': language disorders, maturational lags, sensory aphasias, learning blocks, etc. For the children, the terms are meaningless. All they know is what they think they cannot do, and all too often they are asked to confirm their own suspicions by being asked to do it again!

As children enter secondary school, many have already formed an opinion of their own worth. Some of them believe that their poor handwriting reflects on them and that they are judged by its quality. Whether this is indeed so, and whether this view is instilled by teachers who overemphasise presentation skills at the expense of content, is an area of debate that will remain unexplored here. What is under discussion, is how secondary school teachers can help those who struggle with handwriting and are therefore denied the pleasure of exploring their world on paper; those who later dread filling in application forms; and those who avoid putting pen to paper whenever possible because they are ashamed of the results.

What can be done about the handwriting needs of secondary school pupils? Is it too late to change inappropriate habits that have been allowed to form in the primary school years? What can secondary school teachers do to help children acquire a legible hand and which teachers should undertake the task? Can speed be increased without loss of legibility? Can motivation be increased? These are the questions that the children themselves often raise, and there is no one answer to any of them. To incorporate them in a school management policy and reduce them to viable teaching programmes, it is suggested that there are four main methods of approach; a whole school policy, class lessons, individual teaching, and group sessions.

A WHOLE SCHOOL POLICY

Adequate vision and hearing are essential if pupils are to make good progress in school. Health records should be checked as the pupils enter secondary school and examination of visual and auditory acuity should take place from time to time. Smith and James (1968) inform us that in a class of 40 children, it would be expected that six or seven would be wearing glasses, at least one boy would be colour blind, one child would have a squint, and two more would have eye strain. Bolger (1975) informs us that hearing losses occur at different levels and that auditory discrimination problems may be the cause of *b/d* reversals or similar confusions.

There is no evidence to suggest that practice alone will cause handwriting to improve, as the authors of the New Zealand (1980) study observed when, referring to Barbe's text, they stated, 'practice does not make perfect; it only makes permanent'. The letter-formation patterns need to be shown to the children of course and the provision of a model is often a major instructional vehicle. However, the use of worksheets to establish or change pupils'

127

handwriting will have little value unless there is constant monitoring of letter formation and joins by the teacher.

It would be unreasonable to expect all secondary school teachers to be able to teach or correct handwriting, but it is essential that one or more teachers in each school should be able to assist those who have problems. It is unlikely that all such pupils will be the less able ones; observation of pupils' writing will usually reveal a few otherwise able children who could benefit from assistance with writing speed, legibility or both. A general policy might be developed by members of staff from the English and Special Needs Departments, with full consultation with all school staff before the policy for provision is implemented. Art teachers have often themselves completed courses in calligraphy and may wish to take some responsibility for the teaching of handwriting in general. Writing is a skill requiring movement and rhythm and the physical education or movement specialists might be encouraged to discuss these elements of the writing task.

However poor the handwriting may be, consistency in the general presentation of the work can also help to improve legibility. Praise for improvement in the general appearance of pupils' work can increase motivation and may be the first step toward improved self image for those pupils who lack self confidence. If the demands of the teachers in the school are the same, then the chances of increasing presentation skills must surely be concomitant. The following suggestions for presentation are flexible, as individual schools will negotiate their own standards, and there is no research that can support their inclusion. They are therefore offered as guidelines, serving mainly as a reminder that children often wish to be told what exactly is expected of them. Guideline sheets may be selected as appropriate and attached to each pupil's exercise book (inside the front cover) or placed where the guidelines may be easily observed by the pupil.

With insistence upon standards of presentation, children become aware that what and how they write is important to others. This, with a greater impetus to writing through motivation, can establish a new and important ethos for writing in school. A major attack on graffiti may also be necessary, particularly as this seems to appear in waves as different pop groups hit the screen! Tolerance of graffiti in schools is clearly incompatible with general pride and good standards of presentation.

A secondary school time table usually leaves little time for handwriting lessons. A valuable suggestion from Brenda Brown (1983)

PRESENTATION OF WRITTEN WORK

PRESENTATION OF WRITTEN WORK

DATE

This is to be placed in the top right hand corner of the work, using numbers for the day and the year, the month to be written in full. (N.B. This also helps some children with spelling), e.g.

18th February, 1986.

NAME

If a name is needed it should be placed in the top left hand corner of the work, and written in full, e.g.
Jimmy Jones.

TITLE

The title is to be placed on the second line of the page, should be central and underlined with a ruler.

Please miss a line before starting the work. Always start with a capital letter. If using subheadings, start them by the margin and on a line by themselves, e.g.

RULING OFF

All work should be ruled off after missing one line at the end of the work.

DIAGRAMS

Diagrams or bar charts, etc. must always be in pencil. All arrows or markers must be ruled, labelled neatly, and every diagram must have a heading, e.g.

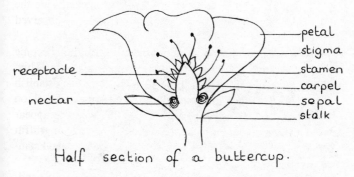

Half section of a buttercup.

August 20th 1987

Presentation of Work

The date has been placed in the top right hand corner of the work. The title is on the next line, and is underlined with a ruler. Miss one line before starting your work.

Capital letters start each sentence, and full stops end each sentence. Use paragraphs when you have a break in your subject.

A Subheading

This should start by the margin and be underlined with a ruler, as above.

Mistakes

If you make a (misteak) mistake, place it in brackets instead of scribbling. Miss one line and rule off at the end of your work.

Jimmy Smith · *19th May 1987*

The Secret

Please miss one line before starting to write. Do not forget capital letters, full stops and paragraphs. If you do work that needs a subheading, start it by the margin and on a line by itself.

Subheading

Continue writing, starting another paragraph. All work should then be ruled off after missing one line at the end of the work.

Use this presentation when you work on paper.

is that there should be a Study Skills course for all first-year pupils. The course should include a range of skills that support performance in school subjects but are not seen as part of those subjects *per se*. It would include instruction in the following: use of the library, conventions of written English, the development of different reading strategies for different reading purposes, techniques for developing and improving spelling, and techniques for developing and improving handwriting.

CLASS LESSONS

There seems to be little reason why classes in most secondary school subjects should not have an occasional session when, for example, some particularly well presented work can be achieved. The work can be edited and displayed, the copying session becoming a handwriting lesson, since, after initial editing, the children are no longer concentrating on content.

History lessons could include the writings and documents of the ages, for how else but through the written word have we learned most about our past? Looking at the language of other countries is fascinating for many children, and attempting to write in Arabic or Hebrew, for example, can also help to develop fine motor skills. ('Looks Irish to me' was one 11-year-old's comment on attempting an Arabic equivalent of his name.)

Religious Education can include the beautiful illuminated manuscripts of Anglo-Saxon and medieval scribes, the children experimenting when writing out a favourite prayer or hymn. It was the growth of Christianity that made more systems of communication necessary, and the study of literacy can combine well with all religions.

To embark upon a topic on handwriting could become a regular feature of History, English, Art or Humanities. The history of the pen, the development of paper, the invention of print and the possibilities of the computer can be explored from many different angles. Jarman (1979) gives valuable information on how to make a quill pen, and supplies a list of addresses and resources for undertaking such a topic. Etymology often appears to fascinate children, and incidentally may help spelling. Children from different cultures can contribute a great deal to such a topic, and give insight into problems of communication between countries with a language barrier.

The computer itself can be used as an aid to handwriting, with the use of graphic tablets such as the Koala Pad. This flat plate-like device attaches to the computer, the child drawing a letter shape on to the pad, and this is reproduced upon the screen (Daiute 1985).

Thus handwriting can be practised across the curriculum and, when used imaginatively, can raise the level of interest of many of the children. The class lessons by rote learning that bored so many of our grandparents are not the only way to develop fine motor skills.

Many authorities on handwriting recommend speed tests or trials to help children develop endurance without loss of legibility (Michael 1984; Pickard and Alston 1985). The trials could take place in Tutor contact time, perhaps once each week, or may even be presented as a game for the younger pupils, with a prize for the pupil who achieves the greatest progress. Tests of one-, two- or three-minutes duration can be given regularly. Sentences like 'The quick brown fox jumps over the lazy dog', or 'The five boxing wizards jumped quickly', use all the letters of the alphabet, and are not difficult to spell. The children can do a letter count after each test, perhaps filling in a class chart to monitor speed changes over a period of time. The importance of maintaining legibility should be stressed and poorly formed letters should not be included in the letter count.

Working out the average number of letters and graphing the results become part of a maths lesson at a later date. Art lessons could include some of the rhythmic exercises first recommended by Marion Richardson (1935), with children experimenting with different writing mediums and developing form with regularity of movement. These exercises can also serve to frame a valued text or work of art (Figures 12.1, 12.2), creating as they do borders of infinite variety and fashion.

Even when a school policy exists and when there is appropriate attention to handwriting in class lessons, some children will have developed such poor letter formation habits and anomalies of grip and style that only individual intervention will help to resolve their problems.

Figure 12.1: Rhythmic patterns frame a valued piece of work

133

Figure 12.2: Rhythmic patterns frame a valued piece of work

INDIVIDUAL TEACHING

Bad habits are difficult but not impossible to change, the basic approaches dividing into three aspects. First, the practical ones of grip, posture, table height, paper and positioning, and lighting. Second, the letter formations themselves, their movements and construction; and third, the style leading on to speed.

Since all children are individuals and handwriting problems differ, the manner in which we need to approach them from a psychological point of view will change according to need. Some children resist change, others welcome it, and the right amount of encouragement at the optimum time is paramount for success. Much, therefore, depends upon the relationship between pupil and teacher, for which there is no easy or instant recipe. Motivation to improve presentation may be increased by giving praise to good points in the writing. Although this sounds somewhat facile, it is something I think we all forget from time to time.

There is always a danger, and it must be acknowledged, that

134

viewing reading, writing and speech as discrete processes focuses attention on the motor skills when handwriting is considered. The interaction of all literacy skills and the part that written language plays in cognitive development must also be taken into consideration. Frank Smith (1983) draws attention to the importance of the interdependence of all language skills when he states 'Thoughts are created in the act of writing which changes the writer . . .'

On many occasions, a model may become the motivation a child lacks as he admires another hand. If the teacher has a good personal style, this can be used to advantage. Otherwise, a good writing scheme or the provision of books on graphology or palaeography may suffice.

The practical aspects can be noted as the child completes a written sample, and the secondary supplement to the Handwriting File (Alston 1985), draws attention to the most relevant when it states. 'Note and record:

(a) left or right handedness,
(b) any discomfort shown during or after completion of the sample,
(c) any unconventional grip,
(d) any unconventional posture,
(e) the type of pen or pencil used,
(f) the position of the paper.'

Any of these may be relatively easy to change and the corrections sustained by gentle reminders. These issues are discussed in depth elsewhere in this book, but it could be that the child may need something as simple as a triangular pencil grip (Easy Grip) for immediate improvement.

When the letter formations themselves present strange and varied faces, then watching the child complete the sample is more important, as incorrect letter formation cannot always be detected by simply examining the script. There is no one ideal hand, but letters and the conventions of how they are formed have evolved over the centuries and lend themselves particularly to a flowing cursive hand. There is little variation in letter formation in handwriting schemes generally. Indeed, considering the consistency of approach to letter formation, it seems surprising that so many children develop poor letter-formation habits.

Peck and Askov (1980) point out that little research has been directed to the production and legibility of letter forms during the past decade.

135

The New Zealand (1980) study recommends the basic letter formation as seen in Figure 12.3. All letters except *d* and *e* start at the top. In co-operation with the child, decide which letters show problems, what improvements can be made, and in which order they can be approached for maximum success and positive feedback. Lehman (1958) indicates the importance of identifying particular faults for teaching when, referring to his own work, he states,

'By directing teaching effort straight at specific faults of legibility, not only was legibility strikingly increased but both speed and quality of handwriting were also — very definitely increased.'

Figure 12.3: Basic letter formations

In Figure 12.4, the writing of an 11-year-old girl, the letters that need priority attention are *f, g, r* and *y*. The similarities of these to other letters need to be pointed out so that the children are learning the minimum number of movements. For example:

f is a tall letter that starts like a *c*,
g is *a* with a tail,
r is half an *n*,
y is *v* with a tail.

Figure 12.4: The writing of an 11-year-old girl

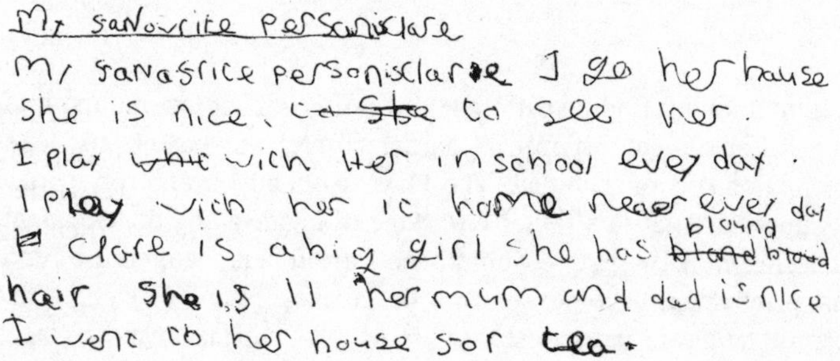

There are, of course, many other faults in this 11-year-old girl's writing, but it is important to show her the positive aspects of her writing so that she does not become demoralised by failure.

Scribbling out to erase can also spoil the presentation of written work, as the observer's eye is more easily drawn to the error. The pupil can be taught to place brackets round incorrect writing and to do this instead of, rather than as well as, crossing out.

The ligature from a letter that ends on the baseline and is then followed by a rounded letter, e.g. *m* followed by *a*, is one that causes many problems. It is used frequently, as in: *ac, ad, ag, cc, ea, ec, ed, eg, equ, ia, ic, id, ig, iqu, ud, uc.* The children need to be shown the similarities in the joins and to practise the movement in letter pairs at first. This can be followed by practice of words that include the letter strings.

It is often the varied letter size that produces the most untidy writing. Figure 12.5 shows the writing of an 11-year-old boy who has varied letter size and no ligatures. The problem of varied letter size can be approached by pointing out and encouraging practice of letters that are similar in size and shape, e.g. *aceo, wvir, suxz, mni, bdhklt, gjpqy.*

Figure 12.5: The writing of a boy who has varied letter size and no ligatures

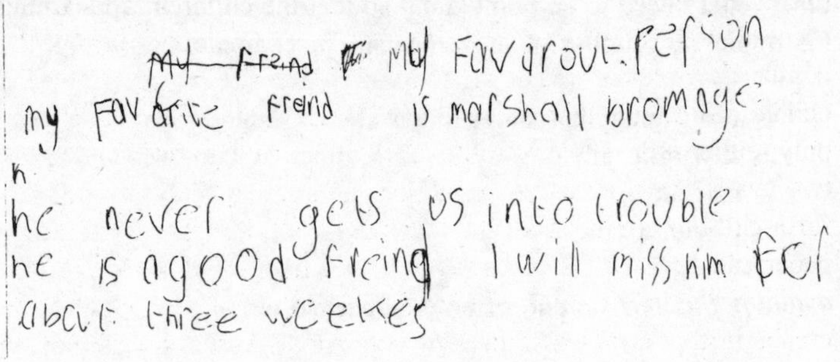

Children enjoy finding different ways of grouping letters, and finding different letter 'families' as the correct movements for letter formation become habitual. The 11-year-old boy has not yet learned ligatures and, at this rather late stage of handwriting development, it seems unlikely that he would benefit from being taught them until his print script becomes less erratic in size. Letters of similar size can be taught in pairs to start with, so that emphasis can be placed on speed and flow, e.g. *oo, or, ee, ou, ai, mi, th, lt, ll, bb, dd.* Pattern shapes can be taught and practised alongside the letter families, and can be used for bordering other art work or writing, e.g.

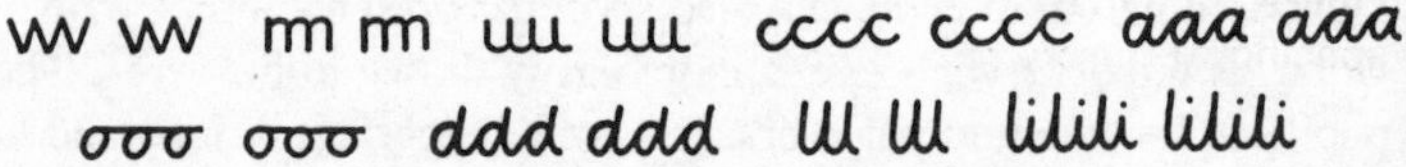

Undersheets with strong black lines can be placed beneath pretty coloured paper. This will assist regularity of pattern and spacing for maximum effect, and paper clips will hold the work in place. The necessity of having parallel strokes in one's writing needs to be pointed out and practised, particularly with regard to letter ascenders and descenders.

Many children have developed the habit of using an occasional capital letter in the middle of a lower-case word. Capitals *R* and *D* are frequent replacements for their lower-case counterparts. In this case, the individual letters need to be taught separately at first. Ligatures are then easier to master if they are introduced in familiar letter strings, e.g. *ri, ro, di, dle, do, da, hard, dry.*

b/d reversals remain a common fault among 11-year-olds with learning difficulties, and can be a problem for some pupils who otherwise have good handwriting. Most teachers have their favourite exercises for assisting with this problem, and different approaches succeed with different children. As *B* and *D* do not appear to be confused, a mental image of a capital *B* often helps to remind the child of the direction of the lower case *b*. Concentrating on one letter only, either *b* or *d*, seems to be more effective than introducing the two letters for contrast. A page from an old text book can be used for a child to colour in all the letter *b*s or all the letter *d*s. Tracing paper can be used for tracing words beginning with *b* or *d* — *but avoiding the introduction of bed, bid, bud, bad or bod*, which may create further problems through confusion. These words can be attacked at a later stage of corrective teaching.

The spacing of letters or words can also cause some children a great amount of confusion, as Figure 12.6 illustrates. Imagine an *O* between words, and the teaching of appropriate ligatures, stressing their correct starting points, will usually help to clear up this problem. The relevance of good spacing and letter form can be emphasised by cutting a word across the middle, e.g. showing first the bottom half and then the top. The top is usually much easier to read than the lower half and helps us to stress the importance of good all-round letter and word formation habits. Enlarging the letters may also help, and Figure 12.7, the writing of a 14-year-old boy, shows a need for this approach. This boy resisted all attempts to change

Figure 12.6: The writing of a pupil who has difficulty in the spacing of letters and words

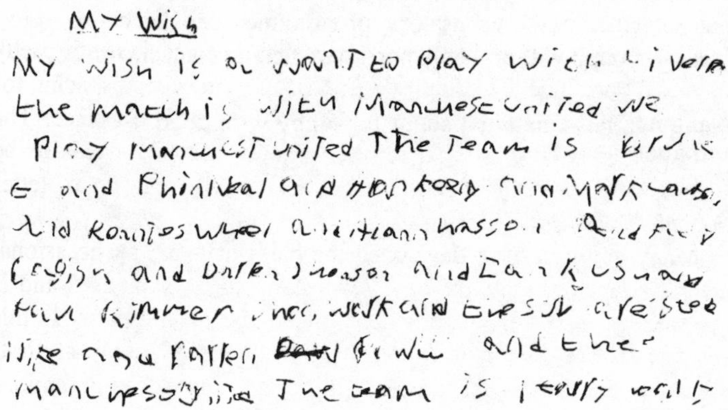

139

Figure 12.7: Enlarging the letters would aid legibility in this 14-year-old's written work

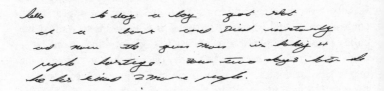

as, unlike the rest of us, he had no problem in reading his own writing. Eventually, he was persuaded to at least enlarge his script, and the results were a little easier to decipher.

On occasion, a child may have perfect letter formation habits but the written result is still unappealing, as Figures 12.8a and 12.8b illustrate. The boy who wrote this piece also had reversal problems, but when asked to complete a sample in his neatest hand, made no errors whatsoever. None of his teachers recognised this writing sample as belonging to Steve. It was solely the pressure of copying, speed writing, and quantity of output that caused the problem, which had become habitual in this middle-band secondary school pupil. He had forgotten that he could write well, and it took a lot of persuasion before Steve accepted that he could write like that at all times if he slowed down a little and concentrated when he was writing.

Some children have motor problems that are only going to be overcome with the help of exercises other than handwriting itself. The advice of a physiotherapist, occupational therapist, or a physical education teacher experienced in Special Education can be sought so that remedial or compensatory programmes can be constructed. Because a pupil will probably not have teaching contact with any one

Figure 12.8a: A habitual script for a boy with good letter formation

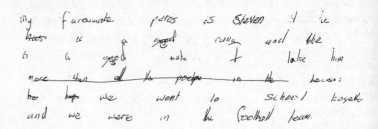

Figure 12.8b: A 'neatest hand' script for a boy with good letter formation

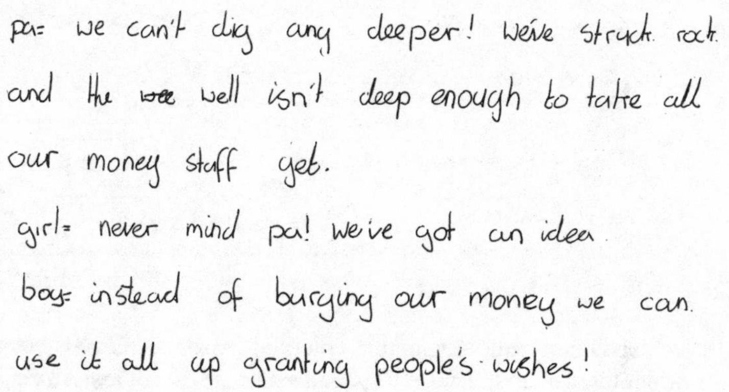

pa= we can't dig any deeper! We've struck rock.
and the ~~wee~~ well isn't deep enough to take all
our money stuff yet.

girl= never mind pa! we've got an idea.

boy= instead of burying our money we can.
use it all up granting people's wishes!

teacher on a daily basis, the help of parents for implementing recommended programmes is invaluable, particularly where regular exercises are essential for progress. In secondary schools, it is rare for any one teacher to teach a child every day, and this is where continuity breaks down. This was the case with Neil, whose writing was causing problems, and who needed motor skill training and exercises to increase hand muscle tone. After consultation with a physical education specialist, spring-clip clothes pegs and other finger muscle strengthening exercises were used in conjunction with some handwriting lessons, and improvement soon followed.

Another common cause for concern in the classroom today is the use, or rather misuse, of correcting fluid. Some children seem to end up with more of this liquid on the script than ink. Figure 12.9 illustrates this problem.

Rather than ban the use of correcting fluid completely, some compromise is called for, and it is suggested that the teacher wields the magic brush. With this approach, the children are shown how to use it effectively on individual letters, while word-errors continue to be placed in brackets. A substitute for correcting fluid is the correcting paper now normally employed by typists and which can be used to cover errors simply by rubbing a pencil over the correcting paper as it covers the part to be obliterated. All display work and other important projects should be drafted to prevent errors but it is not possible to expect pupils to draft writing output on all occasions; indeed, time does not permit drafting or editing on this scale.

141

Figure 12.9: A script that illustrates the misuse of correcting fluid

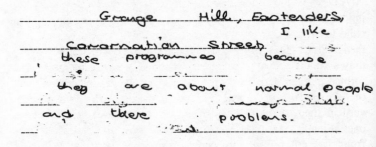

A pencil-case full of tempting coloured pens and pencils spurs some children on to greater efforts; indeed, most cannot resist trying each one in turn and this is to be encouraged. Platignum supply, on request, a poster that displays the company's whole range of products and Osmiroid also have a sales catalogue.

And finally, to write for a purpose always seems to result in better quality presentation. A 'thank you' letter after a visit, a letter of complaint to the local council, an answer to a call from the director of a television programme who is conducting a survey on children's smoking habits, or a reply to those numerous requests for information; all have been used successfully in class lessons and with individual pupils.

GROUP LESSONS

One of the ways of organising something a little different is to start a handwriting club, and for many children this has proved to be the answer to their particular needs.

First there is the problem of making the club sound an interesting and profitable place to be. Prizes and competitions are therefore advertised, which attract the mercenary! Second, the time and venue must be made attractive; a warm inviting classroom on a cold wet lunch time is irresistible to some. Another session after school, once or twice a week, caters for those who go home for lunch, and interested members of staff coerce the remaining reluctant few who need extra teaching input.

A group posture awareness session can be held in conjunction with a paper-position trial, with children experimenting with different combinations to find out which are most comfortable for them.

A task that the children usually enjoy, and which may be revealing, is a laterality test, adapted from Bolger (1975). First ask the child to draw a circle with the right hand and mark the circle '*R*', then a circle with the left hand and mark it '*L*'. Two circles are then drawn simultaneously, and the direction in which each circle was formed marked with an arrow. Next mark the paper with two sets of two small crosses, and ask the children to draw two parallel vertical lines simultaneously from the top crosses to the bottom ones. Finally, repeat this exercise with two parallel horizontal lines from left to right. The natural dominant hand will usually immediately become apparent and the exercise may reveal previously unnoticed midline problems. Figure 12.10 indicates a more competent right hand in the pupil who completed the laterality test.

Next, a writing sample should be collected from each child, so that an analysis of errors can be completed by the teacher later. A standardised method of gathering writing samples assists comparison, either to show progress in a pupil as time progresses or to identify children who need the most help at any particular time. Standard approaches to paper, writing task and timing have been described by Alston (1983, 1985) and, although designed for use with children in the junior age ranges, are equally suitable for use with secondary school pupils.

If a child has great letter-formation problems, then individual sessions must be planned in addition to club activities.

The majority of pupils have greatest difficulty when writing at speed. Sadly, dictation has not completely disappeared from the classroom, and this can cause problems for the writers who do not have handwriting, writing speed and spelling well established. The distinction between writing for someone else and taking notes for oneself needs to be pointed out. The former must be legible and state each word; the latter is for pupils' own use only. Teaching pupils personal shorthand can be an extremely useful exercise, for example @ for at, 4 for for, y'day for yesterday, Mon for Monday, h'writing for handwriting, + for and. Timed test trials in either long- or short-hand modes can become a popular competition, the rule being that any other member of the group can read the written result. The objective is to break one's own record when time is objectively recorded with a timer or similar instrument. The teacher can then observe each pupil as he writes, checking, and revising where necessary, the postural and mechanical aspects of writing, such as

143

Figure 12.10: The laterality test completed by a right-handed pupil

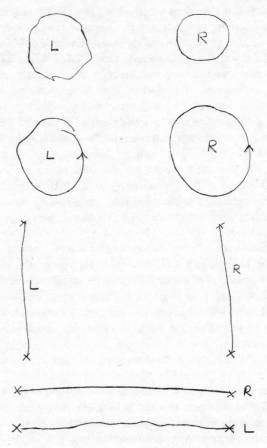

tool grip, sitting position, paper position and letter formation.

The provision of a variety of pens is essential, and a sample of each variety for trial purposes often spurs children into giving up other treats for a week and investing in a good-quality pen. Although it is not usually school policy to encourage use of a pencil, since most secondary school teachers would object, occasional use of pencil is permitted.

For pattern practice, the use of the ball-point pen is discouraged; fibre tip, fountain pen or roller ball usually give better results. Pattern practice is a regular feature of group sessions or handwriting club activities and the end results can be displayed in the form of a

Figure 12.11: A writing sampler

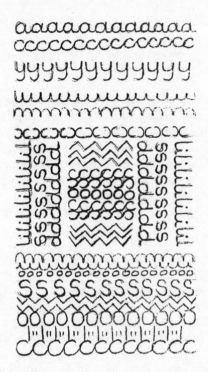

written sampler, rather like the old-fashioned sewing samplers of earlier centuries. A clever use of scissors, glue and a photocopier can give some display work to be proud of, as Figure 12.11 shows. Cheating, by copying the patterns and models of others? Well, why not, if the result boosts confidence and examples of perfection result?

After experimenting with many types of lined paper, the following conclusions have been drawn. First, the paper that produces the neatest work is the most expensive, i.e. the red- and blue-lined handwriting exercise books from Philip and Tacey. Some children do not like this line format as they consider it to be 'babyish', i.e. 'it is used in infant schools.' The cheapest way to provide practice paper is by using the somewhat outdated Banda machine or its equivalent, but ruling the required lines takes a great deal of time and patience. The most popular width of line is the 6-mm middle space, with 14-mm for the combined space for letter ascenders and descenders.

_____

_____

_____

_____

The easiest method for reproduction is by photocopying, but this becomes expensive when reams of paper are used for pattern practice, letter-string formation practice and the rest. The photocopying of line guides on to stiff card, for use beneath unlined paper is recommended. These can be used over and over again, and the card itself, as a backing sheet, can help the flow of writing. If paper clips are used to hold the paper in position, they tend to leave marks on the paper, and children often prefer small bulldog clips for this purpose.

'Handwriting . . . a Second Chance' (Pickard 1986) is a set of worksheets designed particularly for pupils in the secondary age range. The letter-formation worksheets are particularly useful, and the script and general worksheet format are relatively sophisticated and acceptable to those in the secondary age range. Special interest worksheets offer a useful addition for handwriting practice and all have free copyright from the publisher, Learning Development Aids.

If the teacher has a clear hand of her own, she may wish to develop her own practice sheets, as she is then more able to correct the movements of the children. A collection of such sheets will subsequently enable her to provide for the needs of individual children with different problems. A date on every sheet completed by the pupil gives him a clear picture of his own progress.

From time to time throughout his school life a child will explore the ornamental aspects of his writing, and the creative or ornamental pleasures are as important as the communicative ones. Gardner (1973) calls these skills autographic and indicates how they are strongly related to the child's drawing, with both offering an external representation of self expression and individuality. These ornamental aspects are therefore a normal part of development, and, if they do not interfere with legibility, do little harm and help to develop a personal style. In a handwriting club this aspect can be harnessed to other aspects of practice, with the child being encouraged to try styles that he has not previously seen.

A competition, with a theme for each term, can spur some

146

children on to great effort. The winter term theme might be 'The Weather', 'Christmas', 'Keeping Warm', or 'Winter Sports', for example, and work may be copied from text books at first. As skills develop, original work can be encouraged and displayed in an area such as the school library. A first prize of a good quality pen is usually more acceptable when accompanied by a bar of chocolate, not forgetting the occasional treat for the other competitors. There has to be more than one advantage in giving up one's free time!

Discussion about handwriting needs and provision for pupils in the secondary age range is in its early stages. This is somewhat surprising when we consider that a very large proportion of school time is spent on tasks that require writing. Inevitably, several aspects of handwriting remain unexplored, but most, such as the specific problems of left handers, receive attention elsewhere in the text. My main objective has been to show that secondary schools can grasp the nettle of neglect and that there are many ways in which this can be done.

Handwriting helps to form the substructure for writing in general, and the richness of writing and communication is aptly described by Barrow (1979) when he states, 'The nature and purpose of communication is such that ideally if one is in the business at all, one wants to communicate with as much precision, richness, accuracy, fluency, comprehensiveness and fluidity as possible.'

REFERENCES

Alston, J. (1983) 'A legibility index: can handwriting be measured?' *Educational Review, 35* (3).

Alston, J. and Taylor, J. (1984) *The Handwriting File: Diagnosis and Remediation of Handwriting Difficulties*. LDA, Wisbech.

Alston, J. (1985) 'The handwriting of seven to nine-year-olds.' *British Journal of Special Education, 12* (2), 68–72.

Barrow, R. (1979) In Bernbaum, G. (ed.) *Schooling in Decline*. Macmillan, Basingstoke.

Bolger, A.W. (1975) *Child Study and Guidance in Schools*. Constable, London.

Brown, B. (1983) 'Who should teach handwriting in the secondary school?' National Children's Bureau Seminar Day.

Daiute, C. (1985) *Writing and Computers*. Addison Wesley, London.

Easy Grip, LDA, Wisbech.

Faas, L. (1976) *Learning Difficulties: A Competency Based Approach*. Houghton Mifflin, Boston.

Gardner, H. (1973) *The Arts and Human Development*. John Wiley,

Chichester.

Jarman, C. (1979) *The Development of Handwriting Skills*. Blackwell, Oxford.

Lehman, H. Pressey, L.C. (1958) In Hunnicut, C.W. and Iverson, W.J. (eds.), *Research in the Three R's*. Harper, New York.

Michael, B. (1984) 'Foundations of writing.' *Child Education*, January.

Michael, B. (1985) 'Foundations of writing.' *Child Education*, May.

New Zealand Department of Education (1980) 'A study of the handwriting of form 1 pupils in New Zealand intermediate schools.' Wellington, New Zealand.

Osmiroid Educational, Osmiroid, Gosport, Hampshire.

Peck, M. and Askov, E. (1980) 'Another decade of research in handwriting: progress and prospect.' *Journal of Educational Research, 69*, 283–97.

Philip and Tacey, Andover, Hampshire.

Pickard, P., Alston, J. (1985) *'Helping Secondary School Pupils with Handwriting: Current Research, Identification and Assessment, Guidance*. LDA, Wisbech.

Pickard, P. (1986) *Handwriting — A Second Chance*. LDA, Wisbech.

Platignum, Royston, Herts.

Richardson, M. (1935) *Writing and Writing Patterns*. Hodder and Stoughton, Sevenoaks.

Smith, F. (1983) *Essays into Literacy*. Heinemann, London.

Smith, V.H. and James, F.E. (1968) *Eyes and Education*. Heinemann, London.

13

Curricular Developments in Australasia

In this chapter, we examine current curricular developments in Australia and New Zealand. In contrast to the United Kingdom, where concern is being shown by teachers, therapists and examiners but where there is no formal national acceptance that standards are low and help needed, Directors of Education in Australia and New Zealand now advocate and support the implementation of consistent guidelines for teachers and pupils in their schools through formal documents. All the documents to which we refer have been published in the 1980s and reflect a trend of concern for pupils' early establishment of basic writing skills.

The guidelines vary in their recommendations and emphases, and in the degree to which they are intended to be prescriptive. They differ in quite basic principles such as in the script and writing paper formats that they advise teachers to use at different stages of the children's writing development. The State of Victoria presents perhaps the most prescriptive policy, with the Director General of Education stressing the importance of developing a foundation style and supporting the sale of alphabet strips and different lined paper formats by the Victorian Government Bookshop. We hope that readers will find it instructive to compare the six sets of guidelines presented, and that in the future it might be possible to undertake similar analyses for other countries.

In this book, in general, we have been concerned to associate research with practice and to encourage practitioners to examine research before they make prescriptive statements. Although several of the documents refer to research, and New Zealand in particular has conducted its own, it is clear that the term 'research' is sometimes regarded as interchangeable with 'trial' or 'discussion'. With this situation, one can elect to introduce almost any script or paper format without objective research such as that conducted in New Zealand. However, we believe that endeavour to help children to develop appropriate writing habits in the early stages of their educational careers is commendable. The subject is now established as one for discussion at an international level. In itself, this healthy state of affairs is likely to stimulate applied research and encourage interprofessional discussion.

The curriculum documents published by the Education Departments of five Australian states and by the Department of Education in Wellington, New Zealand, are presented. It has been necessary to select from extensive documents the items included in this chapter. In general, the selection has been dependent on their concordance or otherwise with the recommendations of other writers or with the conclusions of established research.

PRIMARY SCHOOL ENGLISH: SYLLABUS WITH NOTES (1981) CURRICULUM BRANCH, EDUCATION DEPARTMENT OF WESTERN AUSTRALIA (Reproduced by permission of the Curriculum Branch of the Education Department of Western Australia)

Handwriting forms part of a more comprehensive curriculum document on Primary School English. The syllabus areas considered are as follows: speaking, listening, drama, reading, literature, writing, handwriting and spelling. For each of those areas, objectives are stated and syllabus outlines are presented.

In the section on handwriting the following is stated: 'Handwriting is a basic skill and tool of communication. It is essential that the child develops a handwriting that is legible and fluent and suited to the demands of the present day.' The objective states, 'The child writes legibly, fluently and attractively', and the reader is informed that 'this will be evident from all the child's written work.'

Four phases to cover the whole of the primary years are considered: Phase One, Readiness to Begin Writing; Phase Two, Introduction and Development of Manuscript; Phase Three, Introduction to Cursive (Transition); and Phase Four, Development of a Mature Style. Within these phases, the reader's attention is drawn to how different aspects of handwriting might be developed.

Amongst the recommendations are the following:

(a) lined paper is not to be introduced until phase three and then only

150

with a letter base line;
(b) rhythm, fluency and lack of tension are stressed throughout the age range;
(c) speed is emphasised at phase four, with the range of 70 to 90 letters per minute suggested as an expected range for children in that phase;
(d) pencils are to be used up to and including phase three, with ball points and fountain pens to be introduced at phase four;
(e) attention to motor co-ordination is recommended.

HANDWRITING K — 7: TEACHERS' NOTES (1980 REVISION) CURRICULUM BRANCH, EDUCATION DEPARTMENT OF WESTERN AUSTRALIA

In the preface to this document the following is stated: 'The Teachers' Notes represent a recommended way of teaching hand-writing and are not prescriptive' and

'If teachers prefer styles or letter formation other than those recommended in the Syllabus or Teachers' Notes, it is possible to adopt these alternatives on a school basis as part of a school policy.'

The beginner script presented in the document consists of manuscript letters with the letter down-strokes vertical and the rounded parts of letters round rather than oval. The cursive script, presented for implementation at stage three, is forward sloping, with rounded letters becoming oval, and with loops attached to the ascenders and descenders of some letters. Criteria by which to judge the child's readiness for transition to a cursive script are offered. Such criteria are not generally offered in documents such as this and discussion about teaching handwriting in terms of performance criteria rather than chronological age is to be welcomed.

It is interesting to note that, in the booklet, 'legiblity' is differen-tiated from 'fluency'. Legibility is described as being dependent upon the following: letter forms (including joinings), spacing, slope, size and proportion of letters, quality of line, and alignment. Fluency is described as being dependent upon: ease and rhythm of movement, posture, penhold, size of letters, quality of pen and paper, and maturity of the writer. Attractiveness is also stressed as an important attribute of handwriting.

151

Teachers of primary school children are advised to encourage good practice through regular diagnosis, encouraging self evaluation, monitoring progress through writing samples, encouraging the child to increase the amount he writes, and by observing posture and pencil hold. It is suggested that the interest of pupils will be maintained if types and sizes of paper and tools are varied and if styles of writing and lettering are explored.

The importance of relaxation for fluent writing movement is stressed and examples of exercise for relaxation are offered.

A valuable section of the document draws attention to the value of involving the children in analysing their own handwriting samples. It is suggested that they can be taught to observe the following simple concepts: size, slope, spacing, shape and speed (fluency). The children can be grouped according to their particular needs or problems so that they can discuss with their peers the difficulties and the means by which they might be corrected. It is suggested that, for certain scripts or at certain times, the teacher might use the writing paper margins to draw the pupils' attention to specific difficulties (e.g. spacing, slope).

The Handwriting Quality Record Sheet (Figure 13.1) is recommended for completion by the child, with assistance from the teacher.

Teachers are encouraged to prepare class handwriting scales against which children may compare their own writing for quality. When a number of writing samples are placed in each of five categories 'very good; good; fair; poor; very poor' and several from each category are displayed, the children can be encouraged to become aware of the reasons why certain samples appear in their particular category.

It is recommended that when children have reached a sufficient level of competence, regular tests should be given in the following manner:

The children are asked to write for two minutes in their best writing, then for two minutes in their 'everyday' writing and finally, as fast as possible for two minutes. Allow rest pauses between. Compare the three samples.

The tester is informed that some variation is to be expected but that the differences should not be too extreme; the pieces should be legible and the script, in general, should be suitable for the purpose for which it is intended.

Figure 13.1: Handwriting quality record sheet

	Feb	Mar	Apr	May	June	July	Aug	Sept	Oct	Nov	Dec
Letters											
Joins											
Spacing: Letters											
Words											
Lines											
Slope											
Size of letters											
Proportion of letters											
Quality of Line											
Alignment											
Setting Out: General											
Headings											
Margins											

Handwriting Quality
Name .... School .... Year ...... Age 1st Jan.....

Special Comments

Though there may be grounds for criticising some of the recommendations offered in this document, e.g. the recommendations for use of blank or lined paper, many areas of the teaching of handwriting have been well delineated and the sections referring to monitoring by teachers and pupils are particularly valuable.

HANDWRITING: SOUTH AUSTRALIAN MODERN CURSIVE. (1984) EDUCATION DEPARTMENT OF SOUTH AUSTRALIA

A handbook and wall charts referring respectively to a Beginners' Alphabet and to the South Australian modern cursive, accompany a comprehensive guide for those concerned with the teaching of handwriting, and with how it might take its place within the context of the Language Arts curriculum. The authors claim that the model has been selected for its suitability in the current situation, i.e. to allow the writers to keep pace with modern and variable writing requirements, and as a suitable model for use with the changes in and variety of current writing instruments. The document is described by the Director General of Education as '. . . the guide for South Australian Government Schools'.

The recommended script is described as one of the modern writing styles, based on '. . . children's early writing behaviour, which indicates that children's natural movements are oval shaped and sloped rather than round and upright'. It is also said to be based upon international writing trends and the existing styles of handwriting in the state. Examples of earlier South Australian school scripts are shown, i.e. copperplate, italic and looped cursive, and attention is drawn to their importance as scripts from which the modern cursive has evolved. It is also claimed that these are the only styles that present a consistency of letter form that leads the writer towards a legible handwriting written at speed. They add to this statement, an assertion that 'Handwriting styles such as Linked Script and Print Script, which use a finger technique rather than a combined finger, hand and arm movement, should be discouraged.'

The authors state that South Australian modern cursive '. . . uses simple letter shapes, formed with traditional handwriting technique in both script and cursive forms. Not far removed from the looped cursive and copperplate styles but written with any handwriting instrument.'

The teaching programme is divided into three stages: Stage One, A beginners' alphabet, including letters without links and capitals; Stage Two, A development of the cursive alphabet, when the exit strokes are added as a precursor to the linked script; Stage Three, When direct linking is introduced, and the cursive script developed. The suggested periods of time in which the stages might be developed are 18 months for stage one and six months for stage two.

Referring to blank or lined paper, the authors state, 'Blank surfaces are best for beginners', and go on to show that by presenting horizontal lines very far apart, e.g. 7.3 cm, the children can write between them but are otherwise not really relating their letters to them, i.e. 'Children follow the path from left to right staying within the lines.' A variety of line widths is presented, with discussion about their selection and purpose.

The formation of each letter, i.e. capital letters, letters without links, letters with links and numerals, are described in detail, and potential problem areas are highlighted. (Exit strokes are described as 'kicks'.)

154

Precise behavioural teaching objectives are presented, so that pupils' knowledge, attitudes and abilities can be differentiated and defined. For example, the importance of the pupils' own involvement in the learning process is emphasised by the objective, 'Children will develop: . . . a willingness to accept responsibility for their own written material'.

There is considerable evidence of teacher influence on this document, and the section dealing with 'Classroom programming issues', lists 14 questions that might be asked about timetable and lesson design, teaching techniques and writing materials, and the methods by which those with illegible handwriting can be helped. The suggestions that follow each of the questions raised are practical and comprehensive. Attitudes receive particular mention at this and other points in the document, with one solution for assistance stating:

Determine whether the child shares your concern and is prepared to make a commitment to relearn technique and/or style.

Negotiate a 'contract' to improve the child's handwriting. Such a contract should give details of: specific objectives, an agreed time after which improvement might reasonably be expected, provision for reporting to the child and parents with samples of work.

Evaluation and assessment are given appropriate attention, with work samples and checklists suggested as suitable for teacher or pupil records. A resource section suggests handwriting activities and resource materials and extends teachers to think in terms of pupils' activities, skills and concepts.

In general, this is an excellent document from which anyone at all concerned with the teaching of handwriting could benefit.

THE TEACHING OF HANDWRITING (1984) DEPARTMENT OF EDUCATION, QUEENSLAND

The pack of materials includes *The Teaching of Handwriting*: a handbook; A Practice Book for Teachers; and 'Changes to the Teaching of Handwriting', an information leaflet for parents. The Primary Handwriting Project Officer is Jan Boys and Barbara Nichol is the Handwriting Consultant.

The Teaching of Handwriting: a handbook

The writers recognise that although there is rapid development in the use of keyboard technology, writing skills are no less needed and the programme they offer is designed to help children to write legibly and cope with the demands of writing at speed. They observe, however, that if children are to develop flexible handwriting skills that will allow them to develop efficient individual styles, consistent instruction based on sound methodology is required. In the handbook, they offer advice on techniques and mechanics of handwriting, primary school teaching methodology and practices through which pupils encountering handwriting difficulties can be helped.

The authors are precise in their discussion on handwriting techniques. Their statement on how writing is produced, for example, is as follows:

(a) We write with a combined finger/hand/arm movement — our fingers and hand place the letter shapes on the page; and our hand and arm move the fingers along like the carriage on a typewriter (hand slides along, does not pivot at wrist)

(b) The basic movements are — index finger pulls down, middle finger pushes away, and thumb flexes at the first knuckle to accommodate the finger movement. Hand and arm move from left to right.

This combined movement produces a relaxed tension — release action, e.g.

Writing posture is discussed in relation to a variety of writing instruments and their suitability or otherwise for different purposes is examined.

Discussion about paper for writing ranges from the merits of blank paper to those of various line widths and guide line relationships. One-lined, two-lined (with a confining line for the lower-case letter bodies) and paper with three lines for each line of letters are presented. The terms 'body', 'head and body' and 'body and tail' help the teacher and child to discuss and distinguish between the letter parts and their letter-to-line relationships.

The Beginner's Alphabet has an exit stroke only in the letter *d* but beginner letters are oval and sloping in readiness for the change to the cursive model. Tom Gourdie is acknowledged as assisting the authors in their choice of script and readers may like to refer to his work in the chapter 'Earlier developments and current models'. The Queensland modern cursive owes some of its characteristics to the modern derivation of the italic style, the teacher's attention, for example, being drawn to the wedge shapes produced within many letters including *n, m, a* and *b*.

Teaching objectives are prescriptive but this is not to infer that the writers of this well-written document do not encourage teachers to recognise differences in children's developmental progress. In the prescriptive mode, they write,

> By the end of YEAR ONE, children should know that: All letters (except *e* and *d*) start at the top. Usually, the pencil is not lifted when making a lower-case letter (except for dots and crossbars). The pencil can be lifted when making capital letters. Big wedges are features of many of the letters, e.g. *a* and *g*. Writing is faster if retracing is kept to a minimum. A finger/hand/arm movement is used to write. Letters have 'heads', 'bodies' and 'tails' and should be placed on the lines in the correct position. The pencil should not be held in the web of the hand.

Evaluative checklists, designed for recording class and group progress, include sections on a range of elements from the writing process and product (e.g. pencil control) to directional movement and letter formation. Referring to a wide range of handwriting difficulties, a section on corrective techniques shows, in turn, different samples of writing, the identified problem in each, what should be taught, and exercises that might help the pupil.

A practice book for teachers: the beginner's alphabet and Queensland modern cursive

This booklet was produced only for teachers. In the early stages of the project, teachers had been invited to complete a questionnaire and by their responses had indicated that they wished to have clear and prescriptive guidelines about the new handwriting model and their role in teaching it. Teachers who had attended a two-day seminar and received the 'Teaching of Handwriting' handbook, later received the 'Practice Book for Teachers', which leads the teachers

157

through the sequence of learning that their pupils will follow. With the question 'Did you notice?' teachers' attention is drawn to points to be stressed when they construct their own teaching programme.

Changes to the teaching of handwriting: information for parents

This information leaflet is intended to be distributed to parents during their child's first week in school. The writers draw the attention of parents to the changes that are occurring in the teaching of handwriting, perhaps compared with how the parents were taught to write. They suggest how the child can be encouraged to develop a range of co-ordination skills, experience using a variety of tools and materials for painting and writing, and develop awareness of the different purposes, such as lists, letters and messages, for which writing can be used.

The three booklets making up this comprehensive scheme give teachers, parents and children a consistent and wide-ranging policy on the teaching of handwriting.

BASIC HANDWRITING (1985) EDUCATION DEPARTMENT, TASMANIA

Marlene Cox is the Curriculum Project Officer who co-ordinated the material for this policy document. K.I. Axton, Director General of Education for the state, states that 'Basic Handwriting' was written in response to requests from many teachers who asked for advice on the teaching of handwriting. There are overall aims that refer to the following: instruction in technique and style, the development of children's concepts and abilities, and stressing the importance of evaluation and monitoring by both teachers and children.

It is claimed that children's natural movements are oval-shaped and sloped. With this view as the basis for the programme, the authors' claim is that the model adopted is one of the modern writing styles developed to provide children with a means for quick and effective communication.

The authors pay attention to children's knowledge, attitudes and abilities. It is of interest to see this example of growing attention to attitudes, the objectives stated here being that 'Children should develop: a positive attitude towards themselves and their handwriting; the desire to experiment in order to develop a personal style; and a willingness to accept responsibility for the quality of their written material.'

Developmental stages are described with the reminder that 'Children vary widely in their rate of general progress . . .'

Handwriting across the curriculum receives support when the authors state 'It is important that the teaching of handwriting is undertaken when any activity that involves handwriting is being undertaken.' They also state, however, that children will at times also need instruction in particular handwriting skills.

The section headed 'technique' is quite detailed, which lays the writer open to error in this rapidly developing but still poorly researched field of study. On pen/penhold, for example, it is stated: 'The pencil should be held lightly between the second finger and the thumb. The first finger should rest lightly on the pencil.' This statement would be in conflict with the views of some current authorities on the subject and should remain the subject of debate until more research is conducted.

Advice on paper position, i.e. a paper tilt of 20 degrees to the left for the right hander and 20 degrees to the right for the left hander, does not take early or recent research (Enstrom 1962, Guiard and Millerat 1984) into account.

Advice on relaxation for the writer is comprehensive and should be welcomed.

The authors state that 'Blank paper is recommended for practice at all stages.' Lines should be introduced when the child understands about the proportions within and between letters. It is recommended that children should be encouraged to write between widely spaced lines, moving gradually to the more conventional 8-mm space. Their recommendation that the child's development should '. . . dictate the most appropriate space for him or her particular stage of development and for the purpose of the writing . . .' is a suggestion still adopted by very few writers and is to be welcomed in this document.

The script is forward sloping and oval from the early stages and the recommendation for the early writing stage is for letters without exit strokes except for letter *d*, in which the inclusion of an exit stroke from the beginning is presumably to differentiate it from a reversed letter *b*. The manner in which letters should join is prescribed but the authors state that 'Ligatures between letters are justified only if they increase the speed and rhythm of writing without detracting seriously from its legibility.' Although it is made

159

clear that some letters such as *b* and *g* should not join to letters that follow, other letters are shown joining to all other letters of the alphabet. This can be misleading when *fb* and *fk*, for example are shown as letter pairs, when in fact they never occur in English spelling.

To assist with planning and monitoring at the pre-writing, writing and experienced writing stages, examples of class or group evaluation record forms are presented. It is also suggested that the pupil should monitor his own progress on a detailed individual record card, to be completed when the teacher and pupil meet together once a month specifically for that purpose.

THE TEACHING OF HANDWRITING (1985) EDUCATION DEPARTMENT, VICTORIA

The new style, Victorian Modern Cursive, is referred to as a 'foundation style' to '. . . provide the basis for further development and personalisation throughout schooling'. The importance of an accepted consistent policy to reduce transition problems experienced by children transferring between schools and school sytems is stressed by Dr N.G. Curry, Director-General of Education.

There is an important section in which research and the recommendations of authoritative writers are reviewed, the suggestion being that the most important recommendations are built into the new 'foundation' style. The authors refer to Victoria research as well as to selected reports from overseas. They conclude the following:

(1) A single consistent style is desirable within the primary school. Some researchers suggest that cursive writing should be taught from the beginning.
(2) Young children can use fine motor skills for smaller writing. It is noted that Victorian preparatory school children can form enclosures in their pictures of less than 20 mm, which is less than the formerly recommended initial writing letter size. They claim that 'Not only are young children capable of smaller writing, but they may find a smaller size more manageable and less tiring.'
(3) Some hand movements lead to greater fluency and legibility. (This conclusion is based on the views of Gourdie and Atkinson 1978 and Gray and Myers 1978, who are referred to as having

identified 'natural' writing patterns among children.) The authors state 'It is considered preferable for a style to place more emphasis on downstroking in its letter formation,' and 'Quick directional changes . . . minimise retrace movements.' Both claims can be shown to influence the new style and, together with the incorporation of a characteristic 'wedge' shape to the letters, lead the writer towards a sloping rather than a vertical script.

Techniques for teaching letter formation, from individual letters to letter clusters, are quite prescriptive. Employment of verbalising or subvocalising techniques is advocated in order to reinforce the letter-movement patterns in the young learner.

Penhold and pen manipulation are discussed. It is suggested that 'The hand should form a "question mark" shape with the index finger approximately two centimetres from the point of the writing implement.' The barrel of the pen, it is suggested, should rest against the long bone of the index finger rather than in the 'V' between the finger and the thumb. A pen grip with the barrel of the pen held in the 'V', between finger and thumb or the web of the hand is suggested as more suitable for the left-handed writer. An alternative grip, the Callewaert grip, in which the barrel is held between the first and second finger is mentioned. Although it is observed that a small number of children seem to use it successfully in secondary schools, the authors conclude that there is insufficient information about this grip for them to recommend it for more widespread use.

The following items may be obtained from the Victorian Government Bookshop:

(1) Student alphabet strips of lower case letters, capital letters or flourished capitals, which can be attached to the writing surface for easy reference when children are writing;
(2) A4 lined (24 mm) paper divided into thirds, suitable for Year 1 children;
(3) A4 lined (18 mm) paper divided into thirds, suitable for Year 2 and 3 children. (The paper is presented to the children with the longer side in the horizontal plane.)

Gwenda Smyth is the editor, Ann James the designer, and Barbara Nichol the calligrapher of this useful publication.

NORTHERN TERRITORY DEPARTMENT OF EDUCATION

The Secretary of the Northern Territory Department of Education has recently endorsed a recommendation of the Northern Territory Board of Studies that the Victorian Modern Cursive style be adopted in Northern Territory schools. There should be a gradual introduction of the styles during 1987, with compulsory implementation occurring in all Northern Territory schools by 1988.

TEACHING HANDWRITING (1985) DEPARTMENT OF EDUCATION, WELLINGTON, NEW ZEALAND

Preparation for the curriculum document 'Teaching Handwriting', began in 1981, when research was conducted in New Zealand intermediate schools. The relatively small school population of New Zealand, compared with many other countries, allowed for a survey representative of the nation's children and decisions about curriculum recommendations were then based on the empirical survey and research conclusions.

Principals of all intermediate schools in New Zealand were asked to identify two form one classes in their schools (pupils aged eleven to twelve years of age and in their seventh year in school) from which handwriting samples could be obtained. To establish random sampling, the classes were selected according to specified letters in the class teachers' surnames. There was some further pupil sampling and selection, in order to keep the writing samples for assessment at a manageable number for research processing purposes.

All pupils in the identified classes supplied two samples of writing; their best or 'neatest' writing (the quality sample) and their 'fastest' writing (the speed sample). For the quality sample, the pupils were asked to copy a piece of prose from a book or journal in '. . . your best writing or printing, whichever you usually do when you want to do your neatest work.' Ten minutes were allowed for this exercise. For completion of the speed sample, teachers wrote 'The quick brown fox jumps over the lazy dog' on the blackboard and the pupils were instructed to write it as many times as possible in a precisely timed three minutes. On each occasion, pupils were given the option of writing or printing, so that for the speed sample they were instructed to 'write or print, whichever you usually do when you want to get something down on paper quickly.'

Two raters examined the samples, identifying writing style and recording whether each sample was legible or illegible and precise writing speed. They were also requested to record whether each pupil's writing deteriorated when the pupil wrote quickly. Letters-per-minute of writing in the speed sample were recorded, as well as details for research classification such as sex, handedness and the Education Board in which the school they attended was located. Five writing styles were employed in sufficient frequency to be identified for research. The five styles are illustrated in Figure 13.2.

Figure 13.2: Five writing styles identified in the New Zealand survey

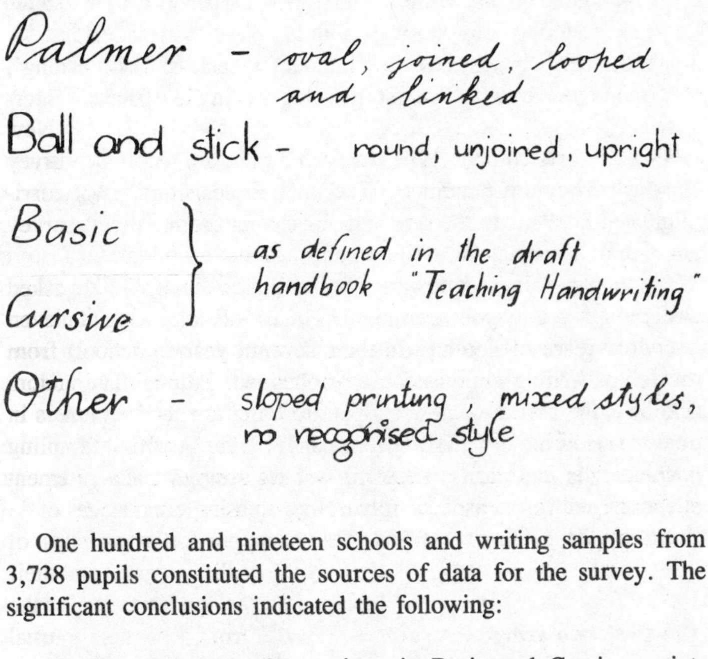

One hundred and nineteen schools and writing samples from 3,738 pupils constituted the sources of data for the survey. The significant conclusions indicated the following:

(1) In the quality samples, writers in Basic and Cursive scripts completed the most legible samples (99 per cent and 96 per cent respectively), with Ball and Stick also showing high percentage of legibility (81 per cent).

(2) Each style was performed in a wide range of speeds, but in terms of mean 'letters-per-minute' over the three-minute period, Basic writers were on average fastest (91 letters per minute) and Cursive and Ball-and-Stick writers wrote at 87 and 86 letters per minute, respectively.

(3) A significant number of writers changed their writing styles

when requested to write at speed, more changes occurring in Cursive and Palmer writers. Fewer changes occurred with Basic and Other writing.

(4) Of writers using the Palmer model, 31 per cent changed style. 22 per cent reverting to Ball and Stick, the model they were taught earlier in their school careers.

(5) Significantly more girls (84 per cent) than boys (59 per cent) had legible quality samples and fewer girls (14 per cent) than boys (20 per cent) showed a deterioration in legibility when they wrote at speed.

(6) More right handers (71 per cent) than left handers (64 per cent) had legible quality samples and the mean speed for right handers (79 letters per minute) was slightly above that for left handers (73 letters per minute). Left handers were less likely than right handers to change their style when writing at speed.

Conclusions from the 1981 research influenced recommendations for the curriculum document 'Teaching Handwriting', which was published in 1985. In the rationale for change from Palmer to Basic and Cursive scripts, the writers point out that an important feature of the looped Palmer style was a full arm movement, unlikely to be easily employed by young children. The new recommendation is for a slightly forward-sloping print script, to be followed by Cursive, formed by adding entry and exit strokes or ligatures. The authors acknowledge that their new scripts are based on the recommendations of Gourdie (1965) and Jarman (1979). A strength of the document, is the clarity with which it encourages teachers to pay attention to different aspects of handwriting at different stages of the children's educational progress. They state the following:

The first two years

The first objective should be to help children to establish the correct grip, to begin letters at the correct point, and to form letters and numerals correctly.

The lower standards

The proposed objective '. . . is to teach children cursive writing by the addition of ligatures.' However, with reservation, the authors state that '. . . the achievement of the objectives depends, of course, on readiness.'

The middle standards

The objectives '. . . are to help the children consolidate their skill so they can write all upper and lower case letters automatically, enable teachers to diagnose the difficulties children are having and to correct them, and help children to develop and maintain the quality of their handwriting.'

Forms one and two

Attention to speed, endurance and purpose are recommended at this stage. Teachers are advised to help children to develop an individual style and to assist and encourage them to write at speed without significant loss of legibility.

Detailed teaching recommendations suggest how objectives might be achieved. The comprehensive list of references and the evidence that the authors have paid attention to earlier research make this a valuable curriculum document.

REFERENCES

Enstrom, E.E. (1962) 'The relative efficiency of various approaches to writing with the left hand.' *Journal of Educational Research, 55* (10).

Gourdie, T. (1965) *The Simple Modern Hand*. Collins, London.

Gourdie, T. and Atkinson, D. (1978) *I Can Write: Teachers Notes*. Macmillan Educational, London.

Gray, N. and Myers, P.W. (1978) 'The running script: draft teachers manual.' Unpublished data.

Guiard, Yves, Millerat, F. (1984) 'Writing posture in left handers: inverters are handcrossers.' *Neuropsychologia, 22* (4).

Jarman, C. (1979) *The Development of Handwriting Skills: A Book of Resources for Teachers*. Blackwell, Oxford.

14

Research: Qualitative and Quantitative Assessment

Checklists have, to a great extent, been of a qualitative nature, with attempts by Stott, Moyes and Henderson (1985) to introduce quantitative measures in alignment, spacing and slant, making some departure from the qualitative mode. However, their truly quantitative measure is that of alignment (measuring each letter from the baseline in millimetres), as the marks awarded for slant and spacing are more arbitrary and less precisely calibrated than might be desirable. It is suggested here that assessment can be placed on a more quantitative plane and that statistical analysis is appropriate for some aspects of handwriting. Statistical evaluation may be employed for changes in pupil performance, (Hancock and Alston 1986) by comparing handwriting performance before and after intervention, or for comparing the performances of pupils within an experimental cohort with those of a matching comparable control group of pupils. It is suggested that cardinal measurement is appropriate for assessing alignment, spacing and slant, and that measurement of these three aspects can be submitted to statistical analysis. Such approaches may be more appropriate when we wish to evaluate the success or failure of teaching programmes for handicapped children or for others who have severe handwriting difficulties.

James, aged eight, was one of a number of children receiving help with handwriting. He is handicapped by myelomeningocele, the severest form of spina bifida, but has no hydrocephalus, which so often accompanies the condition. However, his writing showed many of the characteristics reported by other researchers (Anderson 1976, Cambridge and Anderson 1979) as being experienced by children affected by spina bifida. Among other aspects of handwriting receiving attention, James showed considerable difficulty in placing letters on the writing base line. Figure 14.1 shows his

166

Figure 14.1: Writing alignment, before and after intervention (James)

Before intervention

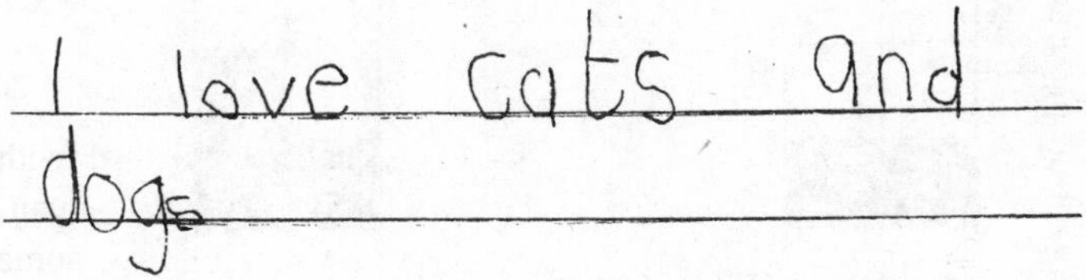

After intervention

writing before and after a six-week intervention period. Two quantitative measures of changes in James' writing are possible; graphic presentation, showing visual evidence of the numerical recording, and statistical evaluation, putting measurement of changes on a conventional statistical plane.

Figure 14.2 gives a graphic presentation of how James aligns his writing and the changes that occur in the intervention period.

Table 14.1 indicates the application of statistical analysis to the 'letter-to-line' deviation.

We might be interested in two aspects of spacing between words. Spacing in general may seem inappropriate and may be too small or too great. Indication to the child about desirable changes can be followed by construction of graphs or histograms from which one can compare spacing before intervention with spacing after teaching has taken place; in this situation, the graph can be discussed with the

Table 14.1: Deviation of letter to line (alignment) before and after intervention (repeated measure t test)

Stage	Mean	n	Standard deviation	t
Before intervention	0.9375	16	0.9287	1.732
After intervention	0.4375	16	0.7274	

Note: One-tailed test, result not significant

167

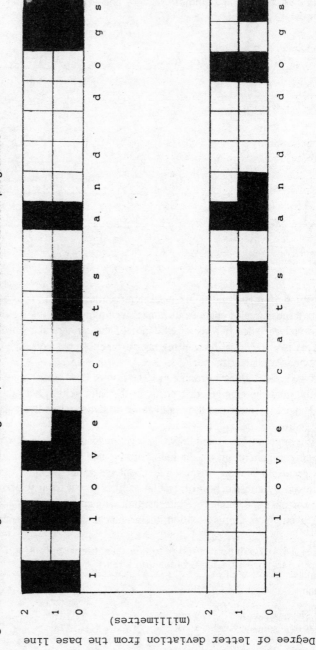

Figure 14.2: Word alignment for writing trials, before and after the intervention programme

Degree of letter deviation from the base line (millimetres)

child or even constructed in the child's presence. We have known the method work well with an otherwise able boy with spatial problems affecting his writing presentation. A further problem, relating to spacing between words, is inconsistency in size of successive spacing. This was also one of James' problems and the numerical application, employing quantitative measurement in millimetres, is presented in Figure 14.3. Changes in consistency in spacing can be evaluated through comparison of statistical variances. The statistical measure, 'variance ratio of F', is appropriate on such an occasion. Its application may be observed in Table 14.2.

Figure 14.3: Variation in spacing between words, before and after intervention

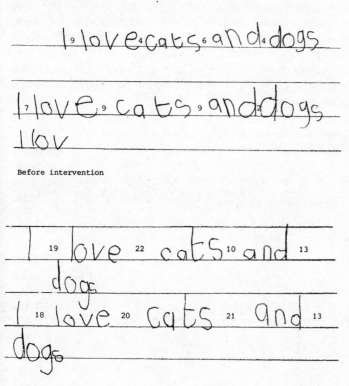

Before intervention

After intervention

QUALITATIVE AND QUANTITATIVE ASSESSMENT

Table 14.2: Spacing between words, before and after intervention (James)

Stage	n	Mean	Variance
Before intervention	8	6.25	7.3571
After intervention	8	17.00	19.4286

Note: One-tail test, $F = 2.6408$ (*df.* 7/7), N.S.

Slant deviations from the more 'normal' relatively upright or slightly forward slant of writing are common, even in adults whose writing is reasonably legible. However, irregular slant is probably the problem that we would more often like to change. Quantitative measurement here can consist of recording deviation from upright and can be measured by use of a protractor. The base line of the protractor is placed at the point where the vertical stroke of each ascender letter meets the base line, and the degree of slant shown on the protractor recorded. The 'variance ratio of F' will also serve our purpose here. Figure 14.4 shows changes in James' writing slant. Table 14.3 submits those changes to the 'variance ratio of F' for statistical analysis.

Figure 14.4: Degree of writing slant, before and after intervention

Before intervention

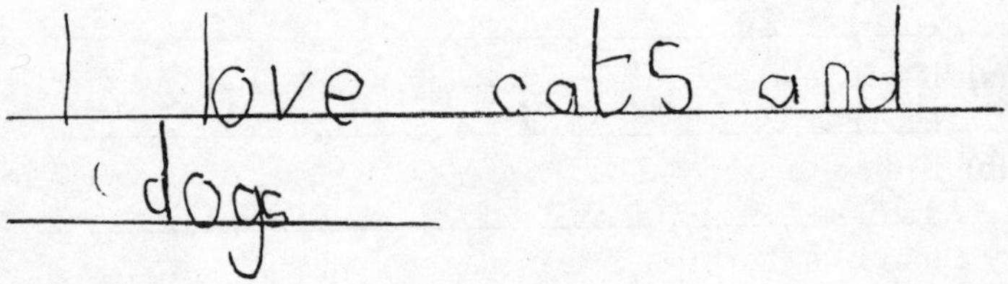

After intervention

170

Table 14.3: Degree of slant before and after intervention

Stage	n	Mean	Variance
Before intervention	18	79.0	56.82
After intervention	18	88.17	10.15

Note: One-tail test, $F = 5.600$ (df. 17/17), $P < 0.001$

Some aspects of handwriting are not so amenable to quantitative measurement as those that have received reference. A method of making numerical awards, based on subjective assessment but using precise criteria, provides a measure which, to some extent, meets the requirements of quantitative objectivity. The method has been employed with comparison of writing tool hold or grip (Alston 1986) and with comparison of letter formation quality, when a pupil writes the same letter on different occasions. However, the method has extensive application possibilities. For the purpose of observing changes in letter formation, a grid with more spaces than would be necessary for each letter of the alphabet is presented. The grid has a letter formation base line so that alignment of the letter can be observed. The child is shown printed letters of the alphabet in random order and, as each letter is presented, is requested to name and sound it. The letter is then covered and the child is asked to write it in a section of the grid. This method of recording letter formation is employed before and after a teaching programme, so that there are two copies of each letter for comparison. The observer, if she wishes, is able to make notes about how each letter was constructed on a separate record sheet. (Figure 14.5 shows the letter grid completed by an eleven-year-old girl.) For the purpose of numerical evaluation, an independent judge is given precise criteria on which judgements should be made. She is then informed that she has six points for each letter, which should be awarded as follows:

(a) if the two letters are of equal quality, award three points to each letter;

(b) if the two letters differ in quality, the six points should be distributed as appropriate, with the better letter being awarded four points and the poorer letter two points.

The results of this numerical evaluation can be submitted to the statistical 'sign' test (Siegel 1956) and the significance of changes in letter formation, reflected in the numerical evaluation, can be assessed.

171

Figure 14.5: Letter formation grid for diagnostic purposes

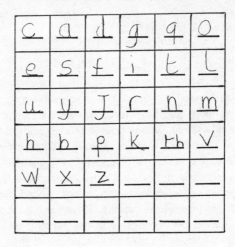

Askov, Otto and Askov (1970) stated, in their review of handwriting research, that in future '. . . perhaps scales should be built on information obtained from factor analysis of handwriting characteristics'. A factor analysis was recorded, as part of the standardisation of *The Handwriting File* (Alston and Taylor 1984). The suggestions for the application of cardinal measurement and statistical techniques to handwriting factors, with the facility to make numerical awards for subjective assessment of handwriting characteristics, indicate that progress in the assessment of handwriting has been made.

REFERENCES

Alston, J. and Taylor, J. (1984) *The Handwriting File: Diagnosis and remediation of handwriting difficulties*. LDA, Wisbech.

Alston, J. (1986) 'The effects of pencil barrel shape and pupil barrel preference on hold or grip in 8-year-old pupils.' *British Journal of Occupational Therapy, 49* (2).

Anderson, E.M. (1976) 'Handwriting and spina bifida.' *Special Education: Forward Trends, 3* (2).

Askov, E. Otto, W., and Askov, W. (1970) 'A decade of research in handwriting: progress and prospect.' *Journal of Educational Research, 64,* 100–11.

Cambridge, J. and Anderson, E.M. (1979) 'The handwriting of spina bifida children.' ASBAH, London.

Hancock, J. and Alston, J. (1986) 'Handwriting skills in spina bifida children: monitoring and measurement.' *British Journal of Special Education, 13* (4).

Siegel, S. (1956) *Nonparametric statistics for the behavioural sciences.* McGraw-Hill, New York.

Stott, D.H., Moyes, F.A. and Henderson, S.E. (1985) *Diagnosis and remediation of handwriting problems.* Brook Educational, Guelph, Ontario.

15

The Physically Handicapped Child: Special Needs for Handwriting

The 1981 Education Act in the United Kingdom and the 1975 Education for All Handicapped Children Act, United States of America, drew our attention to the importance of the precise assessment of children's educational needs and, to some extent discouraged us from identifying them within their type of handicap. However, amongst physically handicapped children, handicapping conditions are usually identified by their physical characteristics and, for some conditions, research has shown that the children as a group may be particularly susceptible to difficulties that impede educational progress. Some conditions, for example, have associated neurological, joint and muscular abnormalities which can affect handwriting and, in turn, affect the children's educational development. Many physically handicapped children are now educated in ordinary schools where the class teacher may be expected to identify problems and make appropriate provision. Paramedical support in the form of assistance from occupational therapists, physiotherapists and speech therapists may be available. However, the ease with which such help can be obtained tends to differ from one local authority or geographical area to another and it is important that the class teacher should be equipped to identify those children for whom she needs to seek help and perhaps to identify the area in which the help is required. Not all physically handicapped children need help and, within each condition, the degree of help required will vary enormously. One does not wish to magnify problems or draw unnecessary attention to them but simply to alert the teacher to possible problem areas and the manner in which they can be avoided. Some categories of handicap are presented, with their accompanying notes, and attention is drawn to texts from which additional information about physical handicap in general, and about specific handicapping conditions, can be obtained. If teachers in the United Kingdom are concerned, the assessment sequence recommended by the Warnock Committee (1978) and endorsed by the 1981 Education Act should be initiated. At stage three or four of the assessment sequence, an appropriate assessment team can be brought together. Local authorities in the United Kingdom and the United States of America are now quite accustomed to assembling the appropriate professionals for each case conference. The teacher should be part of the case conference team and has her first access to help through her headteacher.

SPINA BIFIDA

Spina bifida is perhaps the most educationally researched physically handicapping condition. Initially, we gained information about the children's handwriting from the work of Elizabeth Anderson, who identified particular component skills of handwriting in which problems for the children seemed to occur.

Compared with matching control group children, when pairs were matched on intelligence, age and sex, those affected by spina bifida showed the following characteristics in their handwriting:

(1) When asked to write individual lower-case letters and digits, affected children seemed to know their letters and digits slightly better than the control children, but the quality of penmanship tended to be poorer.
(2) When asked to copy a sentence in their best writing, and being unobtrusively timed, the control group children, on average, wrote significantly faster, producing roughly three sentences for every two written by the affected children.
(3) When alignment of words, spacing of words and letters, individual letter formation, uniformity of letter size, uniformity of slant, and quality of stroke were considered, the affected children were significantly poorer than the matching children, with the largest differences being in alignment and the spacing of words and letters.
(4) The affected children showed greater difficulty in forming letters and symbols accurately and some showed clear evidence of ataxia and tremor.

When discussing possible origins of difficulty in affected

175

children, Anderson (1976) referred to the following: receptor efficiency; sensory organisation; effector efficiency; motor organisation, including the use of visual, kinaesthetic and internal feedback.

(a) Receptor efficiency relates to the adequacy of eyes, ears and other senses. Anderson's research showed that one in ten of the children were affected by nystagmus (irregular and uncontrollable movement of the eyes) or squint. However, she concluded from her evidence that the sensory problems seemed unlikely to be the major factor affecting handwriting.

(b) Research by Tew and Spain has respectively shown 'figure ground' and 'figure identification' perceptual problems in affected children. Anderson concludes that perceptual or 'sensory organisation' problems are clearly possible contributors to the spacing and alignment difficulties that the children show.

(c) Effector efficiency refers to the ability to execute the required movement and the written product that was intended. Neurological research has identified the important role of the cerebellum in this domain. Incoming information is co-ordinated by the cerebellum, a brain structure situated in the hindbrain and at the top of the spinal cord. Many affected children are known to have an Arnold-Chiari formation or misshapen cerebellum, with cerebellum elongated and displaced downwards into the cervical canal, which forms the upper area of the spinal chord. Cerebellar damage is known to be associated with disturbance in the range, direction, force and rate of movement and good handwriting is dependent on adequate performance in all these component movement skills.

(d) Adequate motor organisation, requiring the use of visual, kinaesthetic and internal feedback, influences the manner in which movement in space is organised and executed. Ataxic, or unco-ordinated movement and tremor can be observed in the handwriting of many affected children.

The children are often affected by unstable spine or curvature (scoliosis) and have difficulty in developing good balance. The use of one hand for propping the body is a commonly observed feature and may affect the ease with which the child develops a leading or dominant hand for writing tasks. Anderson concluded, from her study of seven- to ten-year-olds fitted with valves or shunts, that 15 per cent were left handed and 30 per cent were of unresolved laterality or were able to employ either hand for one-handed tasks. The development of a leading hand is also related to awareness of the two sides of the body and to the ability to co-ordinate the two for bilateral tasks. Directional skill seems to be dependent on body awareness and laterality and may be considerably delayed in affected children. Spina bifida has several degrees of severity, and children with myelomeningocele, the most severely affected, may need to be fitted with a valve or shunt to release the pressure of cerebrospinal fluid in the brain. These children are likely to be the most severely affected from a writing point of view. However, the association between apparent severity of handicap and handwriting difficulty is by no means to be taken for granted. Figure 15.1 shows the writing of a nine-year-old girl, affected by spina bifida myelomeningocele.

Figure 15.1: The writing of a nine-year-old girl, affected by spina bifida myelominingocele

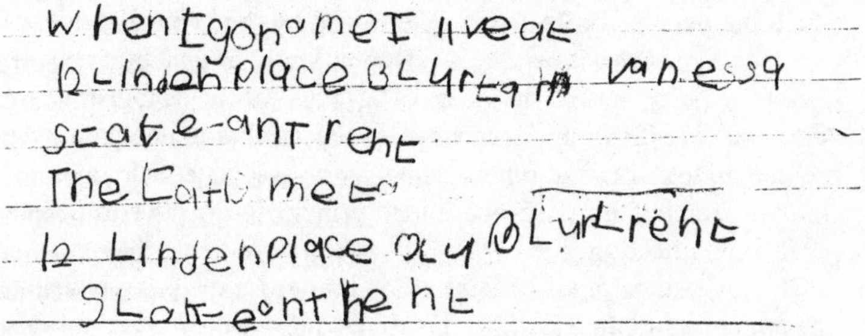

When Elizabeth Anderson wrote in 1976, she was careful to point out that 'Although two in three of the children had marked writing problems, it would be wrong to conclude that all those with spina bifida and hydrocephalus will be poor writers.'

Selective surgery for affected children was adopted by Lorber in 1971 and was given official endorsement by the Department of Health and Social Security in 1973. Because, from this time, the most severely affected children were unlikely to have been given surgical intervention for survival, the population of spina bifida children changed and those born after the early 1970s tended to be higher in intellectual ability and educational performance. Research by Sklayne and Lonton (1981) showed changes in intellectual ability, reading and mobility but there is currently no report on handwriting performance.

EPILEPSY

In this section, we refer to those children who have epilepsy as the only or major aspect of their handicapping conditions. However, those affected principally by other conditions may have epilepsy as an associated problem. Children affected by cerebral palsy, for example, may also have epilepsy, as may others where the handicapping condition has a neurological involvement. In mental handicap, where the causes may be from a variety of origins, epilepsy may also be present.

Epilepsy is caused by an unusual or excessive discharge in the brain. The discharge is initially a neurochemical one but the result is synonymous with discharge from an electric current. The way in which the person is affected is determined by the site and extent of the discharge. Classification of different kinds of epileptic convulsion may vary and a number of groups of neurologists have discussed classification. Here we are concerned with describing the problem to teachers and others who may be associated with affected children; for this purpose, we intend principally to refer to Scott's (1978) classification.

The lay person tends to think of epilepsy as a major convulsion, 'the epileptic fit'. In this case, the affected person has a major brain discharge, originating in the brain-stem area, and rendering him helpless during the stages of 'tonic' (high muscle and limb tension) 'clonic' (excessive and repeated movement of the limbs) and 'sleep'. Clearly, he will not be writing during these phases. However, in 1976, Hackney and Taylor, referring to children with epilepsy in ordinary schools, wrote '. . . his hand control seems to vary from day to day . . . before a fit his writing is all over the place . . . writing kept coming out wrong'. When referring generally to epilepsy, they state that lack of motor control 'may occur in some children before, during or after a period of epileptic activity'.

There are types of epilepsy other than the grand mal convulsion. Petit mal shows itself in a number of forms. The most common occurs when the child loses consciousness, i.e. experiences an 'absence' for a number of seconds and may stare vacantly or flutter his eyelids. Such apparently minor symptoms may not be observed in the ordinary classroom when the child is with 20 or 30 other children. If he is writing, however, then the attack will usually be observable in the writing. During the attack he may falter in conversation, in handwriting or in any other aspect of his classroom performance. It may even be possible, from writing observation, to

Figure 15.2: The writing of a 15-year-old girl affected by petit mal epilepsy

The Best of all

I sometimes think I'd like to be A little Eskimo.
And drive a team of dogs before my sleigh upon the snow.
or walk the streets of China, where gay lanterns glow at
night, And have a pair of chop sticks and A
pigtail and a kite.
or if I lived in India
A Potter I would be,
And make a row of pots with clay
For everyone to see

And if I went to Africa
Wild animals I would track,
or ride the desert mile on mile
upon a Camel's track
But all the same were very sure,
Although our islands small
To be an English boy or girl
Is much the best of all

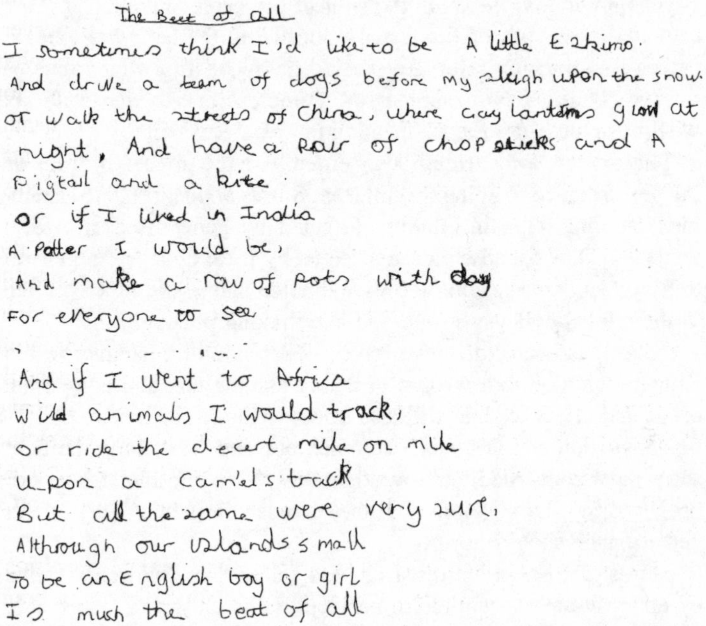

make some kind of assessment of how frequently the attacks occur. The number of 'absences' a child might experience in one day varies considerably, with some having as few as ten and others experiencing 100 or more. Figure 15.2 shows the writing of a 15-year-old girl affected by petit mal epilepsy. The occurrence of an absence can be observed in overwriting of letters or groups of letters.

Also classified as petit mal type attacks are myoclonic jerks or muscle spasms, appearing as purposeless movements of the arms or legs or both. The 'akinetic' spasm, also coming under the petit mal heading, is seen as a sagging of the knees but perhaps with a fairly rapid recovery.

Both grand and petit mal are generalised fits affecting the whole brain and neurological performance. Some attacks, however, are localised, often to the temporal lobes, where auditory and related skills are situated. Localised functions can, of course, affect any skill that has its function based in that part of the brain. The Jacksonian attack is specific to the motor area of the brain with the subject remaining conscious but losing control of the fine or gross motor movement. It would be possible for him to go on writing during such an attack and certainly with an unaffected limb. Psychomotor fits, in which the subject performs 'automatisms' are also common types of fits, usually located in the temporal lobe. A newer classification refers to 'partial' or 'focal' fits, which may be further classified into 'simple' or 'complex' ones, but we do not wish to involve the reader in this kind of discussion.

Researchers are currently concerned with the effects of drugs on the performance of epileptic children. Stores and Hart (1976) examined reading skills in children affected by generalised and focal epilepsy. They found children affected by focal epilepsy in general to have depressed reading scores and noted that most of the children in their focal epilepsy group had been taking phenytoin.

There has been little research or observation on handwriting in epileptic children but we can probably assume that anti-convulsant drugs that affect reading will also affect writing. The area of epileptic convulsion and drugs is a complex one and workers in the field seem most concerned that investigations relating to blood levels of drugs, drug intoxication and the manner in which they affect performance should occur.

Stores (1978), in his research, has shown that children affected by epilepsy are susceptible to an identifiable cluster of observable behavioural symptoms. For example, referring to the Rutter Children's Behaviour Questionnaire, they may, on occasion, be identified by their teachers as 'squirmy, fidgety, rather solitary or resentful'. If self concept is associated with handwriting, and it probably is, it is possible that, concomitant with the behavioural symptoms, writing may be variable and inconsistent. In all such situations, a consistent handwriting programme is likely to make the writing more stable and resistant to the variables associated with fits, anti-convulsant drugs and behavioural adjustment.

CEREBRAL PALSY

The term cerebral palsy refers to a number of conditions that affect movement. In themselves, the conditions are not progressive. However, if the person affected by spasticity in particular does not receive appropriate physiotherapeutic support, then the condition could seem to get worse and movement become more restricted.

Spasticity is the form of cerebral palsy in which the muscles are very tense and limbs often permanently in a flexed position.

Figure 15.3a: The writing of an eight-year-old girl (Jane), affected by spastic quadriplegia

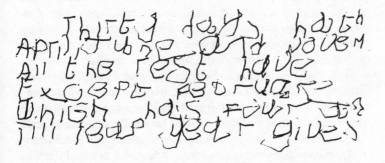

Figure 15.3b: Jane's writing after a little help and reminders that letter formation and care are important.

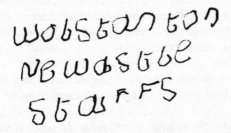

Movement is therefore considerably restricted and tends to occur in a jerky manner. Attempts at movement therefore over-shoot the intended target and movement that would normally be smooth in the writing process becomes somewhat staccato. Children who have upper limbs affected may begin with the thumb adducted into the palm of the hand. The use of a baton, such as that used in Conductive Education can be helpful in rectifying this problem. Figure 15.3 shows the writing of an eight-year-old girl with spastic quadriplegia, i.e. who is affected in all four limbs.

Hemiplegia indicates that only half of the body is affected and often results in the child 'carrying' the affected arm or hand and perhaps 'dragging' the affected leg. Therapists encourage the use of an affected hand as much as possible, perhaps as a 'helping hand' if the unaffected hand has accepted the leading role. If the hand that would, due to brain organisation, normally be the leading hand, is affected, then problems of making a naturally less competent hand

181

more competent and establishing a sense of laterality can occur. Identification and solutions referred to in Chapters 8, 11 and 12 will be appropriate.

The athetoid child has uncontrollable movements that make attempts at handwriting or keyboard skills extremely frustrating. Attempts at straight lines become writhing ones and rather snake like. When the children reach what would normally be cursive (joined up) writing, the cursive writing may become even more illegible than print. For this reason, the change to cursive writing is sometimes discouraged. Children affected by athetosis often wish to write in the normal manner and need help if the movements are to become at all within their control. A weighted arm band (e.g. a series of calico segments filled with sand and tied round the wrist with tapes) can help. A means of fixation, such as holding on to the rung of a stable ladder-backed chair may also give stability.

In ataxic children, the area of the brain principally involved in the abnormality is the cerebellum. This is situated at the base of the brain and is normally responsible for co-ordinating general balance and the rate, direction and distance of both fine and gross movements. In these children, the movement is irregular and imprecise for the normal writing activity. Figure 15.4 shows the writing of a 13-year-old boy identified as affected by ataxia. The writing is inconsistent and shows evidence of tremor.

Figure 15.4: The writing of a 13-year-old boy, affected by ataxia

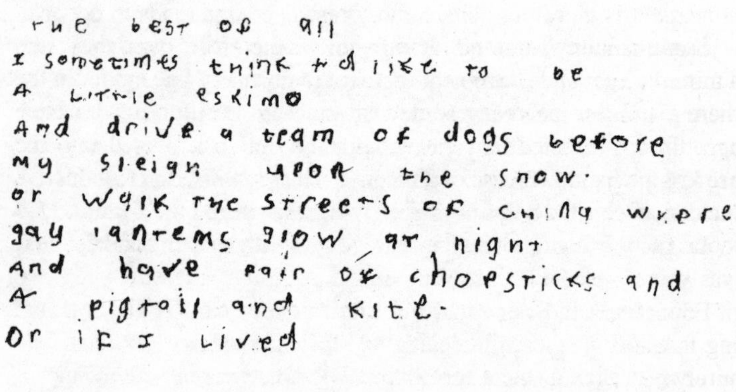

Friedreich's ataxia is a separate condition in which movements become increasingly more difficult to control. The symptoms tend to be similar to those in non-progressive ataxia but increasing in severity. A consistent handwriting model, with economy of movement, is helpful to affected children and pen or pencil adaptations such as the triangular grip may also help.

There are children who do not show a clear-cut cerebral palsy such as those described above, but who nevertheless have writing problems that seem to be physical in origin. They may be said to have, for example, cerebellar lesions and could be regarded as being minimally cerebral palsied. Figure 15.5 shows the writing of a 15-year-old boy, identified as affected by a cerebellar lesion. There is evidence of inconsistent movement and tremor.

Figure 15.5: The writing of a 15-year-old boy, identified as affected by a cerebellar lesion

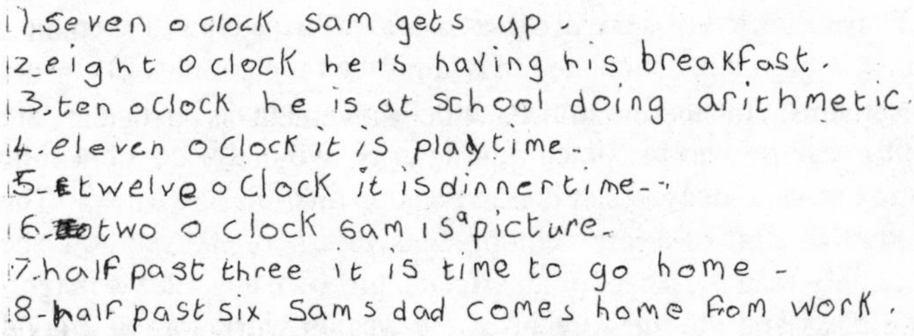

1. seven o clock sam gets up .
2. eight o clock he is having his breakfast.
3. ten oclock he is at school doing arithmetic.
4. eleven o Clock it is playtime.
5. twelve o Clock it is dinner time - -
6. two o clock sam is a picture.
7. half past three it is time to go home -
8. half past six Sams dad comes home from work.

Some children, with no identifiable handicapping condition, have a minimal tremor in their writing, though there is some evidence that there are fewer children affected in this way than perhaps a decade ago. Probably the better monitoring of babies at birth so that babies are less likely to be starved of oxygen is responsible for this reduced incidence of children with handwriting tremor.

In 1970, a comprehensive report on children with cerebral palsy was written by Dr M.M. Wilson and published by the Department of Education and Science. The reader might be forgiven for suggesting that the views expressed in 1970 about affected children must surely be out of date. However, many of the educational difficulties referred to in the report would be equally applicable when we refer to the children today.

Amongst the difficulties reported are: persistence in reversals well beyond infant or junior class; mirror writing; difficulty in hand/eye co-ordination; failure to space words; letters and figures upside down; inability to judge distance or direction in space; and loss of place on page when reading.

The writer refers to the serious handicap that inability to write can be, particularly for athetoid children who are considered to be often of reasonably high intelligence.

OTHER PHYSICALLY HANDICAPPING CONDITIONS

With the exception of a few conditions, e.g. haemophilia, cystic fibrosis and diabetes mellitus, physically handicapping conditions place children at risk for difficulty with handwriting. The difficulties might be in writing control, speed or endurance when the writing task is over a longer period of time. Difficulties may only come to light when there is proper monitoring of the child's writing performance.

Those affected by juvenile rheumatoid arthritis tend to keep their writing inordinately small and may limit the range of movement and direction of letters. This limitation is likely to occur because movement is painful and restricted, and is to be avoided if possible. The writing is sometimes so small as to be quite illegible to teachers. One member of staff of a large comprehensive school showed how she could only read the script of an affected girl by using a large magnifying glass and yet the content of the written work was of a good academic level. Wrist supports and arm and finger splints are often used to assist movement and to reduce pain.

Boys affected by muscular dystrophy (the affected are usually boys and they usually have the very severe Duchenne type) are likely to have increasing difficulty with handwriting, as muscles and joints become increasingly affected by the condition. Recognition of those affected by the condition usually occurs in the pre-school years. An early introduction to good handwriting habits is likely to keep the children writing in a reasonably normal manner during their primary school years. The adapted methods of physiotherapy, employed in a number of schools and regions, and developed particularly for these children, are likely to influence writing skills as well as other and more general physical functions. Figure 15.6 shows the writing of a 14-year-old boy affected by muscular dystrophy, who has received regular treatment from the specialist management team (Bennett 1985) at Hebden Green School, Cheshire.

The condition of children affected by brittle bones (osteogenesis

Figure 15.6: The writing of a 14-year-old boy affected by Duchenne muscular dystrophy

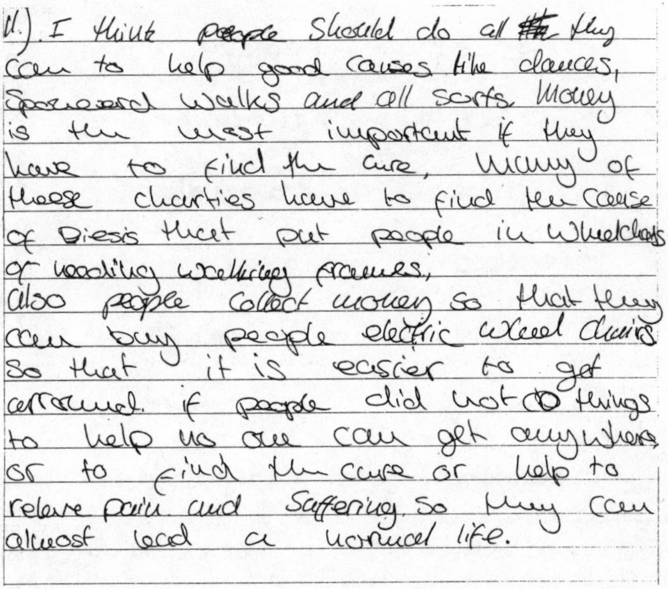

> B(i.) I think people should do all the they can to help good causes like dances, sponsored walks and all sorts. Money is the most important if they have to find the cure. Many of these charities have to find the cause of Diseis that put people in wheelchairs or woolding walking frames.
> Also people collect money so that they can buy people electric wheel chairs so that it is easier to get arround. If people did not do things to help us we can get anywhere or to find the cure or help to relive pain and suffering so they can almost lead a normal life.

imperfecta) varies considerably. There are those within the normal range of stature, though perhaps slightly shorter than usual, and others who are of extremely short stature, confined to a wheelchair, and often very restricted in shoulder, arm and hand movements. Many of the children are affected by ligament laxity (Alston 1983), which can affect hands and arms; the balance between ligament laxity and muscle tension and development determines the speed and endurance that can be applied to the writing task. For these children, the decisions about the relative emphasis upon handwriting and keyboard skills are important. Although handwriting competence is desirable for all children, and should receive special attention in the infant and early primary school years, there may be an optimum point in primary school education when the relative importance of the two media of communication must be considered. The purpose of this decision is to equip the child with a form of communication that will allow him to develop to full potential in the secondary school setting, i.e. when speed and endurance in writing will determine the degree to which he is able to take notes in class, record homework requirements, and participate with others in the examination process.

Figure 15.7: The writing of Damien, a severley handicapped boy affected by brittle bones (osteogenesis imperfecta)

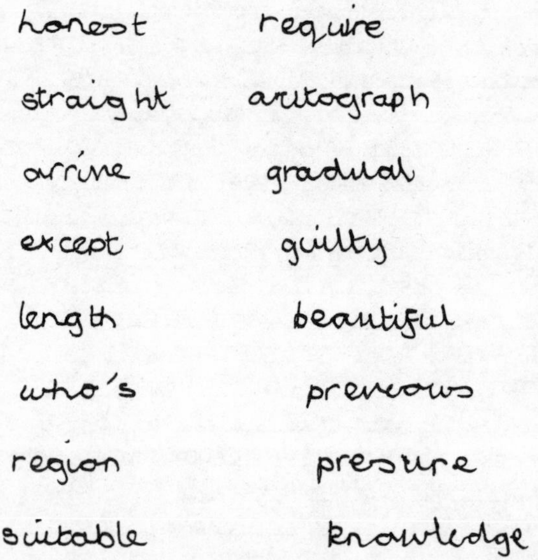

honest	require
straight	autograph
arrive	gradual
except	guilty
length	beautiful
who's	previous
region	presure
suitable	knowledge

Figure 15.7 shows the writing of Damien, a 9-year-old severely handicapped boy with brittle bones. His spelling age of 13 years seven months (Vernon 1977), indicated that he needed a speedy method of recording his written work, compatible with his high level of educational potential.

All physically handicapped children need precise assessment, preferably from members of a multidisciplinary team of therapists. Teachers are likely to be co-ordinators of advice and can suggest how recommendations can be put into practice. Attention should particularly be paid to the following:

(a) seating and writing surface,
(b) selection of writing tool,
(c) paper size and position, and
(d) the written task, so that capabilities and endurance are realistically assessed and monitored.

The tilting of the writing surface towards the body of the writer often results in a considerable improvement in writing performance.

The reference to relative importance of handwriting and

keyboard skills, discussed in the section referring to brittle-boned children, is applicable to many physically handicapped children. Attention to precise assessment becomes particularly important as more children, through recent legislation and recommendations (Education Act 1981, Chapter 60; All Handicapped Children Act 1975) become educated in ordinary schools.

REFERENCES

Alston, J. (1983) 'Children with brittle bones: an examination of their educational needs and progress.' *Special Education: Forward Trends, 10* (4).

Alston, J. (1985) 'Brittle bones: a handicap with special occupational therapy needs.' *Occupational Therapy, 9* (2).

Anderson, E.M. (1976) 'Handwriting and spina bifida.' *Special Education, 3* (2).

Anderson, E.M. (1977) *The Child with Spina Bifida*. Methuen, London.

Anderson, E.M. and Plewis, I. (1977) 'Impairment of motor skill in children with spina bifida cystica and hydrocephalus: an exploratory study.' *British Journal of Psychology, 68*, 61–70.

Bennett, P. (1985) *An Effective Physical Regime for Duchenne Muscular Dystrophy Children*. Huntleigh Technology and Hebden Green School, Winsford, Cheshire.

Cambridge, J. and Anderson, E.M. (1979) *The Handwriting of Spina Bifida Children*. Association of Spina Bifida and Hydrocephalus, London.

Department of Education and Science (1983) *Education Act 1981* (Chapter 60). HMSO, London.

Hackney, A., and Taylor, D. (1976) 'Epilepsy and the ordinary school.' *Special Education, 3* (1).

Hackney, A. and Taylor, D. (1976) 'A teacher's questionnaire description of epileptic children.' *Epilepsia, 17*, 275–81.

Scott, D. (1978) *About Epilepsy*, Third Edition, Duckworth, London.

Sklayne, K.D. and Lonton, A.P. (1981) 'The effects of selective surgery on the intelligence and self concept of children with spina bifida and hydrocephalus.' Paper from the Dublin Meeting of Society for Research into Hydrocephalus and Spina Bifida.

Stores, G. and Hart, J. (1976) 'Reading skills of children with generalised or focal epilepsy attending ordinary school.' *Developmental Medicine and Child Neurology, 18*, 705–16.

Stores, G. (1978) 'School-children with epilepsy at risk for learning and behaviour problems.' *Developmental Medicine and Child Neurology, 20* (4), 502–8.

United States Congress (1975) Education for all Handicapped Children Act. Public Law 94–142, USA

Vernon, P.E. (1977) *Graded Word Spelling Test*. Hodder and Stoughton, Borough Green, Kent.

Warnock, H.M. (1978) *Special Educational Needs: Report of the*

THE PHYSICALLY HANDICAPPED CHILD

Committee of Enquiry into the Education of Handicapped Children and Young People. HMSO, London.
Wilson, M.M. (1970) *Children with Cerebral Palsy*. HMSO, London.

16

Handwriting and School Achievement: A Cross-Cultural Study

Muriel Tarnopol and Nusia de Feldman

HANDWRITING PROBLEMS INTERNATIONALLY

Handwriting problems have been frequently examined in the learning disabled population in every country, as evidenced by the inclusion of paper-pencil tests in the diagnostic batteries of clinics in 27 countries (Tarnopol and Tarnopol 1976, 1981). Classroom teachers have referred students on the basis of unclear, confused, disordered and laboured handwriting in the hope that evaluation and appropriate remedial techniques will make an appreciable difference for their students.

In the San Francisco metropolitan area, teachers and psychologists have reported that it appears that students from other countries have better handwriting, are less frequently left handed or ambidextrous, and have parents who stress good handwriting and monitor homework assignments. That writing may be influenced by complex variables outside of the classroom has long been taken for granted. Simple curiosity to establish what some of these may be led to a series of studies in cities internationally. The objective of these was to compare the incidence and prevalence of left-handed and ambidextrous students, study sex differences, investigate handwriting styles (cursive, printing or mixing both), categorise handwriting quality (excellent, good, fair or poor), document language(s) spoken in the home and the socioeconomic status of the parents, if the mother is at home and who helps with the homework and in what subjects, and a wide variety of other possibilities.

The first study began in 1975 with graduate students in the San Francisco metropolitan area and continues to the present time wherever it is possible to test students in groups during regularly scheduled classes. The first study with a limited number of variables was followed by other studies of graduates enrolled in universities, and these were later supplemented with studies in elementary, middle and high schools with greatly expanded variables (Tarnopol and Tarnopol 1981).

Not all students tested were able to take the same battery due to absences, local administrative problems and situations beyond our control. Below the university level, classes were randomly selected by local education authorities. As much as was possible, they tried to comply with our request that all socio-economic levels be represented and that classes selected for testing were to include even distribution of all ability groups represented in each city. Local education authorities were responsible for these aspects of each study, as plans had to be completed before testing began.

This study is still in progress and readers are advised to take the information presented 'as is' with the understanding that the findings indicate 'trends' in each city and should not be considered conclusive evidence of what is going on in each country in the area of handwriting, laterality, curriculum and other variables.

Certain terms are used interchangeably such as laterality/ handedness, handwriting/penmanship, writing style/penmanship style, and handwriting/penmanship quality.

GRADUATE STUDENTS IN EDUCATION COURSES

Handedness, penmanship style and penmanship quality were investigated for the following groups of students enrolled in graduate courses in education: right and left handers, cursive writers, printers, those who mixed both, and men and women. These students, both experienced and inexperienced teachers, were tested in their classes with standardised instruments currently in use in the United States for the diagnosis of learning ability and disability (see Appendix 1). The tests measured spelling, arithmetic computation, vocabulary, and visual motor integration. A twelve-point scale for rating penmanship was created, which assessed the following:

(1) consistent use of margins,
(2) correct use of space on the page,
(3) letter placement on the lines,
(4) uniform letter height,
(5) uniform letter size,
(6) letter size not too small,

(7) letter size not too large,
(8) pencil pressure not too heavy,
(9) pencil pressure not too light,
(10) correct eraser use,
(11) letters not reversed or inverted,
(12) letters correctly joined in cursive writing or lines correctly touching in printing.

Students receiving ten to twelve points were rated excellent (1). Those with seven to nine points received good (2) ratings, while those with four to six points were rated fair (3). Poor (4) ratings had from nought to three points.

Test results for graduate students

Table 16.1 presents the raw score means of the variables. It was found for these students, who had a mean age of 30 years, that there were no significant differences of the raw score means for penmanship quality, handedness or handwriting style. However, significantly more men who printed compared with women who printed ranked in the fair and poor categories.

Table 16.1: Graduate students enrolled in education courses, 1975–80

Variable	n	Mean raw score	SD	SS	Percentile	AE
Spelling	311	41.4	5.4	116	86	—
Arithmetic	281	31.4	6.6	114	82	—
Vocabulary	165	78.7	9.5	NA	—	19 years
Visual motor	197	22.2	1.8	10	57	adult
Penmanship	311	2.4	0.9	NA	—	—
Age (years)	311	30.5	7.6			
Teaching (years)	160	4.2	5.7			

For these adults, spelling, arithmetic, vocabulary, visual motor and penmanship means were correlated, as presented in Table 16.2.

We did not infer that because there were no significant differences of the raw score means, these parameters had no influence whatever over academic variables. Since raw-score mean values may obscure relations that exist at the upper and lower levels of accomplishments, it would be necessary to examine other aspects of these variables also.

Table 16.2: Correlation matrix for graduate students, 1975–1980

Variable	Arithmetic N	r	Vocabulary N	r	Visual motor N	r	Penmanship N	r
Spelling	279	0.39*	164	0.61*	196	0.18	311	0.43*
Arithmetic			162	0.41*	195	0.37*	269	0.25*
Vocabulary					147	0.24	153	0.26*
Visual motor							184	0.25*

Note: * = 0.001 level of probability

Major findings in studies of graduate students from 1975 to 1985

By the end of 1985, 609 graduates had been tested for academic achievement, handedness, penmanship quality and style of penmanship. For the right- vs. left-handed students no differences were significant. One per cent of the students claimed they were ambidextrous and 11 per cent stated that they were left handed.

It made no significant difference if the graduates wrote in cursive or printed or mixed both. However, printers achieved a mean raw score in arithmetic of 32.0 compared with cursive writers (30.7) and those who mixed both (30.8). Cursive writers and printers had slightly higher vocabulary, although not signficantly, than those who had mixed both (cursive = 78.6 and printers = 79.7 vs. mix both = 76.9).

Significantly more men than women printed and were rated fair and poor in penmanship. This finding generally was consistent with studies we conducted in elementary and high schools in non-Asian countries. Also, a clinical observation observed in groups during testing was that more men than women showed signs of fatigue when taking the visual motor test. This was evidenced by verbal groaning on the part of some men, shaking hands, fingers and arms, profuse perspiration, and verbally stated indications about how much they disliked 'handwriting' and how they found it unpleasant. These clinical signs appeared in elementary and secondary boys also. If girls and women found handwriting difficult, their feelings were well suppressed, perspiration during writing tasks was not observed, and they appeared to have no need to vigorously shake their fingers and hand, or swing their arms out from the shoulder.

We did not find left-handed adults significantly represented in the group of poor writers or printers, nor did we find that they were different in visual motor ability. It has been observed that left-handed subjects are at a disadvantage when taking the visual motor test that involves copying geometric designs (Beery 1967). The adults in these studies did not appear disadvantaged in this skill.

HIGH SCHOOL GIRLS IN SAN FRANCISCO FROM 1980 TO 1984

In 1980 the Academic Council of a parochial high school for girls identified a number of critical deficiencies in the entering class of ninth graders. This freshman class was characterised as having poor penmanship and note-taking abilities, low testing skills, difficulty in following directions, and trouble paying attention. The faculty also complained that homework was poorly done, difficult to read, incomplete and often late. Spelling, writing and penmanship were poor. Basic reading and mathematics abilities were low and complicated by inadequate comprehension. The faculty asked for consultation about the causes of these inadequacies, curriculum modification, and in-service training for these problems.

A proposal to test the entire class by the end of the first two weeks of their ninth grade year and again at the end of their twelfth grade year was accepted. The broad objective was to assess the kinds of difficulties this particular class faced, and to document important academic and social variables, permitting analysis of change and the rates at which change occurred. Information of varying detail was collected that described each student according to various stable personal characteristics such as age, handedness, writing style, penmanship quality, performance of academic abilities sampling spelling, arithmetic, vocabulary, visual motor integration, human figure drawing, etc.

The ninth grade class

One hundred per cent ($N = 210$) of the class was tested. The grade placement at the time of testing was 9.1, as indicated in the test manual (Jastak and Jastak 1978). The mean age of the girls was 14 years four months, with a minimum of age 13 to a maximum of 15 years nine months, which was surprising to the faculty. The girls were age and grade appropriate in spelling and vocabulary. They were low in arithmetic, visual motor integration and human figure drawing.

Penmanship ranged from excellent to poor with a mean of good. Sixty three per cent of the students received excellent and good ratings, 31 per cent were fair, and six per cent were poor. Table 16.3 presents a summary of the academic levels of the entering class.

Table 16.3: High school ninth grade girls (n = 210), 1980

Variable	Mean	SD	Min.	Max.	Range
Penmanship	2.2	0.9	4	1	3
Spelling (WRAT)					
raw score	33.6	5.2	18	45	27
standard score*	111	9.3	83	138	40
grade rating	9.3	11.4	5.7	11.9	6.2
Arithmetic (WRAT)					
raw score	25.7	4.3	15	40	24
standard score*	96	10.0	70	128	47
grade rating	7.4	14.0	3.9	12.0	7.8
Vocabulary (WRVT)					
raw score	52.9	11,6	24	79	55
age equivalent	14.4		8+	19	11 years
Visual Motor (DTVMI)					
raw score	19.8	2.4	12	24	12
age equivalent	12.7		6.5	14.6	9 years
Human Figure Drawing (HFD)					
raw score	23.1	2.8	13	29	15
Age	14.4	0.5	13.0	15.9	2.9 years

Note: Visual motor (DTVMI) (copying 24 geometrical designs) has a ceiling of 24 correct, equal to 14.6, 1982 norms. Human figure drawing (Koppitz scoring) has a maximum of 30 points. *Standard scores are based on national norms, the mean = 100 and SD = 15

Almost 12 per cent of the girls were left handed and one per cent was ambidextrous. Forty-eight per cent used cursive exclusively, 37 per cent printed and 15 per cent mixed both. Ten per cent embellished their penmanship with hearts dotting the letter i, as illustrated in Figure 16.1. It was surprising to note that these girls consistently did this on all writing, including tests. Variants of this style of writing rarely appeared in the students who used cursive consistently.

The faculty expressed no concern that more than half the girls printed or used a mixture of both, or that some took the time during any written task to decorate individual letters, even during tests!

Figure 16.1: An example of embellished penmanship

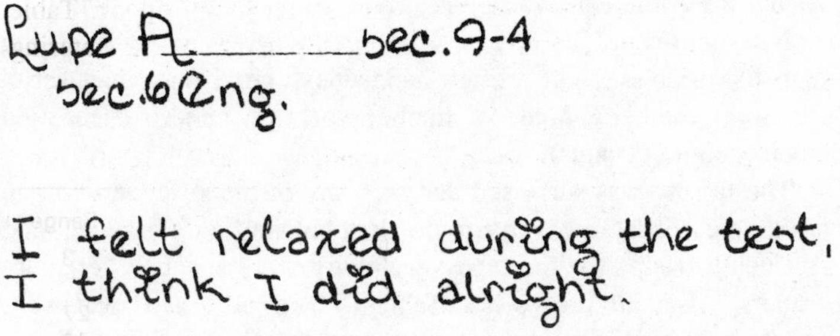

Lupe A_____ sec.9-4
  sec.6@ng.

I felt relaxed during the test,
I think I did alright.

Attitudes expressed by teachers indicated that they saw these characteristics as indications of individuality, which some even welcomed. Such a shift away from formal, Spencerian writing that they had been taught was desirable, they indicated, in this decade of 'the individual'. It did not seem to occur to them that there may be a relation between speed and fatigue in penmanship due to this style of writing that may be problematic for girls with fair and poor penmanship.

Fifty one per cent of the girls came from homes where foreign languages were spoken. It was not surprising that the vocabulary raw score mean did not favour these students, as seen in Table 16.4. There were no differences in penmanship, in visual motor skills or in spelling. Ability in arithmetic was higher in the foreign-language speaking group, but not significantly, as was that in human figure drawing.

Table 16.4: Ninth grade girls from English-speaking vs. foreign-language speaking homes in San Francisco

Variable	$n = 103$, (49%) English		$n = 107$, (51%) Foreign language	
	Mean	SD	Mean	SD
Penmanship	2.2	0.9	2.2	0.9
Spelling standard score	110.8	9.7	110.3	11.1
Arithmetic standard score	94.9	10.5	96.1	9.4
Vocabulary* raw score	55.8	10.3	50.0	12.0
Beery VMI	19.7	2.3	19.9	2.4
Draw-A-Person	22.6	2.3	23.5	2.4
Age	14.3	0.5	14.4	0.5

Note: *The vocabulary means are significantly different in favour of the children from English-speaking homes ($P = 0.001$)

The correlation matrix for ninth graders indicated that penmanship correlated with spelling and arithmetic, and that spelling correlated with arithmetic, vocabulary, and visual motor integration.

No significant differences were found between the following pairs of variables, right- vs. left-handedness, cursive vs. manuscript (printers), mother at home vs. mother works, or father's occupation (socioeconomic status).

The faculty was surprised that so many of the girls were low in arithmetic, visual motor integration and human figure drawing, and that penmanship, spelling and vocabulary were adequate for ninth graders. Also, the ranges (see Table 16.3) in all tested areas were a disturbing finding and far greater than they had anticipated.

Table 16.5 Significant coefficients of correlation for ninth graders

r	Variables	N	P <
0.49	Penmanship vs. spelling	210	0.001
0.30	Penmanship vs. arithmetic	210	0.001
0.39	Spelling vs. arithmetic	210	0.001
0.43	Spelling vs. vocabulary	210	0.001
0.25	Spelling vs. Beery	210	0.001
−0.26	Spelling vs. age	210	0.001

The senior class

The class was post-tested one week before graduation. Grade placement at time of testing was 12.9. Only 160 girls remained of the 210 who were freshmen. Table 16.6 presents the achievements of the class at the end of the four-year period.

As expected, the mean raw scores for spelling, arithmetic, vocabulary, visual motor and human figure drawing were higher for seniors than freshmen. However, it is more appropriate to adjust raw scores for both groups by expected raw scores, as presented in Table 16.7. A t-statistic was constructed for each variable to assess the statistical significance of the difference of actual minus expected raw scores between the two groups. All the t tests were very highly significant, indicating that, though the seniors did show raw-score improvement, they lost ground to the general population of students as a whole. Penmanship was not included in these statistics because there were no published norms or scores for this scale for comparison.

Did the quality of penmanship relate to the achievement of the

Table 16.6: High school senior girls ($n = 160$), 1984

Variable	Mean	SD	Min.	Max.	Range
Penmanship	2.2	0.9	4	1	3
Spelling (WRAT)					
raw score	37.7	4.8	24	50	26
standard score	111	7.2	90	121	40
grade rating	10.2	10.9	7.2	12.9	5.7
Arithmetic (WRAT)					
raw score	28.4	5.0	17	41	24
standard score	100	10.1	78	125	47
grade rating	8.3	15.9	4.6	12.4	7.8
Vocabulary (WRVT)					
raw score	62.5	9.8	35	83	48
age equivalent	16		10+	19+	9 years
Visual Motor (DTVMI)					
raw score	20.7	2.1	15	24	9
age equivalent	13.1		7.9	14.6	6.7 years
Human Figure Drawing (HFD)					
raw score	23.7	2.6	15	29	14
Age	18.1	3.8	17.0	19.0	2.0 years

Table 16.7: Deviations from expected raw scores

Variable	9th Graders Actual-Expected	SD	12th Graders Actual-Expected	SD	t*	$P > t$
Spelling	+0.6	5.2	−12.3	4.8	24.7	~ 0
Arithmetic	−4.8	4.3	−14.1	5.0	18.8	~ 0
Vocabulary	−1.1	11.6	−10.5	9.8	8.43	< 0.0001
Visual Motor	−2.2	2.4	− 1.3	2.1	3.8	< 0.0005

Note: *The t-statistic tests the difference in the actual-expected columns for the ninth and twelfth grade groups.

seniors? As illustrated in Table 16.8, there were no significant differences for arithmetic or for figure drawing. Vocabulary differences were not significant, but the nine girls who were poor in penmanship were lower in vocabulary, as they also were in spelling and visual motor skills.

The correlation matrix for excellent writers indicated that spelling vs. arithmetic ($r = 0.57$, $P = 0.001$), spelling vs. vocabulary ($r = 0.56$, $P = 0.001$), and visual motor vs. arithmetic ($r = 0.41$, $P = 0.002$) were correlated. For the good writers, spelling vs.

Table 16.8: Penmanship quality and mean raw scores for seniors

Variable	Excellent (n = 45, 28%)		Good (n = 62, 39%)		Fair (n = 44, 28%)		Poor (n = 9, 6%)	
	RS	SD	RS	SD	RS	SD	RS	SD
Spelling	38	5.3	39.5	4.1	35.7	4.5	35	3.6
Arithmetic	27.6	5.4	28.9	5.2	28.7	4.5	28.1	4.2
Vocabulary	62	10.3	63.7	8.8	62.2	10.5	59.2	9.7
Visual motor	21.2	1.8	21.1	1.8	19.9	2.1	18.8	2.8
Human figure	23.8	2.7	23.9	2.6	23.4	2.5	23.8	1.9
Age	18.1	0.4	18.0	0.4	18.0	0.3	18.1	0.5

arithmetic ($r = 0.52$, $P = 0.001$) were the only subjects that correlated, as was the case with the fair writers ($r = 0.45$, $P = 0.001$). Correlations for the poor group were not established because of the small number.

The nine girls with poor penmanship ratings stated on their questionnaires, which all the seniors completed the last week of school, that they had strong feelings about the written aspects of their school experience. One wrote, 'I hate everything about writing. My hand gets tired. The teachers mark me down for bad, sloppy penmanship. I can't write fast enough. I don't like the way my papers look but I don't know what to do about it. I really hated high school.' Another girl complained, 'I am always last to finish. I feel stupid and my writing looks stupid, no matter how hard I try.' One senior wrote, 'For twelve years I tried to please my teachers and use good handwriting and could not. I am tired of school and did not learn anything!'

Handedness and academic achievement in senior girls

To determine handedness, girls were asked to check (tick) on each test whether they were using either their right or left hand or both. Girls were observed by the examiners, and all left-handed and ambidextrous writers were confirmed also by classroom teachers. To be classified as either right- or left-handed, the girls had to take all five tests, answer their questionnaires, and deliver their written sample with the same hand. Ambidextrous students were observed to change hands from test to test and within the various tests. There were only two of these students and teachers and the school psychologist were aware of them before this study began. Table 16.9

Table 16.9: Handedness, academic achievement and penmanship in seniors

Variable	Right (n = 135, 84.4%)	SD	Left (n = 23, 14.4%)	SD	Ambidextrous (n = 2, 1.2%) Case 1	Case 2
Spelling	37.4	4.7	39.3	4.8	28	43
Arithmetic	28.4	4.9	28.6	6.1	23	29
Vocabulary	62.3	9.4	64.3	11.8	51	51
Visual motor	20.7	2.0	20.7	2.4	19	24*
Human figure	23.6	2.5	24.7	2.8	22	25
Penmanship mean	*2.1	0.9	2.0	0.9	Poor	Good
Age	18.1	0.4	18.1	0.4	18.9	17.8

*Categories	Right N	%	Left N	%
Excellent	37	27.4	7	30.4
Good	52	38.5	9	39.1
Fair	38	28.1	6	26.1
Poor	8	5.9	1	4.3

Note: None of the differences of the means is significant

summarises handedness, penmanship and school achievement for the seniors.

Cursive writers, printers and students who combine both

The faculty was surprised when they learned that twelve per cent of the seniors used only cursive, compared with 48 per cent of the freshmen. As presented in Table 16.10, the 19 cursive writers are not significantly different from the other groups. They had slightly better penmanship and arithmetic. The visual motor skills of the three groups were almost identical. No significant correlations for the cursive writers were noted.

Fathers, mothers and academic achievement and penmanship

Thirty-four per cent of the fathers were professionals, 33 per cent white-collar workers, and 12 per cent blue-collar workers. Data was missing for 20 per cent of the fathers. Differences were not significant for fathers and their occupations.

Thirty-one per cent of the mothers were at home, 65 per cent were blue- and white-collar workers and only one mother was professional. Differences were not significant for mothers as presented in Table 16.11.

Table 16.10: Penmanship style and academic achievement in seniors

Variable	Cursive writers (N = 19, 11.9%)		Printers only (N = 47, 29.4%)		Combine both (N = 94, 58.7%)	
	RS	SD	RS	SD	RS	SD
Spelling	38.8	5.1	38	4.7	37.3	4.8
Arithmetic	30.1	4.2	28.8	5.2	27.9	5.1
Vocabulary	60.8	11.9	62.8	9.9	62.7	9.5
Visual motor	20.4	2.4	20.4	2.1	20.8	2.0
Human figure	23.2	2.1	24.5	2.5	23.5	2.7
Age	18.1	0.4	18.1	0.4	18.0	0.4
Penmanship	1.9	0.8	2.4	1.0	2.0	0.8
	N	%	N	%	N	%
Excellent	6	32	10	21.3	29	30.9
Good	9	47.4	15	31.9	38	40.4
Fair	3	15.8	15	31.9	26	27.7
Poor	1	5.3	7	14.9	1	1.1

Table 16.11: MHS Seniors' fathers, mothers and academic achievement

Fathers	Deceased (N = 2,		Blue collar (N = 19,	White collar (N = 52,	Professional (N = 55,
Variable	1.2%)		11.9%)	32.5%)	34.4%)
Spelling	29	—	38.3	38.3	37.1
Arithmetic	18	20	28.8	28.1	28.9
Vocabulary	47	—	62.4	62.5	62
Visual motor	19	21	21.5	20.5	20.4
Human figure	21	25	23.3	23.2	24.1
Penmanship					
			N (%)	N (%)	N (%)
Excellent	1	—	6 (31.6)	17 (32.7)	12 (21.8)
Good	—	1	9 (47.4)	19 (36.5)	21 (38.2)
Fair	—	—	4 (21.1)	11 (21.2)	19 (34.5)
Poor	—	—	0	5 (9.6)	3 (5.5)

Mothers	Deceased	At Home	Blue & White Collar	Professional
Variable	(N = 1, 0.6%)	(N = 49, 30.6%)	(N = 104, 65%)	(N = 1, 0.6%)
Spelling	27	37.8	38.1	28
Arithmetic	20	29.1	28.5	23
Vocabulary	47	61.8	63	51
Visual motor	19	21.1	20.7	19
Human figure	21	23.9	23.8	22
Penmanship				
		N (%)	N (%)	N
Excellent	1	13 (26.5)	28 (26.9)	1
Good		18 (36.7)	43 (41.3)	
Fair		15 (30.6)	28 (26.9)	
Poor		3 (6.1)	5 (4.8)	

Notes: N = 32 (20%) of fathers were missing, N = 5 (3.1%) of mothers were missing

Three students reported that two fathers and one mother were deceased. Penmanship did not appear to be affected. Two of the girls had excellent scores and one had a score of good. However, it was of interest to note that the three girls showed diminished raw scores compared to the means of blue-collar, white collar and professional parents in spelling, arithmetic and vocabulary. Visual motor was within normal limits as was human figure drawing.

Language spoken at home, penmanship and academic achievement

The teachers had stated that they rarely saw penmanship problems in their San Francisco students who were from Asian-speaking language groups. At this school, these included Filipino, Tagalog, Ilocano, Chinese, Japanese and Indonesian students, who numbered 24 students. Table 16.12 illustrates the incidence and prevalence of the penmanship categories according to the language spoken at home. Not one of these girls received a poor rating in penmanship, and only two were rated as fair.

Other language groups that had no students in the poor category were Greek, French, Russian, Dutch and Maltese. These groups combined had four girls in the fair category; 29 per cent of the English-speaking and 30 per cent of the Spanish-speaking students contributed the largest number ($n = 32$) of girls with ratings of fair.

Table 16.13 presents the raw score means for the English vs. foreign-languages spoken at home groups and their categories of penmanship.

Comparison of means by analysis of variance for several classification variables

Analysis of variance (ANOVA) techniques were used to assess the significance of the differences in scores among the seniors when analysed according to several classification variables. The variables used in the analysis were spelling, arithmetic, vocabulary, visual motor and human figure drawing raw scores and penmanship raw score. Classification variables were satisfaction with high school (yes, no or partially), number of books read in one year for pleasure that were not required (none, one, two, three, four, five, six, seven, eight or more) and language spoken at home, which included

201

Table 16.12: Language spoken at home and mean raw academic scores of seniors

			Asian (N = 16, 12.5%)						
Variable	English (N = 86, 53.7%)	Spanish (N = 23, 14.4%)	Filipino (N = 7)	Tagalog (N = 7)	Ilocano (N = 2)	Chinese (N = 6, 3.7%)	Italian (N = 6, 3.7%)	Arabic (N = 5, 3.1%)	German (N = 4, 2.5%)
Spelling	37.1	35.5	40	43.6	35.5	40	39	35.4	32
Arithmetic	28.1	26.7	28.3	30	27.5	35	28.2	27.2	29
Vocabulary	64.4	58.2	57.4	66.7	67	56	67	54.8	58.5
Visual motor	20.8	20.5	21.4	22	18	21	21	19.2	20.3
Human figure	23.8	23.4	23.9	23.7	24.5	22.8	24.5	23.8	22.3
Penmanship	N (%)	N (%)	N (%)	N (%)	N	N (%)	N (%)	N (%)	N (%)
Excellent	22 (25.6%)	8 (34.8%)	4 (57.1%)	6 (85.7%)	—	4 (66.7%)	1 (16.7%)	1 (20%)	—
Good	35 (40.7)	7 (30.4)	3 (42.9)	1 (14.3)	—	1 (16.7)	4 (66.7)	1 (20)	—
Fair	25 (29.1)	7 (30.4)	—	—	—	1 (16.7)	—	2 (40)	2 (50%)
Poor	4 (4.7)	1 (4.3)	—	—	—	—	1 (16.7)	1 (20)	2 (50)

Variable	Greek (N = 3, 1.9%)	French (N = 2, 1.2%)	Russian (N = 2, 1.2%)	Dutch (N = 1, 0.6%)	Japanese (N = 1, 0.6%)	Maltese (N = 1, 0.6%)	Indonesian (N = 1, 0.6%)
Spelling	39.7	45.5	46	—	42	35	43
Arithmetic	35	31.5	28	34	—	25	40
Vocabulary	54	60	69	—	65	67	48
Visual motor	21	20	22.5	18	—	16	22
Human figure	26	23	24.5	—	—	22	26
Penmanship	N (%)	N (%)	N (%)	N	N	N	N
Excellent	0	1 (50)	1 (50)	—	—	1	—
Good	1 (33.3)	—	1 (50)	—	1	—	1
Fair	2 (66.7)	1 (50)	—	1	—	—	—
Poor	0	—	—	—	—	—	—

Table 16.13: Seniors English only vs. foreign languages spoken at home

Academic variable	All seniors ($N = 160$)	English spoken only ($N = 88$, 55.0%)	Foreign languages ($N = 69$, 43.1%)
Spelling	37.7	37.1	39.4
Arithmetic	28.4	28.1	32.3
Vocabulary	62.5	64.4	60.6
Visual motor	20.4	20.8	21.1
Human figure	23.7	23.8	23.4
Penmanship	2.1	2.1	2.0
	N (%)	N (%)	N (%)
Excellent	45 (28.1)	22 (25.0)	22 (33.8)
Good	62 (38.7)	36 (40.9)	23 (35.4)
Fair	44 (27.5)	26 (29.5)	16 (24.6)
Poor	9 (5.6)	4 (4.5)	4 (6.2)

English, Spanish and other languages cited in Table 16.12. In addition, the same variables were regressed on the number of daily hours of television watching. The results are summarised below.

Satisfaction with high school has no apparent effect on the various raw score measurements. The number of books read has, surprisingly, no significant effect on any variable except human figure drawing raw score. Even this significance level is weak ($P = 0.092$) and possibly spurious. Language spoken at home is significantly associated with spelling ($P = 0.002$), arithmetic ($P = 0.012$) and vocabulary raw score ($P = 0.037$). Table 16.13 indicates that only vocabulary raw score is significantly different for English and non-English-speaking students, as previously stated. The apparent difference in conclusion probably follows from the fact that the ANOVA considered a more detailed language classification, and that some groups exhibited higher mean scores than the English-speaking group. The means for the Spanish-speaking group were generally slightly lower than those for the English-speaking students, while the Tagalog- and Chinese-speaking groups tended to have higher mean raw scores.

The number of daily hours of television viewing was not associated one way or another with any variable other than arithmetic raw score, as presented in Table 16.14.

Table 16.15 illustrates satisfaction with high school.

CARACAS BOYS AND GIRLS IN 1984

A study of elementary school children in grades two and five was

Table 16.14: Seniors — How much time daily watching television?

Variable	None (N = 17, 10.6%)	One hour* (N = 68, 42.5%)	Two hours (N = 37, 23.1%)	Three hours (N = 16, 10%)	Four hours (N = 11, 6.9%)	Five hours (N = 1, 0.6%)	Six hours (N = 3, 1.9%) #1	#2	#3
Spelling	36.3	38.7	36.5	36.8	37.1	35	36	44	45
Arithmetic	27.9	30.0	27.6	25.6	27.2	21	17	25	35
Vocabulary	62.4	64.8	59.8	58.8	59.9	61	67	70	72
Visual motor	20.7	21.2	19.8	20.8	20.3	16	21	21	23
Human figure	23.6	23.7	23.6	25.1	21.2	26	21	22	24
Age	18.1	18.1	17.9	18.0	18.4	17.7			
Penmanship	2.3	2.0	2.2	2.1	2.0	4.0			
	N (%)	N (%)	N (%)	N (%)	N (%)	N			
Excellent	4 (23.5)	23 (33.8)	8 (21.6)	4 (25.0)	5 (45.5)	—	1	—	—
Good	4 (23.5)	27 (39.7)	18 (48.6)	7 (43.8)	3 (27.3)	—	—	1	—
Fair	9 (52.9)	16 (23.5)	8 (21.6)	4 (25.0)	1 (9.1)	—	—	—	—
Poor	—	2 (2.9)	3 (8.1)	1 (6.3)	2 (18.2)	1	—	—	1

Note: * N = 7 (4.4%) were missing

Table 16.15: Seniors — satisfaction with Mercy High School

Variable	All (N = 160)	Satisfied (N = 107, 70.4%)	Partially satisfied (N = 38, 23.7%)	Not satisfied (N = 5, 3%)
Spelling	37.7	37.6	37.7	35.6
Arithmetic	28.4	28.9	27.4	26.2
Vocabulary	62.5	62.4	62.8	59.2
Visual motor	20.7	20.7	20.6	19.8
Human figure	23.7	23.8	23.6	23.6
Penmanship	2.1	2.0	2.3	2.2
Age	18.1	18.1	18.0	17.8

undertaken in Caracas, the capital of Venezuela. This addition to our international study was made possible by Nusia de Feldman, who translated the tests we were using into Spanish, and who also organised and carried out the bulk of the testing in the schools. The children were tested with level one of the Wide Range Achievement Test in Arithmetic. It was not possible to administer the spelling section of this test. They were also administered the same human figure drawing and visual motor integration tests (see Appendix 1) as the other students we were able to examine.

The variables, in addition to raw score means for the tests, included handedness, penmanship style (cursive, printing and those who combine both), quality of penmanship, sex, and other characteristics. It was not possible, due to scheduling and other constraints, to collect data reflecting the wide range of variables we were able to study in San Francisco. However, enough information was gathered to present a lively description of these students and their handwriting.

Caracas second graders

Caracas eight-year-olds were tested at the end of the second grade. Table 16.16 presents the mean raw score achievement of the boys and girls with the same information from their age-mates in San Francisco, Southampton, Taipei, Hiroshima and Tokyo. There is no penmanship rating for Republic of China and Japanese second grades due to inherent difficulties of using a rating scale for differing orthographies. However, the visual motor and human figure drawing scores offer a measure of hand-pencil co-ordination, which is valuable.

Table 16.16 indicates that Caracas second graders compare

Table 16.16: Caracas second graders compared with second graders in international study

Country (City)	Venezuela (Caracas)	United States (San Francisco)	England (Southampton)	Republic of China (Taipei)	Japan (Hiroshima)	(Tokyo)
Number tested	169	44	229	99	47	214
Mean age	8.3	8.2	8.3	7.9	8.3	8.2
Grade*	2.9	2.9	2.10	2.5	2.8	2.7
Tests+						
Arithmetic WRAT	29.1	27.5	28	27	29	29
Visual motor DTVMI	13.6	14.3	14	15	17	15
Human figure HFD	20.5	20.1	22	23	24	23
Penmanship	2.1	2.1	2.2	NA	NA	NA

Note: * Grade placement at time of testing from WRAT Manual, 1978 Edition. + All scores are raw score mean. NA = not available for comparison due to different orthographies.

Table 16.17: Caracas fifth graders compared to fifth graders in international study

Country (City)	Venezuela (Caracas)	United States (San Francisco)	England (Southampton)	Republic of China (Taipei)	Japan (Hiroshima)	(Tokyo)
Number tested	155	46	247	42	45	148
Mean age	11.4	11.0	11.3	10.8	11.3	11.2
Grade*	5.9	5.9	5.10	5.5	5.8	5.7
Tests+						
Arithmetic WRAT	35.5	38.5	34	41	43	43
Visual motor DTVMI	16.1	18	17	20	21	19
Human figure HFD	21.1	23	24	24	25	24
Penmanship	2.1	1.9	2.1	NA	NA	NA

Note: * Grade placement at time of testing from WRAT Manual, 1978 Edition. + All scores are raw score means. NA = not available for comparison due to different orthographies.

Table 16.18: Caracas second graders ($N = 169$)

Variable	Mean	SD	Minimum	Maximum
Arithmetic (WRAT) 1978				
Raw score	29.1	9.6	23	33
Standard score	119.8	1.9	81	130
Percentile	59.5	2.1	10	98
Grade rating	3.5	3.9	2.6	4.5
Visual Motor (DTVMI) 1982				
Raw score	13.6	2.8	8	21
Age equivalent	7.5	2.0	5.1	13.1
Percentile	34.5	2.7	1	98
Standard score	8.2	3.9	1	17
Human figure (HFD) 1968				
Raw score	20.5	10.9	11	26
Penmanship	2.1	0.9	4	1
Age	8.3	5.9	7.2	10.8

Note: Grade placement at time of testing was 2.9 (end of the school year). Visual motor (DTVMI) copying of 24 geometrical designs has a ceiling of 24 items correct, equal to 14.6 age equivalent score, 1982 norms. Human figure drawing (Koppitz scoring) has a maximum of 30 points. Standard scores are based on national norms, the mean = 100, and the standard deviation = 15, for WRAT arithmetic. Standard score means = 10 based on national norms for the DTVMI and the standard deviation = 2.9

favourably with San Francisco and Southampton children in the same age range in raw-score mean values for penmanship quality, for arithmetic, visual motor and human-figure drawing.

Caracas fifth graders, as presented in Table 16.17, maintain their good penmanship rating but appear to lose ground compared with their English and American counterparts in other areas. Children in the cities of Taipei, Hiroshima and Tokyo gain significantly at the fifth grade level in arithmetic and visual motor skills. English and Asian children attain the highest human figure drawing raw score means for eleven-year-olds. The raw score means for the Taipei second and fifth graders reflect the achievement of these students in the middle of their second grade year while the non-Asian children's scores are based on testing at the end of this year. Hiroshima and Japanese classes were also tested before the end of their second-grade year. It is assumed that if the Asian children had been tested at the same point in the academic year as the non-Asian children their raw score means would reflect higher achievement.

Tables 16.18 and 16.19 give the means, standard deviations and ranges for Caracas second and fifth graders. Standard scores in arithmetic indicate that second graders compare very favourably with American children in this age group; however, their visual motor abilities lag by approximately one year. As fifth graders,

Table 16.19: Caracas fifth grades (N = 155)

Variable	Mean	SD	Minimum	Maximum
Arithmetic (WRAT) 1978				
Raw score	35.5	3.4	28	43
Standard score	93.5	11.1	70	124
Percentile	36.5	23.9	2	95
Grade rating	5.0	7.6	3.5	7.3
Visual Motor (DTVMI) 1982			9	24
Raw score	16.1	3.3	9	24
Age equivalent	9.3	2.6	5.4	14.6
Percentile	31	25.5	1	9
Standard score	7.6	3.2	1	16
Human figure (HFD) 1968				
Raw score	21.1	2.3	14	27
Penmanship	2.1	0.9	4	1
Age	11.4	8.1	10.1	15.0

Note: Grade placement at time of testing was 5.9 (end of the school year).

there is a standard score drop that is significant in arithmetic. At this grade level, the lag in visual motor skills widens to approximately two years, while the gain in human figure drawing is less than one raw score point. There is no change in penmanship from the second to the fifth grade for the average child.

Penmanship quality, handedness, style of writing and sex differences

Twenty-one Caracas boys (11.7 per cent) were left-handed compared with eighteen girls (12.7 per cent). One boy and one girl (1.3 per cent) were ambidextrous. Eighty-eight per cent of the boys were right-handed (n = 156) compared with 87 per cent (n = 114) of the girls. More girls printed (13.4 per cent) compared with boys (8.9 per cent). Fewer boys (3.9 per cent) mixed both compared with girls (6.3 per cent).

Significant differences were found in penmanship quality for boys and girls. Forty-two per cent (n = 75) of the boys versus eleven per cent (n = 29) of the girls ranked in the combined fair-poor categories.

Tables 16.20 and 16.21 present sex differences for the Caracas and Southampton students. In each city, boys are very significantly rated fair and poor.

The fact that 87 per cent of the Caracas boys use cursive

Table 16.20: Sex differences in Caracas second and fifth graders in handedness, writing and penmanship

Variables		No. of males (%)		No. of females (%)	
Right hand		157	(87.7)	123	(86.6)
Left hand		21	(11.7)	18	(12.7)
Both hands		1	(0.6)	1	(0.7)
Cursive writers		156	(87.2)	114	(80.3)
Printers (manuscript)		16	(8.9)	19	(13.4)
Mixes both		7	(3.9)	9	(6.3)
Penmanship					
Excellent	(1)	40	(22.3)	43	(30.3)
Good	(2)	64	(35.8)	70	(49.3)
Fair	(3)	57	(31.8) } (41.9%*)	27	(10.0) } (11.4%*)
Poor	(4)	18	(10.1)	2	(1.4)

Table 16.21: Sex differences in Southampton second and fifth graders

Variables		No. of males (%)		No. of females (%)	
Right hand		210	(87)	208	(89)
Left hand		29	(12)	24	(10)
Both hands		2	(0.8)	1	(0.4)
Cursive writers		36	(15)	30	(12.9)
Printers (manuscript)		152	(63)	139	(59.7)
Mixes both		53	(22)	64	(27.5)
Penmanship					
Excellent	(1)	49	(19)	74	(32)
Good	(2)	83	(34)	92	(39.5)
Fair	(3)	81	(37) } (50%*)	55	(24) } (20%*)
Poor	(4)	31	(13)	12	(5)

Note: * Differences are significant (based on a t test) at a level of 0:001.

only compared with 15 per cent of the Southampton boys and 80 per cent of the Caracas girls use cursive compared with 13 per cent of the Southampton girls, raises the issue of the curriculum. It was surprising to find such differences from city to city. It suggests that these choices are not a reflection of a natural inclination by sex but are more influenced by what individual teachers decide or the local curriculum advises. We have found that even when the local curriculum favours printing vs. cursive or vice versa, individual teachers in Southampton, Caracas and San Francisco will make unilateral decisions to teach a different style of penmanship than most of the teachers are presenting. During the data-gathering period for penmanship style, we were surprised by the absence of discussion about the different possibilities from both teachers and administrators. Often psychologists would have information about the relative disadvantages of one style over the other, particularly in the area of the perceptual confusion they noticed which they thought appeared more in printing than in cursive styles. However, teachers of the reading and learning disabled in each of these cities, and everywhere we have presented data on these variables, have very definite opinions on the reasons for teaching cursive only to these categories of learners.

Because it was not possible to administer the spelling test, reversals and inversions had to be tabulated from the arithmetic tests. As presented in Table 16.22, there were no significant differences for boys and girls in arithmetic raw score, standard score and percentile mean. Girls ranged in percentile from a low of two to a high of 98, while boys ranged from the fourth to the 96th percentile.

We considered disregarding the sign in arithmetic to be an indication of impulsivity, one of the characteristics of learning disability. Fifty-six per cent of the girls made no error involving disregarding the sign compared to forty-one per cent of the boys. One error of this nature was made by thirty-two per cent of the boys compared with thirty-one per cent of the girls. Twenty-one per cent of the boys disregarded the signs twice compared with ten per cent of the girls. Eight boys compared with six girls did this three times and three boys each made these errors four times. No girls did this.

Ninety-nine per cent of the girls compared with ninety-seven per cent of the boys made no number reversals. Two boys made one, one girl made two, and three boys each made three reversals on their test. Ninety-six per cent of the girls compared with ninety-two per cent of the boys made no number inversions. Eight per cent of the boys compared with four per cent of the girls inverted numbers. It is of interest to note that no girls disregarded the signs four times, reversed three times and inverted five or six times.

Considering that the mean arithmetic raw scores between boys and girls (boys = 31.6 and girls = 31) actually favour boys, although the differences are not significant, one wonders what would happen to the arithimetic mean if boys and girls could be trained to guard against impulsivity (disregarding the signs), and to double check all problems for reversals and inversions. Might it also not be possible to train them to double check their penmanship and correct reversals, inversions and general sloppiness (or impulsivity)? Some penmanship programmes in use today actually attempt to do this.

Table 16.22: Caracas second and fifth graders — arithmetic, disregarding the signs, reversals, etc.

Variables	Males	(SD)	Females	(SD)
Arithmetic (WRAT)				
Raw score mean	31.6	4.8	31	4.6
Grade equivalent	4.2		4.2	
Standard score mean	98.8		99.2	
Percentile mean	48		48	
Percentile range	4 to 96		2 to 98	

	No. of males	(%)		No. of females	(%)	
Arithmetic disregarding the signs						
None	74	(41.3)	(73%)	79	(55.6)	(86.6%)
One	57	(31.8)		43	(31)	
Two	37	(20.7)		14	(9.9)	
Three	8	(4.5)	(27%)	6	(4.2)	(14%)
Four	3	(1.7)		—		
Arithmetic number reversals						
None	174	(97.2)		141	(99.3)	
One	2	(1.1)		—	—	
Two	—	—	(2.8%)	1	(0.7)	(0.7%)
Three	3	(1.7)		—	—	
Arithmetic number inversions						
None	165	(92.2)		136	(95.8)	
One	3	(1.7)		2	(1.4)	
Two	3	(1.7)		1	(0.7)	
Three	6	(3.4)		2	(1.4)	(4%)
Four	1	(0.6)	(8%)	1	(0.7)	
Five	—	—		—	—	
Six	1	(0.6)				

Table 16.23 presents the scores of Caracas children by hand and style of writing. The 39 children who are left-handed do not appear significantly different from their right-handed classmates in any of the tested areas. However, they have slightly higher scores in arithmetic, visual motor and human-figure drawing. There were no significant differences in the penmanship raw scores. Thirty-three per cent of the left-handed and right-handed were in the combined fair and poor groups. About five per cent more right-handed children used cursive compared with left-handed students and five per cent more left-handed than right-handed used printing.

In Caracas, the school achievement of the eleven per cent who printed was significantly higher in arithmetic. These children were also higher in visual motor and human figure drawing compared

211

Table 16.23: Scores of Caracas second and fifth graders by hand, cursive writers, printers, and those who mix both

	Right-handed			Left-handed			Cursive			Print			Both		
	N	Mean	SD	N	Mean	SD	N	Mean	SD	N	Mean	SD	N	Mean	SD
Arithmetic	280	31.4	5.0	39	32.2	5.1	270	30.8	4.4	35	35.8	4.3	16	34.7	4.5
Visual motor	280	14.8	3.3	39	15.3	2.8	270	14.5	3.2	35	16.4	3.3	16	15.8	4.0
Human figure drawing	280	20.8	6.6	35	21.5	2.6	270	20.6	6.5	35	22.0	2.5	16	20.1	2.4
Penmanship	280	2.1	0.9	39	2.2	0.9	270	2.1	0.9	35	2.0	0.7	16	2.2	0.8
	N	(%)		N	(%)		N	(%)		N	(%)		N	(%)	
Excellent	74	(26.4)		9	(23.1)		72	(26.7)		8	(22.9)		3	(18.8)	
Good	113	(41.1)		17	(43.1)		107	(39.6)		19	(54.3)		8	(50.0)	
Fair	74	(26.4)		10	(25.6)		78	(27.0)		7	(20.0)		4	(25.0)	
Poor	17	(6.1)		3	(7.7)		18	(6.7)		1	(2.9)		1	(6.8)	
Penmanship style	N	(%)		N	(%)										
Cursive	238	(85.0)		31	(79.5)										
Printing	29	(10.4)		6	(15.4)										
Both	13	(4.6)		2	(5.1)										

with the cursive writers, although these differences are not significant.

The correlation matrix for the second and fifth graders indicates that penmanship correlates with arithmetic, visual motor and human-figure drawing raw scores as presented in Table 16.24.

Table 16.24: Caracas second and fifth graders. Significant coefficients of correlation

r	Variables	N	P
0.33	Arithmetic raw score vs. Human figure drawing raw score	323	(0.001)
0.39	Arithmetic raw score vs. Visual motor raw score	321	(0.001)
0.20	Human Figure raw score vs. Visual motor raw score	317	(0.001)
0.24	Penmanship vs. Arithmetic raw score	323	(0.003)
0.27	Penmanship vs. Visual motor raw score	321	(0.001)
0.30	Penmanship vs. Human figure drawing raw score	323	(0.001)

SUMMARY

Readers are asked to bear in mind that these different studies are based on an attempt to learn what is happening internationally in handwriting. We did not report here on a study of 200 Italian second and fifth graders that was completed recently and which is still in the process of statistical analysis, or on other studies in progress in California. It is our goal to be able to bring these different studies into concordance in the near future.

What has been learned is that there is disparity between stated goals in local education and what actually happens in the classroom. Readers are reminded to look at the data 'as is' and are asked to offer suggestions for future studies of cross-cultural influences on handwriting.

A brief view of three major groups reported here follows.

The university graduates

Significantly more men print than women, and rank in the fair and poor categories for penmanship. There were no significant differ-ences for the cursive, print or mix both groups, the left- and right-handed, or for penmanship quality. The mean penmanship quality for graduate students was 2.4 compared with 2.2 for ninth and twelfth graders, and 2.1 for second and fifth graders.

Only men during the test battery complained about fatigue and their dislike of writing tasks. One 40-year-old man stated as he handed in his spelling test, 'It's pretty bad, isn't it!' I never passed the course in handwriting for my teaching credential.' When asked how he got credit for the course, which was at that time a requirement for the credential, he replied, 'I got my sister to take the test for me. She can really write well!'

Penmanship correlated with spelling ($r = 0.43$, $P = 0.001$) and with arithmetic ($r = 0.25$), vocabulary ($r = 0.26$) and visual motor ($r = 0.25$) at the 0.001 level of probability.

The high school students

We found that contrary to our expectations, teachers as a whole at the high school level were not able to objectively evaluate the penmanship of their students, or their academic functioning in a number of critical areas. Teachers believed that foreign-language speaking students had better penmanship, which this study did not confirm. At this level, it was noted that there was a major shift away from cursive writing in the ninth grade to printing or a combination of cursive and printing that high school teachers in this San Francisco school accepted. The correlation matrix for high school seniors indicated that penmanship vs. spelling were the most strongly correlated subjects ($r = 0.49$, $P = 0.001$). There was no change in penmanship quality over the four years (ninth graders raw score = 2.2 and twelfth graders = 2.2), at least as far as the twelve-point rating scale that we developed and used could distinguish.

High school girls just before graduation, who had poor penmanship, indicated that this troubled them and for some influenced their enjoyment and achievement in school. Six per cent were in this category and their visual motor, vocabulary and spelling levels were low. Five of them had marked low self esteem, as evidenced by their human figure drawings and comments they wrote on the questionnaires and various tests.

The elementary school children

Children in Caracas were compared with their age-mates in San Francisco, Southampton, Taipei, Hiroshima and Tokyo in arithmetic, visual motor integration and human-figure drawing. Non-Asian second and fifth graders (eight- and eleven-year-old mean ages) had higher raw scores for visual motor and human-figure drawing skills. At the fifth grade level, arithmetic was significantly in favour of the Asian cities. Penmanship was compared for the non-Asian students (Caracas = 2.1, San Francisco = 2.1, and Southampton = 2.1) at the second grade level. The only change at the fifth grade was in the San Francisco classes (from 2.1 to 1.9).

Left-handed students in the non-Asian cities are not, contrary to what was expected, hampered in academic functioning. In fact, they had slightly higher scores in arithmetic, visual motor and human-figure drawing. There were no significant differences in penmanship. Left-handed students in Caracas were in the same penmanship categories as the right-handed in approximately the same percentages.

There appears to be no consensus in the non-Asian cities about what the children should be using as far as cursive, printing or mixing both. The chief determiner of what is taught is the teacher, not the guidelines from the local education authorities.

The most significant finding of these studies involving non-Asian children is that males at every age appear to rank in the fair and poor categories of penmanship, complain more frequently about their dislike of 'handwriting', tire more visibly, and express strong dissatisfaction when their handwriting is in printing, mixed both, and is poor. Said one older boy as he handed in his spelling with marked dysgraphia, 'How I wish I could learn cursive. It's grown up writing and I hate printing.'

REFERENCES

Beery, K. (1967) *Developmental Test of Visual Motor Integration*. Follett, Chicago.
Beery, K. (1982) *Revised Administration, Scoring and Teaching Manual for the Developmental Test of Visual-Motor Integration*. Follett, Chicago.
Jastak, J. and Jastak, S. (1978) *The Wide Range Achievement Test Manual of Instructions*. Jastak Associates, De Wilmington.
Tarnopol, L., and Tarnopol, M. (1976) *Reading Disabilities: An International Perspective*. University Park Press, Baltimore.
Tarnopol, L. and Tarnopol, M. (1981) *Comparative Reading and Learning Disabilities*. Lexington Books, D.C. Heath, Lexington, Massachusetts.

APPENDIX 1

Attwell, C.R. and Wells, F.L. (1972) *Wide Range Vocabulary Test*. Psychological Corporation, New York.

Beery, K. (1982 revision) *Developmental Test of Visual Motor Integration*. Follett, Chicago

Jastak, J., Bijou, S. and Jastak, S. (1980 revision) *Wide Range Achievement Test*. Jastak Associates, De Wilmington

Koppitz, E. (1968) *Psychological Evaluation of Children's Human Figure Drawing*. Grune and Stratton, New York

17

Conclusion

Within these pages, numerous questions have been asked and, on occasion, attempts to provide answers to the questions have been made. We have examined legislation and curricular recommendations and selectively presented normative information about child development and graphic skills. We have tried to show links between physical and neurological development, laterality and handedness, and have considered the development of a wide range of graphic performance in young children. We hope that we have led the reader to a point at which links between child development and handwriting performance can be made. Reference is made to children within the normal range of educational development and also to those affected by a number of different physically handicapping conditions.

Guest authors have generously made their knowledge and research conclusions available to us. Their contributions were invited so that perspectives from the different professions could be brought to the subjects of handwriting research and practice. Together they have drawn on their experiences arising from work with children of a wide age range and from their training and backgrounds in education and associated therapies.

Elizabeth Whitmarsh brings her training in special education and the experience of teaching children with special needs in a large comprehensive secondary school.

George Pasternicki has been interested in writing-paper format and in general writing performance for some years and brings the special perspective of the educational psychologist to the chapter he has written.

We are particularly grateful to Jenny Ziviani, Muriel Tarnopol and Nusia de Feldman who, as well as offering experiences from their own specialist areas of interest, have helped us to bring a world-wide perspective to the book. Jenny brings her occupational therapy skills to the chapter she has written. She is one of those rare people who are not only good practitioners but who have also subjected much of what they practise to experimental research.

Muriel Tarnopol, a teacher of many years experience with pupils of all age groups, was also director of In-Service Projects for Classroom Teachers of Educationally Handicapped Minors, a federally funded appointment. She is known world-wide for her writing about reading disability and comparative reading and learning difficulties. As a consultant in special education to public and private schools, she brings those advisory skills to her writing as well as her facility to conduct research and to interpret and disseminate its conclusions.

Nusia de Feldman is Professor in the Department of School Psychology at Universidad Central de Venezuela. She is also Chief Psychologist of the Instituto Diagnostico in Caracas. She conducted the Venezualian handwriting research.

The comparative research conducted by Muriel Tarnopol and the co-authors to whom she refers indicates that questions about handwriting characteristics and performance are being asked throughout the world and that although some aspects of handwriting performance can be shown to relate to either curricular legislation or guidelines, many cannot. As the authors state in the summary of the chapter, '. . . there is disparity between local education stated goals and what actually happens in the classroom'.

We believe that if progress is to be made, it is essential that teachers should participate in this discussion. We are encouraged by the United Kingdom document, 'The Responses to Curriculum Matters 1,' and remind the reader of the statement to which we drew attention in Chapter 1.

Objectives at the age of 11

All children should have had extensive experience of planned intervention and support, in accordance with their individual needs . . . these will encompass: handwriting, spelling, punctuation . . .'

We encourage teachers to question teaching approaches and policies and to remember that it is often through their children's writing that they and others form opinions about intellectual capacities; it is important that the children should be helped to present themselves as well as they are able.

Questions that might lead to different curricular provision include:

(1) Have we examined handwriting models, schemes and related research so that we can make a considered decision about our handwriting policy?
(2) What is our policy on the teaching of handwriting and how can we ensure that it is consistently implemented throughout the school?
(3) Could we discuss a handwriting policy with the schools from which our children come and to which they will go when they leave us?
(4) Does the policy we implement at a particular stage of the children's development have implications for how pupils will adapt to the handwriting needs of the secondary school?
(5) Can we prevent our children from developing handwriting difficulties?
(6) Can we initiate a handwriting checklist that will help us to identify problems when they arise?
(7) Can we, through class, group and individual teaching arrangements, ensure that help can be given to those who need it?
(8) Who are the left-handed children in our school?
(9) Are our provision and recommendations for left-handed children appropriate for their needs?

We hope that through discussion presented at different points in the text, readers will be provoked to ask further questions. Some will believe that they have the answers and others will see opportunities for further research. Above all, we hope that researchers will consult practitioners and go on to disseminate research findings to them, but also that practitioners will be inspired to initiate their own research so that research and practice become more closely associated. Through this kind of co-operation and through interdisciplinary dialogue and practice, good standards in the teaching of handwriting in schools can be established or retained. With the growth of interdisciplinary awareness, a greater number of practitioners and researchers will be in a position to help the not inconsiderable number of children who are currently known to be handicapped by handwriting difficulties.

REFERENCE

Department of Education and Science (1986) *English from 5 to 16: the responses to curriculum matters 1*. HMSO, London.

Index